TOSHACK'S
— WAY —

My Journey Through Football

TOSHACK'S
WAY

My Journey Through Football

JOHN TOSHACK

WITH DAN SUNG

First published as a hardback by deCoubertin Books Ltd in 2018.

First Edition

deCoubertin Books, 46B Jamaica Street, Baltic Triangle, Liverpool, L1 0AF.

www.decoubertin.co.uk

ISBN: 978-1-909245-71-6

A CIP catalogue record for this book is available from the British Library.

Cover design and typeset by Leslie Priestley.

Printed and bound by CPI.

In memory of Bill Shankly.

Contents

Foreword by Xabi Alonso

I WAS SIX YEARS OLD WHEN REAL SOCIEDAD WON THE COPA DEL REY.
I don't remember watching the game and I was too young to remember the
street parties but everyone in San Sebastián knows the footage of that penalty
shootout like they were there in Zaragoza in the stadium themselves. Every player
who stepped up to take one of the kicks against Atlético Madrid that day, and the
goalkeeper Luis Arconada, are heroes to Sociedad fans, and we consider John
Toshack one too.

John is a very important figure to both Real Sociedad and to the city of San
Sebastián. He is very popular because of his personality. It is always noticed when
John is around because he has so many different perspectives and opinions about
so many things because of what he achieved. He loves it there too. As well as
managing the club three times, for a total of more than eight years, he also had a
column in the local newspaper and wrote a great book in Spanish about his first
years in the city called Diario del galés – diary of a Welshman – which most of us
from there have read. He is a very charismatic person for us.

I was lucky enough to play for some very, very good managers during my career
and I would include John as one of those, for sure. He was so important for me.
He gave me my first chance to prove myself and, as a football player, you need
someone that first time to trust in you and to see something different that you
might bring to the game. Not every manager has the ability to do that. In my case,
it was John who was crucial to my career because, if he hadn't put that trust in me,
I don't know what would have happened.

I was just 18 when I started working with John and, actually, the situation at

Real Sociedad at the time was quite complex. I was on loan at Eibar along with a young striker called Joseba Llorente and the manager of Real Sociedad was my father. The team was not doing so well. My father resigned and John was called back to San Sebastián for the third time in his career with the job of rescuing the club from relegation, and his first move was to bring back Llorente and me from our loan.

John saw something in me and he put me in the team as a central midfielder, which was incredibly brave considering the importance of the position. He tried to make me a little bit quicker than I was but it really didn't work. I was no quicker at 18 at the beginning of my career than I was at 35 at the end of it, or at any point in between, but that didn't matter. I had other qualities and that's what John saw. If you're not fast, then you need to have that vision, that clear anticipation about what's going to happen. Then you work and the routine gives you more fluidity to take those decisions and your mind becomes quick and so does what you do with the ball, even if your legs are not.

John gave me a lot of responsibility and that made me want to prove myself and improve. It was a big call for John. We stayed in La Liga and those first months were incredible for me. John was able to unite the foreign players, the Basque players and the youngsters under one banner very quickly because of his experience in football as well as the region.

John and I have followed similar paths in our careers at times and, for sure, the strong connection between Liverpool and Real Sociedad played a part in my move to Anfield. To me, Liverpool was familiar because of what John had done as a player there and because of the story of his gesture in that special game when he returned with Swansea, as a manager, just after Bill Shankly had died.

Liverpool was a different place when I was there. I was with Rafael Benítez and the long line of Boot Room managers was over by then, so I didn't recognise the training methods which John had used when I got to Melwood. I wouldn't have known the history of Liverpool like I did without John and he came to watch me play at Anfield some years after we had worked together. It was amazing to be there together with him in that context.

Prologue:
Learning more from
defeat than victory

IT WAS AT THE CLIFTON HOTEL, IN SOUTHPORT, IN MARCH 1982, WHEN Peter Robinson and John Smith offered me the job as manager of Liverpool Football Club for the first of two occasions in my career. After three European Cups, four league titles and nearly seven years in charge, Bob Paisley was set to step down and, having taken Swansea City from the depths of the Fourth Division to the top of the First within four years, I was a natural choice to take charge of the club where I'd made my name as a player and won nine winners' medals in the process.

I'd left Liverpool still a young man at just 27 years of age with what would normally be plenty of years as a player still ahead of me, but circumstances had dealt me a different set of cards, setting me on the path to management instead.

For all the work I'd done in South Wales, for everything I'd built down there, Liverpool was a very special club to me. Anyone who'd played under Bill Shankly and Bob Paisley had been very lucky. It had been a footballing education there like no other and, if I'm honest, a lot of what I did at Swansea I did with the thought at the back of my mind that one day Liverpool would come back for me. On that day in 1982, they had.

I hadn't always gotten on famously with Bob but it was him who'd recommended me for the position and, when I walked out of that meeting, I left thinking that Bob would finish out the season and I'd take over the following year. But that's not the way things worked out. Almost immediately, Bob woke Liverpool up from the club's less than glittering form that season and, in doing so, I can only guess that he woke something in himself as well. With his ambition renewed, he went on to mastermind another two league titles and as many League Cups. Meanwhile, everything for me went downhill at Swansea. At the time of that meeting, my stock as a manager had never been higher. Swansea were riding high in the First Division and considered dark horses in the title race. Just eighteen months later, everything would fall apart but, to paraphrase Bill Shankly, sometimes you can get more out of a defeat than you can a victory.

Very often, I find myself repeating Shanks's words. Anything he might have missed was more than made up for with Bob Paisley at his side; man-management and tactical nous together. They were so different and an ideal pair.

Bob knew Shanks like the back of his hand. He knew how to get what he needed from him. They never had a coaching badge between them at Liverpool but the basis of everything I've ever done in coaching, I learned at Liverpool between 1970 and 1978. I've never seen anything to change my mind since. It's paying attention to the small things, what Shanks called 'The Recipe'. He had a phrase that he would always come back to time and time again – the most important things in football were important fifty years ago and they'll be important fifty years from now.

I had four good years under Bill Shankly at Liverpool. We won the league, the FA Cup and the UEFA Cup too, but that was the second great side he'd built and, after fifteen years in charge of the club, in the summer of 1974 he decided enough was enough and stepped down. It might not have been the madness you get as a coach at Madrid these days but the pressure of running a big club takes its toll. Bob Paisley, of course, stepped up from his role as number two and guided the club to an era of even greater glory, of which I was glad to be a part as well, and I was lucky to be there for much of that because, even from early on, I felt that Bob wasn't quite on my side. He never disliked me in a personal way. I just think that maybe he preferred other players. That's the feeling that I had.

Bob didn't have anything to do with signings when I joined the club. He was Shanks's number two, a physio and a coach, and I never felt like I was quite his cup of tea. Certainly for a few years, I never had his confidence, and that was confirmed when he signed Ray Kennedy from Arsenal in 1974 and subsequently tried to move me on. But I got back into the side and I scored some important goals, which endeared me a little bit more to Bob. He saw that understanding I had with Kevin Keegan and he knew it would be beneficial to the club, even if it hadn't been his original plan. He had a good mind for the game. He was a shrewd judge of a player and he knew how to get what he wanted out of a team. Even if the two of us didn't get on that well, I wasn't blind to what a good manager he was.

It's hard to say how successful I would or wouldn't have been if I had become the boss at Liverpool in 1982. After Bill and Bob, I'd certainly have had some big shoes to fill. What I do know is that without their guidance, I'd never have got that phone call in 1984 after I'd finished at Swansea that sent me on a different path altogether, managing different clubs and countries across Europe and North Africa.

You can't be quick on all decisions. Some take longer than others, some are more difficult, but you have to make them. If you're in football management, you can't sit on the fence too long or you'll fall off. Anyone will accept it if you need another 24 hours to think, but the time comes when we all have to make decisions and, when I look back on it now, I've never been frightened of making them, whether it was to go to Real Madrid, to return to San Sebastián, to take the Wales job or even to leave it after just one game in charge. When you look back over my career, you can maybe say that one call or another might not have been the best idea, but I like to think I got a lot more right than I did wrong.

As it turns out, saying yes to that phone call in 1984, taking that offer to work abroad for the first time in my life – that was one of the easiest decisions I've ever had to make. I never thought about how long I'd be away or where it might lead. I just knew at that moment that working abroad was what I wanted to do. That I'd end up working across three continents, in ten different countries, winning trophies in five of them, managing Real Madrid twice and becoming the only manager to win all three Spanish cups with three different teams, it never crossed my mind that such achievements would be possible. I just knew I wanted a change. I wanted some sunshine and Portugal had all of that for me. But that was 1984; there's plenty to tell before then . . .

1
Beginnings

RELATONSHIPS SHAPE THE PEOPLE WE BECOME.

My managerial career was shaped by my experiences as a player and the characters that guided me, firstly at Cardiff City and then at Liverpool. Both clubs offered the best education I could have wished for.

My father was a Scotsman, Bill Shankly was a Scotsman, and my Cardiff manager, Jimmy Scoular, was a Scotsman too. They had the same values. They came from villages. They had that same strong, proud, no-nonsense work ethic. There's certainly something in that Scottish temperament that makes for great managers. Not all Scots are great managers and not all great managers are Scots but, if you look over the years at Shankly, Matt Busby, Jock Stein and Alex Ferguson; you've got four there who are right up the top. I'm Welsh all the way but maybe the Scottish influence rubbed off on me.

I've worked in a lot of different countries and I've been asked whether my sense of adventure stems from my father. It was a big decision for him to choose to leave his family and settle in South Wales, as he did, with little scope for communication with the farm where he grew up back in Dunfermline. Returning to Scotland then felt like a trip to the Arctic.

One trip a year was all he could afford. We used to go up as a family for two weeks every summer: me, my parents and my brother, Colin. We'd rent a Standard Vanguard and take it on a fourteen-hour drive from Cardiff. There were no motorways. We'd leave at four o'clock in the morning, stopping in a layby for a hot meat pie at lunchtime somewhere near Lancaster. Then it would be up over Shap in Cumbria, across the Kincardine Bridge and over the Firth of Forth, before finally arriving at the farm at seven in the evening. There was a real spirit of adventure. Motorways now make the journey a lot easier.

In 1958, when I was nine years old, the Commonwealth Games were being held in Cardiff and the city centre was decked out in ribbons with all the flags of the nations flying on the lampposts. I'd have preferred to stay to watch the sport, but my father's holiday time was limited so up we went to Scotland where, instead, I played football with my seven older cousins.

At the age of eleven, I was fortunate enough to have witnessed Jock Stein's first foray into management when he took the job at nearby Dunfermline and my cousin Johnny took me along to watch them play.

My father, George Toshack, was a pilot in the Royal Air Force and based at St Athan in the Vale of Glamorgan when he met my mother, Joan Light, who was a Cardiff girl. They were married in December 1947 and I was born just over a year later in March 1949. I don't think they'd known each other more than eighteen months and there was never any question of my mother moving to Scotland.

My father was well respected. Before the war, he was a carpenter par excellence. He came to know everybody in the trade in South Wales and Cardiff and everyone knew him. I can see this classic photo of him wearing a tie, his carpenter's apron and a pencil behind his ear. The people who worked for him spoke so highly of his abilities.

I worked out pretty quickly I would not be a carpenter, having hammered a nail through my own thumb. My father took me back to my mother and told her I was costing him money. He suggested it might be safer for me to do something else. That was that.

We might have had very different professions but the way my father went about his business had a big influence on me. He taught me the importance of discipline in the workplace; a pride in performance. I think this is something that has slowly ebbed away from football and maybe this explains why I've fallen out with a few people along the way.

For a young footballer, my father also had what I think is the perfect approach as a parent. You see a lot of parents on the touchline these days shouting away at their kids and giving them a grilling before and after the games on what they need to do and where they've gone wrong, but you need to let a good coach do the work. My father knew better than to interfere. He was more likely to be hiding behind a tree to make sure I was focused on my game.

My mother was very proud of me in a more open way than my father. She didn't mind everybody knowing that she was my mother. She'd always be quick to point out to people what I'd been up to. My dad didn't like too much fuss. My mother was a wonderful woman, she really was. The most important influence they had on me together was to give me the space to make decisions for myself. I think they were aware of the kind of boy I was and I don't suppose I was ever going to let anyone decide anything for me. I always had a clear idea of what I wanted but, all the same, they could have got in the way of that and they never did, and that's easier said than done as a parent.

Decisiveness is an absolutely key attribute of a football manager. When you're in charge of people, you'll find you're faced with decisions virtually every minute of the day. Whether it's about player selection, buying and selling, working with injuries, organising pre-season friendlies, anything; you need to say yes or no. Perhaps some of those smaller details are taken away from managers in the modern era but, ultimately, the buck still stops with you and you need to have the courage of your own convictions and be able to make up your mind. And, for me, from an early age, I wasn't frightened to make a decision.

The experience you gain from making your own decisions is something that has gradually been taken away from footballers now, and that's had a big knock-on effect for those looking to get into management. When I was playing, there were no agents telling you what they thought you should do and taking their 15 per cent. I had just my father, my mother, my brother and myself, and the final decision – and the responsibility – was mine alone.

The change began thirty years ago. Players now are so cosseted there's a whole part of them that never grows up. I might ask a player what he thinks about the interest we're getting from another club to buy him and he'll start telling me what his agent thinks. I'm not interested in what his agent thinks. I want to know what he thinks.

It's very difficult to see yourself as others see you, but if I had to define myself it'd be as someone who has never been afraid of making a wrong decision or a mistake. I just felt, from an early age, a sense of authority. Life is about making decisions. You can't say maybe. Maybe is, for me, not a word that tells me anything. If someone answers something I ask with a maybe, I feel like retracting the question.

If I've been able to do that, that's partly because I'd been making up my own mind for a long time. I was captain of the school baseball team, captain of the cricket team and captain of the rugby team too, so I grew up getting used to making decisions.

I played football all the time, whenever I could. I'd even get my mother to make me sandwiches so that I could spend the time I was supposed to be eating lunch at school playing football instead. Eventually, one of the older boys told my sports teacher about me and I was picked for the Under-11 school side at Radnor Road Juniors when I was just eight years old. My sports teacher, the late Roy Sperry, must have had a lot of confidence in me because elevating a kid by a few years to a new level wasn't normal practice. By then, I already knew that football was what I loved most of all. I played all sports but soccer always had that edge over everything else. If I lost at those other games it didn't really bother me but when I lost at soccer it hurt.

My parents, though, were insistent that I achieved some kind of academic grounding. I passed my eleven-plus and went to Canton Grammar School, but the problem we had there was that the school didn't play football. It was rugby only. So on Saturdays, I played rugby for the school in the morning and soccer in the afternoon for Pegasus, the local team in the Cardiff District League; when I dislocated my shoulder playing rugby for the school it meant I missed a trial for the Cardiff Schools' football side, which put me off rugby a little bit. When the chance came round again, I got my go at the city-wide team and I got in along with a Canton Grammar School pal of mine called Dave Gurney. That made our school think twice about playing soccer and very soon Canton was fielding a team in the grammar school tournament, the Ivor Tuck Cup.

At fifteen, I set a record in the town team and racked up 47 goals in 22 games by the end of my first season. I made it to the Welsh Boys' side where I scored a hat-trick in my first game, a 3–1 victory against Northern Ireland at Swansea in the Victory Shield.

Suddenly, invitations to trials at Football League clubs began to arrive. A few of the lads in that Welsh Boys' team with me – Roy Penny, Cyril Davies, the Slee brothers – and I were invited up to Tottenham for a trial in the autumn of 1964 with Bill Nicholson's Spurs. Spurs had an ex-international called Arthur Willis who had played for Swansea and eventually settled in Wales, and he was always on the lookout for new Welsh talent for the club. Willis had been one of the key players in Tottenham's push-and-run team that had first won the title in 1951. And, at the time, Tottenham had Terry Medwin, Cliff Jones and Mel Hopkins –

all Welsh internationals who were playing in that double-winning team of the 1960s. So, Arthur took all of us young boys up to London and we spent a week training at White Hart Lane and staying in the White Hart pub itself, right on the corner of the ground. We were back home maybe four or five days before I got the letter in the post. It said thank you for your time but, unfortunately, you don't come up to the high standards required of Tottenham Hotspur Football Club. It was a real blow at the time. Every time I scored a goal for Liverpool against Tottenham, I'd remember that.

I was invited up to try out for Don Revie's Leeds side and Stan Cullis's Wolves as well, but I rejected both offers after that experience at Tottenham. I wanted to stay at home in Cardiff and take the extra year at college my parents wanted me to, so I signed amateur forms at Cardiff City, aged sixteen, in 1965.

Signing for Cardiff was a big deal personally. I'd stood on the top of the Bob Bank stand and watched them play every week for as long as I could remember. Football was the be all and end all right from the beginning. I'd arrive home from school and get straight out on the street. I played with a tennis ball against the side of a house across the road. It was football, football, football, and then here was this chance to make it my life for the club that I loved. It was also a chance to play alongside the man who, for me, was the very best in the game – John Charles.

I remember having seen John on television playing for Wales. I remember him going to Juventus. I had old cine film footage of him that I'd watch over and over again. I totally idolised him. And then, there I was, playing a couple of matches with him in the Cardiff City second team. I trained with him. I observed him. I observed how he headed a ball. I cleaned his boots.

Mel Charles was John's brother and he was a fine player too. I still laugh now when I remember how Mel would get his words all muddled up. He'd have the dressing room rolling on the floor when he complained that his Hercules tendon was sore or when he crossed the Tyne Bridge for the first time and commented, 'Look at that bridge! There's some agriculture that's gone into that!'

There were a lot of players who smoked in those days and they'd offer the cigarettes around, but John would only offer one to Mel and Mel would only offer one to John. They wouldn't offer them to anyone else. John used to joke that Mel was so tight that he wouldn't send his kids to school because they had to pay attention. When you saw the pair of them together, they were amazing specimens and, of course, my game was based around a very similar style of play to them with their ability in the air. John was at the stage in his career where he'd finished in Italy. He'd left Juventus, returned to Leeds and then headed back out for a spell at Roma, before signing for Cardiff to play professional football in Wales for the first time in his career. By this time, John had developed problems with injuries. His knees had started to cave in, but he always had a bit of time for me and I was very grateful for that. He eventually took over the Welsh Under-23 side in which I played, so he managed me a bit too.

For me, John Charles always was the greatest footballer. We talk about the likes of Cruyff, Messi, Pelé and the rest, but there weren't and still aren't many players who could play both No. 9 and No. 5, and still be the best in both positions. I remember whenever Wales played at home and Juventus were not prepared to release him to play, the Welsh FA would ask them not to say anything until the day of the game, because if people thought John was coming there'd be gates of 40,000. If he didn't come, the attendance would drop dramatically. That was the pull that he had.

He made an enormous impression on me. He used to give me little tips in training sessions, like the sort of movement I should be making when the ball comes in from a cross; if the keeper follows it, you knock it back where it came from to make him change direction. It's harder for the keeper that way. These are things I've since passed on as a manager to my players. John was always telling me what it was like at Juventus and what it was like living in Italy. Considering my wanderlust later in life, I'm sure John's words had an impact on my mindset.

Another major influence on me at Cardiff was Jimmy Scoular, the manager. Jimmy was a tough customer. He'd made a career as a no-nonsense tackler with a temper to match, and he wasn't about to change his ways now that he'd moved into management.

Cardiff had been relegated from the First Division in 1962 and Jimmy had arrived at the club just one year before I had to turn its fortunes around. He'd favoured a youth policy at the expense of some of the older stalwarts still left over from Cardiff's days in the big league, but had quickly realised that he still needed to keep a few of those old heads around for their experience and bit more balance. I don't feel embarrassed to say that, as a sixteen-year-old, I was frightened of Jimmy. I think it's a good thing that players sometimes are a little intimidated by their manager. A healthy respect goes a long way. It means you can't take liberties.

You didn't mess about with this fella. If he told me to do something, then I did it. Fortunately, Jimmy liked me. I think the fact that my father was a Scotsman, and grew up just over the Forth from where Jimmy had in Livingston, helped a little bit. Jimmy didn't always see eye to eye with John Charles, though. He and Mel weren't always his favourites. I think Jimmy became frustrated with the injuries that the two picked up, and it was one of those injuries that gave me my first chance.

I was sitting in technical college on a Monday morning in October 1965 when one of the junior professionals at the club, David Houston, came running in to say that John Charles and one of the other key players, Barrie Hole, were both injured and that I had to fly out to Liège for the second leg of our Cup Winners' Cup tie against Standard. Cardiff City may not have been in the First Division but, since 1961/62, UEFA had offered a single spot in the Cup Winners' Cup to any Welsh winners of the Welsh Cup, and Jimmy had quickly realised how important both the experience and the gate receipts could be to the club if we were playing in Europe each season. In the nine years that Scoular was at Cardiff, he made sure Cardiff City won the Welsh Cup seven times.

I was less worried about making my debut than I was thinking what Jimmy might do to me once he found out I didn't have a passport. I'd never flown anywhere in my life. In the end, I had to go down to the post office and apply for one of those temporary versions. I forged my dad's signature because I couldn't find him in time but I don't suppose Interpol are going to be after me for that one fifty years later.

I was an unused substitute in the end but there was drama for me off the pitch when, along with two other Cardiff lads, Georgie Johnston and Bernard Lewis, I ended up in the local jail for disturbing the peace. The three of us were sitting by the hotel pool eating some very overpriced sandwiches when Georgie and Bernard decided it would be a good idea to pick up one of the chairs and throw it into the water as a protest. I can't remember which of the two it was that ended up hurling the thing in but, when I looked up at the window behind us, there was someone on the telephone to the police, who promptly came and picked us up. I thought my career was over before I'd even kicked a ball when Jimmy Scoular walked into the constabulary to get us out. Jimmy was furious on a good day, so you can imagine him at that particular moment.

There were a few rogues in that Cardiff City side; a few older ones that led me astray, and I think Jimmy knew his players and what had happened. So, he gave me another chance and a few weeks later, in a match against Leyton Orient, on 13 November 1965, I walked onto the pitch as player at Ninian Park, the ground I'd been going to all my life as a fan, not one mile from the house where I grew up. Twenty minutes in, I replaced Graham Coldrick, who'd picked up a knock to his knee, and, at 16 years and 236 days, I became the youngest player to step out as a Cardiff Blue – a record that stood until Aaron Ramsey took that honour some forty years later. Five minutes before the end, I scored my first professional goal at the Grange End. The irony is that Paul Went, the Orient lad marking me, was only just sixteen himself.

Not many managers would place so much faith in a sixteen-year-old and it's something I've never forgotten in my own management career. I don't think I really had the characteristics that Jimmy Scoular would normally want in a player, but he still trusted me. Maybe I lacked a bit of the aggression that players needed in those days to survive, but that's normal for a teenager playing against seasoned pros looking to kick lumps out of you. I always felt it was about brain more than brawn. If I thought my way around the field with intelligence, I could overcome the more physical aspects of the game. I don't think I've ever been an openly aggressive player like others might have been, but I learned to look after myself on the pitch. Jimmy had the sense to let me start to do that and I have an awful lot to be thankful to him for.

I stayed at Cardiff for five years. We never really achieved that much in the league, certainly to begin with. We only avoided relegation to the Third Division by a single place in my first two seasons and managed a mid-table finish after that, partly thanks to the strike partnership I formed with Brian Clark. He arrived at the club in 1968 after his time at Huddersfield had not gone so well. There were quite a few forwards at Cardiff when I started off – George Andrews, Terry Harkin, George Johnston. There had to be lots in those days because we were still playing very front-heavy formations. When Clarkey came in there was a change to a more defensive shape but it didn't matter, because the two of us really hit it off and scored goals by the hatful. We had two or three good years where we looked like we were going to get up to the big league but it never quite happened. We got very close in the Cup Winners' Cup too, which gave me a ton of European experience at a very early age – we were involved in the competition five times during the years I was there. Liège did for us that first year in the first round in 1965/66, but we were only inches from the final the next time we qualified in 1967/68.

It began with victories in the first two rounds against Shamrock Rovers and NAC Breda. Then, in March 1968, we took one of the longest ever away trips in the Cup Winners' Cup when we played Torpedo Moscow. It was the middle of winter and Moscow was covered in snow and ice, so the venue was switched to Tashkent, now the capital of Uzbekistan, over 2,000 miles further away from the Soviet capital. We played a league match at Middlesbrough on the Saturday, travelled down to London, stayed there that evening, flew out to Moscow the next day, trained in a gymnasium underneath the Lenin stadium, and then got on the plane on the Monday for Tashkent, within a couple of hundred miles of the border with China and Afghanistan; part of the old Marco Polo run on the Silk Road.

It was one of the poorest places anyone could ever imagine. We took tins of corned beef and bread with us and we'd queue up outside Jimmy Scoular's room for our rations. We lost the game by a single goal and then won the home leg by the same margin. This was in the days before penalty shootouts decided these things, so it went to a third game at a neutral venue – which turned out to be Augsburg in Germany – where Cardiff came out winners. So, Second Division Cardiff City found itself in a semi-final against a very good Hamburg side with West German internationals like defender Willi Schulz and striker Uwe Seeler, who scored over 400 goals for his club and 43 for his country. We fought hard and came out with a 1–1 draw in the first leg away. It looked like we were headed for another replay with the score at 2–2 at Ninian Park but Seeler fired off a bit of a nothing shot from distance in the dying minutes. Our keeper, Bob Wilson, didn't quite get his whole body behind it and it was Hamburg who went through.

The next year we went out to Porto in the first round after receiving some pretty horrific treatment over there. I think they must have started the building work in the hotel we were staying in especially for our arrival and some of the players were attacked by Porto fans on the pitch at the final whistle. It could be very hostile away in Europe in those days but it was all part of an important learning curve for me and, it didn't matter the competition, I was scoring goals for fun: 17, 31 and then 22 in consecutive seasons.

I'd had offers from other clubs such as Bobby Robson's Fulham, but none of them seemed quite right. Cardiff was my hometown club. I used to walk to work; the training ground was only twenty minutes from my house. I never wanted to do anything else other than play for Cardiff City. But then you play more games, you're involved in more big matches, and you see how professional football works. You want more of that and you want to know whether you're good enough to play at a higher level.

Liverpool were watching me and I knew the club's chief scout, Geoff Twentyman, had been to Ninian Park on a couple of occasions, though I didn't take much notice of him because it was normal to see scouts around. There were scouts at all sorts of games, but when I saw Jimmy Scoular walking up the hill to our house that Sunday morning in November 1970, I knew what he was coming over to say. Liverpool had offered £110,000 for my services and that wasn't the kind of money that Cardiff could turn down.

It was difficult because we were going really well in the league and we were in with a great chance of finally getting promotion to the First Division. Some people have since said that when Cardiff City sold me, they stopped trying. They threw away their chances of going into the top flight. I have a different view on the matter now than I did at the time, having been a manager and seen so many similar situations that I've had to deal with myself. But I was a player in those days. In the end, I just felt it was good for Cardiff, getting £110,000, which was a club transfer record for both Liverpool and Cardiff, and it was good for me because I was getting a chance to go to one of biggest clubs around – so everyone, in theory, was happy.

Bill Shankly was a massive draw. Shankly embodied Liverpool. I felt I could trust his judgement and it was a big confidence booster for me to think that somebody like him wanted me. So, I thought this was the right opportunity.

Dialogue with Bill was sometimes challenging, however. Everyone was so much in awe of the man. We hung on his every word. He only ever talked about football. Fortunately, he liked me. He signed me and I was one of his favourites. He was in the army, in Barry, in South Wales, and he used to box a lot. He knew I was Welsh and so he'd tell me about his time there and how he used to go up to the Rhondda Valley to watch boxing. He had an obvious affinity with the place and the people, and I think that's probably part of the reason he took a shine to me. He was the best man-manager I ever met and later a wonderful friend and mentor during my run as manager of Swansea City. I cried unashamedly on the morning I heard he'd died.

When I made my debut for Cardiff as a sixteen-year-old, I was earning £12 a week with an extra £8 for a first-team appearance and a bonus of £4 for a win and £2 for a draw. By the time my move to Liverpool came, I was up to £40 per week. At Liverpool, I earned £80 per week plus add-ons, which included a crowd bonus of £2 for every thousand tickets sold over 48,000 spectators. Anfield held 54,000 at the time. Shanks once asked all the players to go home over the summer and come back after the break and tell him how much they thought they were worth to the club, and what their pay increase should be. It was the summer of 1973 when we had just won the UEFA Cup and the league championship – Liverpool's first major honours for seven years. I asked for a pay rise of £70 per week. He gave me £90. I went out of his office delighted but, by the time I reached the car park, I realised he'd had me down for a rise of £100. I couldn't turn back, though. Years later, when I was manager, I brought that incident up with him. 'Aye, John, son,' he said, 'I saved ten pounds a week on you but you weren't the only one.'

You're not defined as a manager by your playing career or by those that you've previously played under. There are a lot of top managers who never played at all. Neither is it just a case of playing under a decent manager in order to become a good one. At the end of the day, you've got to be yourself. You can remember things that happened, you can remember training sessions and you can remember what a certain manager did in certain situations, but temperament plays a big part.

There are a lot of great players that have gone into management and haven't been able to handle defeat in the proper way or haven't been able to accept players with less ability than themselves when they played. As it turned out, I didn't have to wait too long as a player before I found out whether I had what it took to sit in the hot seat myself.

Roy Sperry, Jimmy Scoular, John Charles, Bill Shankly and my father: they've all passed away now but they are often in my thoughts and very much alive for me with the words they have said and the impact they had. I owe them so much.

2

Liverpool and the Kop

A PERSISTENT INJURY CAN PLAY HAVOC WITH YOUR CAREER. ONE moment, you know exactly who you are and where you're going. Then injury turns up and it knocks you sideways – your confidence, your ability, your position in the team and the livelihood of both you and your family. But the reality is that an injury, like all big life events, does not necessarily have to be a negative.

When I signed for Liverpool as a 21-year-old, in November 1970, I'd picked up an injury to my ankle the day before with Cardiff and I was terrified that the deal would fall through, but Shanks assured me that it didn't affect his plans. I played my first game for Liverpool against Coventry just three days later when I shouldn't have. They really wanted to get me fit to play. So, I played and I struggled a little bit, and Bill and Bob Paisley could see it.

The step-up at Liverpool was a lot to take in. I arrived at Lime Street Station with Sue, my wife at the time, and Shanks was there with the media to greet me at the platform. 'You've gone from Sunday school to church,' he said to me in that gruff Ayrshire accent of his. 'Do you want a steak, son? I'll take you to the best steak restaurant in town,' and off the three of us went to the Lord Nelson Hotel where Shanks would often treat the team.

Making that step-up, you've got to have doubts about yourself, whoever you are; anyone's going to get them, and having that niggling injury didn't help. Of course, in those situations, it's important if you can that you get off to a good start, but it wasn't the best game. We drew 0–0 and Everton were next up in the Merseyside derby at Anfield. There was little time to settle in. Everton were First Division champions, with Howard Kendall, Joe Royle, Alan Ball and the like, while we had one of the least experienced Liverpool teams ever, including other derby debutants like Brian Hall, Steve Heighway, Alec Lindsay and John McLaughlin. Everton were in mid-table but they were still favourites.

The first half was a cagey affair, as is often the case in big games like this, and we went in at half-time with no score. By the hour mark in the second, though, we were two goals down; the first a sublime chip from Alan Whittle to catch Ray Clemence off his line and the second a close-range header at the back post from a towering Royle. We were shell-shocked. Then Heighway got one back from a typically dazzling dribble all the way up the wing, along the byline and into the net. With fifteen minutes to go Stevey pushed up the left once more, crossed the ball and I outjumped Brian Labone to put us on level terms. Then, shortly afterwards, I flicked on for Chris Lawler to fire in our winner with just five minutes to go; 3–2, one of the all-time great derbies. A game like that, you never forget.

There was no pampering at Liverpool. It was sink or swim. The doubts don't disappear completely when you score a goal against Everton but it helps, and to get off the mark, particularly in a game of such importance, it really helped a lot. It wasn't just me who felt the joy of the moment. We were a young side; the beginnings of the second great team that Bill Shankly and Bob Paisley would build. Shanks had won promotion back to the First Division for Liverpool in 1962 after nearly a decade away, then two league titles in 1964 and 1966 and an FA Cup in between, but that first team reached a critical stage in early 1970, a watershed moment they'd call it. It was a game where Liverpool lost 1–0 in the FA Cup sixth round to Second Division Watford and Bill and Bob decided it was time to rip it all up and start again. Out went Ian St John, Ron Yeats and Roger Hunt, and in came Emlyn Hughes, Heighway, myself, Ray Clemence and Larry Lloyd. He signed a group of us all from teams outside the top flight; Emlyn came from Blackpool, myself from Cardiff, Clemence from Scunthorpe, Lloyd from Bristol Rovers, and there were more later.

The scouting had been carried out by the famous Geoff Twentyman, who trawled the lower divisions for players that other clubs had missed. We were in our early twenties when the new generation came in, and those first days of 1970/71 were an eye-opener for us all. We only finished fifth in the league that year, but we conceded fewer goals than anyone else and remained unbeaten at home; good signs of something solid to build on and the kind of form that saw us get very close in a couple of cups.

Liverpool had also finished fifth in the 1969/70 season, which meant the club had qualified for the Inter-Cities Fairs Cup. It was the last year that the competition was played before it was replaced by the UEFA Cup, and the club had made it into the third round by seeing off Ferencváros of Hungary and Dinamo Bucharest in the months before I'd arrived. I scored the only goal away from home against Hibs, which gave us the platform to put another two past the Edinburgh side at Anfield in a game which I missed through an injury.

Now, playing in Europe was not a new thing for me but our quarter-final opponents were a different level. While Liverpool were on the brink of a great generation, Bayern Munich were about to be just as successful with the great Sepp Maier in goal, Franz Beckenbauer and Hans-Georg Schwarzenbeck at the back along with Paul Breitner next to them, and then Uli Hoeness and Gerd Müller hammering shots at your goal. All six would go on to win the 1972 European Championship in Belgium and the World Cup with West Germany in 1974, as well as a hat-trick of Bundesliga titles from 1972 to 1974 and three European Cups back-to-back between 1974 and 1976 for Munich. This was an incredible side. I'd faced a few of them in Frankfurt as a twenty-year-old for Wales in a 1969 friendly. Somehow we'd escaped with a 1–1 draw. Two years on Müller, who scored that day, had just won the World Cup Golden Boot, the European Golden Shoe and the Ballon d'Or. All the talk in the newspapers was about Munich and how Liverpool was going to cope with Müller but, in the end, the tie was over before we got on the plane to Germany for the second leg.

Alun Evans had been signed by Shanks from Wolves in 1968 as a successor to Roger Hunt. The club had paid £100,000 for him as a nineteen-year-old, which made Evans the most expensive teenage footballer in Britain – a lot of money considering he'd only scored four goals for Wolves. He played in almost every league game in his first season, scoring seven times, and just when he was getting things going the next season he was attacked in a nightclub in Wolverhampton and had a pint glass smashed into the side of his face, which left him with deep cuts around his right eye and a lot of scarring. That was something that caused him a lot of problems, and there had also been all the responsibility and expectation on his shoulders, which was a bit too much for him – he never really recovered while he was at Anfield. Not a tall lad, he was very busy; I had been signed to play alongside him but it never really happened. He was out for the first four months of the season after a knee operation held him up for a lot longer than anyone anticipated. So, when he started that night against Munich, his first full game back after the lay-off, no one was expecting too much from him. It proved to be his finest moment in a Liverpool shirt.

Evans scored a hat-trick against one of the most difficult opponents you could ever meet. The first was a big hit on a cross from Heighway, the second a knock-down from me from a free-kick and the third a poacher's finish after Emlyn Hughes had a shot parried by Maier. The Bayern coach, Udo Lattek, had blamed the frozen pitches in Germany for Bayern's below-par performance. They hadn't played for three weeks but it didn't matter. It was a big win and a 1–1 draw at the Sechzger Stadium in Munich finished it off for us when Shanks got Ian Ross to man-mark Beckenbauer all night and stop them creating anything like the four goals that the Germans would need. Bayern, for me, with Beckenbauer and Schwarzenbeck to play against, were among the toughest opponents I ever faced. They were very strong and I was comparatively young at that stage. I remember coming off and thinking it had been a bit too much for me, and it was the same feeling when we faced Leeds United in the semi-final.

Leeds against Liverpool was a big fixture at that time. Shanks was just rebuilding his team, whereas Don Revie's great Leeds side still had a bit left in them. We were new to that level and we were finding it tough going against them. Norman Hunter and Jack Charlton, the centre-backs I had to deal with, were at the peak of their powers and tough customers, very strong in the tackle. They were so solid in the first leg at Anfield, so hard to break down, and it was a single header from Billy Bremner that gave Leeds the advantage. It was the only goal scored in a grinding tie. Both sides were knocking on the door in the second leg at Elland Road. Ian Callaghan and I hit the woodwork but it was no good, and it was Leeds who went on to beat Juventus in the final and become the last winners of the competition before it was changed into the UEFA Cup the following year.

April 1971 wasn't the end of all our cup dreams, though. We still had a date with Arsenal at Wembley in the FA Cup final to look forward to. We had taken out a few smaller sides until the sixth round when we were drawn at home against Tottenham Hotspur. The Londoners were stubborn opponents, determined not to lose at Anfield, and the game went to a replay at White Hart Lane. In the end the tie was decided by just one goal; but it was the performance of Ray Clemence that will be remembered from that ninety minutes. You'd look back down the pitch and he'd be putting in save after save to keep us in it. There was a period of sixty seconds where the Spurs striker, Martin Chivers, who already had 31 goals that season, saw three dead-certain strikes saved by our keeper. One was virtually point-blank range. It was Steve Heighway who did the damage for us off one of my knockdowns and it meant a semi-final showdown with our city rivals, Everton; the first all-Mersey affair at this stage in the competition for twenty years.

The city was buzzing with all the talk around the game but I was just as interested in the other semi-final, Arsenal vs Stoke City, because my cousin, John Mahoney, played centre-midfield for the Potters. 'Joshy', as we called him, and I knocked about plenty as young lads, playing football. A few years later, from 1973, we were both turning out for Wales together but in 1971 it was a Toshack/Mahoney FA Cup final that I wanted. We'd kicked a ball around as boys imagining just this when we'd visited his family in Manchester, pretending to commentate on the game.

Liverpool's preparation for the game against Everton was hardly ideal. We were only back from our second-leg Fairs Cup game in Munich about 48 hours before we travelled to Old Trafford to face the Toffees. The game in Germany had been delayed, so there was only enough time for light training on the Friday before we were off to Manchester the next morning. After just ten minutes, Everton's Alan Ball opened the scoring and we struggled to offer any threat until after the break. Brian Labone was marking me. I wasn't making it easy for him but I didn't have it my way in the air as much as I'd wanted. In fact, at half-time, Shanks told us to play it on the ground more, but when Labone limped off after 51 minutes, what authority Everton had with their lead began to disappear. Just a few moments later, Heighway put the ball through to Alun Evans to level and then on 73 minutes, a high cross came in close to the Everton keeper Andy Rankin and, without Labone protecting him, he had to come for it and I went in to challenge.

I had two ways of going up for a header. If the ball was coming in from the right, I'd have my left eye looking out at the goal and the keeper. If he wasn't coming, I'd go full throttle to head it at goal, but if he was, I'd go up with my left arm raised a bit, protecting me and, rightly or wrongly, making it difficult for the keeper to get a clean catch on it at the same time. Out of the corner of my eye, I saw Rankin making his move. I knew he was coming for it, and he clutched at it but couldn't hold on and the ball dropped to Brian Hall, who was as surprised as anyone to see it land perfectly in front of him. He just hooked it in and the Stretford End exploded. From there, it was 'You'll Never Walk Alone' through to the final whistle.

Arsenal did for Stoke after a replay the next Wednesday but, for me, in my first season, to be going to an FA Cup final was still an incredible achievement. My immediate memories from that date, 8 May 1971, meander to colours and textures. We played in heavy, red, long-sleeved, woollen shirts on a roasting-hot day at Wembley, up beyond 32 degrees, and Arsenal had these lightweight material, yellow tops with short sleeves. I turned my ankle in the first ten minutes. Bob soaked it with a sponge at half-time but I didn't want to take my boot off because I had a feeling I'd never get it back on again if I did.

Liverpool had had a few strikers who'd been injured. Tony Hateley had left in 1968; Bobby Graham and Alun Evans were finishing about that time and I was the new kid on the block who was struggling to make an impact. I felt the pressure. I was always aware at Liverpool how fierce the competition was. They'd sign a new striker every summer, and to begin with I hated it, but I got used to the idea and, of course, it was most often to keep the current players on their toes as much as it was to replace them. I knew I must have been a decent threat though, because the Arsenal goalkeeper Bob Wilson had been told to come out and help his centre-backs in the air whenever possible. He was out like lightning for everything, so much so that Steve Heighway caught him out for Liverpool's goal. It was in the second minute of extra time after the first ninety had ended goalless. Wilson miscalculated and this gave Steve the space he needed to score at his near post. Unfortunately, Arsenal's Eddie Kelly levelled it ten minutes later and then Charlie George scored his famous double-winning goal and lay down on the turf, leaving a tired Liverpool nine minutes in which we couldn't make the difference. It was disappointing, but we were a new team and we were still finding our feet.

That first season, we'd overachieved in many ways. That Wembley day had come just a little too early for us, really. With a little more experience (and short-sleeved shirts) we might have taken it home. The club was planning for the future and a big part of that would be the signing of Kevin Keegan. I came into Anfield one day and Kevin was sat on a dustbin outside the dressing room waiting for someone to come and find him. I knew who he was because I'd seen him in the press conference after he signed from Scunthorpe, so I introduced myself. He went down on the coach to Wembley for the Arsenal game with all those who weren't playing, and stayed in the team hotel. The following season, our partnership came to life.

Pre-season was very methodical at Liverpool. First was fitness training, then they'd have a thirty-minute practice match after ten days where they'd leave the grass long so it made the game slower. Three days later, they'd cut the grass shorter and we'd play sixty minutes. Then shorter again and for ninety minutes, giving everyone a chance to ease themselves in.

One summer's day we were playing one of those pre-season practice matches, the first team against the reserves. Normally, the reserves would win because they were so determined. They'd try that little bit harder and the first-teamers didn't want to get themselves injured.

Shanks had signed Kevin Keegan to replace Ian Callaghan in midfield originally, but he'd seen something in the first of those thirty-minute matches and put him up top with me. We beat the reserves 3–0 – something that normally didn't happen – and, afterwards, Shanks asked Kevin how he'd feel about starting that season as a striker. In our opening league game against Nottingham Forest, I got the ball to the byline, cut it back, Kevin scored and our dynamic duo was born.

It was never the plan to sign Toshack and Keegan so they could play up front together for Liverpool. It just happened by accident. The most difficult thing of all in management is to get your team scoring goals. You can organise teams and you can get teams to be difficult to beat but normally you have to buy a goal. It's very difficult to teach your team to score. You can work on finishing all day and you can get players who strike good balls and finish well, but the art of being in the right place at the right time, you've either got it or you haven't. It's almost impossible to teach players that. They need maximum concentration. They need to know their teammates very well. They need to be able to smell where the danger is, where a chance is going to appear before everyone else realises it and, when the ball comes, they have to be able to finish well too.

I've never seen anybody work so hard at their game as Kevin did. To come from Scunthorpe, to play six years at Liverpool, become captain of England, sign for Hamburg and become European Footballer of the Year; you don't get that without his kind of attitude. He never, ever stopped. He had everything. He was a professional and played every ninety minutes like they were his last. He made bad balls into good ones; long balls that looked as though they were going out, that a lot players wouldn't even bother to chase, he'd get after them and keep the ball in play. People always talk about Kevin on the ground and Toshy in the air but, if you look at the goals we scored, it was all round – left foot, right foot, everything. Too often, people remember the surnames of Toshack and Keegan but it was Toshack,

Keegan and Heighway. Every aspect of attacking play between the three of us, we had it. There were players that I couldn't get the better of in the air, but Kevin and Steve could find a way. Sometimes Steve had problems wide on the left, but then Kevin and myself could get through the middle. And Kevin sometimes found himself man-marked out of a game, but I had the measure of my centre-back in the air, or Stevie would create something. It was very hard for any team to keep us out.

I remember playing against Chelsea in a league game at Anfield in 1973. They had this big lad called Micky Droy. He was huge. One newspaper later summed him up nicely as 'six-feet four-inches of hard-core centre-back, who had an unsentimental way with a headed clearance and who, from 1971, gave fifteen years of no-nonsense service to a mortifyingly declining side'. Any ball that came straight down the middle, I had no chance. He'd win the lot. So, I went out to wide areas of the field and Micky would follow me. Now, I wasn't involved too much in that game but nor was Micky, and we won 1–0. Kevin did the damage, with him and Stevie a threat in the space that was left behind. I remember Micky saying to me as we came off the pitch, 'Ah, you never scored today, Tosh,' and I replied, 'No, well done, Mick, you've had a good match.' Players seemed quite happy when I hadn't scored, even if their team had lost the game. Very often, it's what you do indirectly that counts and we never had to talk about it, Kevin, Stevie and myself. We were all intelligent enough, football-wise, to know where, when and who could make the best inroads. I seemed to have a lot of success in Europe because, in those days, they maybe weren't as strong as some of the big centre-backs at home.

It was the beginning of the 1972/73 season when things began to get tricky for me at Liverpool. We had lost the league the previous year by a single point on the final day of the season with a draw at Arsenal, when I'd had a perfectly good goal disallowed for an offside that never was. Our form at the beginning of that 71/72 campaign had been mixed. Initially, I was in and out of the team a bit while Shanks was searching for his best pair up front. I'd started well but the goals had dried up a little and I was dropped in December while Alun Evans and Bobby Graham were tried with Keegan, but neither of them hit it off with him. In the meantime, I scored six goals in the three reserve games I played, which was enough to show the coaches what they were missing and I was reinstated towards the end of January. Whether it was my presence or not, I couldn't say for certain, but it was around that time the team finally gelled. That second side that Shanks had been building really came together and off we went on a fifteen-game unbeaten run that saw us shoot up the table from tenth into second position by April. We were knocked out of the cups over that difficult autumn and winter, including the Cup Winners' Cup, which we had qualified for because Arsenal were already playing in the European Cup. I wasn't in the team when we'd met that brilliant Bayern Munich team for the second year in a row. They were out for blood this time and dispatched Liverpool in the second round with a 3-1 scoreline in Germany in the second leg, after a stubborn 0-0 at Anfield where they were determined not to give it away this time.

We only conceded five goals after January in that 1971/72 season and two of those came in our FA Cup defeat to old enemies Leeds United in a fourth-round replay at Elland Road. Unfortunately, one of the other remaining three was in our penultimate game against the team just behind us but on the same points in third place, Brian Clough's Derby County. Derby's defenders, Roy McFarland and Colin Todd, for me, were the best centre-half pairing in the league that season. They were super players and the old Baseball Ground was always a shocking place to play football. In the winter, it was an absolute bog right through the middle. Your feet would sink in the mud. They wouldn't allow games on it these days; it was like playing on quicksand. In the spring sunshine that mud would bake hard and the ball would bounce around all over the place. Derby took the two points, as it was, with just the one goal in the second half of a niggly kind of game; not exactly one for the purist, but that was enough for Brian Clough's men to take on holiday to Spain while they watched and waited for Liverpool and Leeds to play out their final games in hand. Leeds needed a draw or better at Wolves and we needed them to lose as well as two points of our own at Highbury.

Arsenal had just lost the cup final to Leeds two days before but if they were tired they didn't show it. A point for them would mean that even a loss to Spurs in their final game would give them a finish above their north London neighbours, which was maybe what gave them the strength. All the same, we were the better side that day. Unlike when we had faced them at Wembley the year before, this was a game we deserved to win. We nearly did when Emlyn hit the crossbar in the first half and Kevin missed with an overhead kick on the rebound which only just went wide. The big moment, though, was in the final minutes of the game. We didn't know it at the time, we were just playing for our lives to get the points, but Leeds were getting beaten at Molineux 2-1. The championship was there for the taking when I put the ball in the net via a shot from Keegan. I was so used to Kevin's play already that I ran in at the far post in case he dragged his initial shot off-target, which he duly did. I think I was onto it before the linesman really knew what was going on and it was unfairly chalked off. It was the 89th minute and we'd come agonisingly close. To this day, in my mind, I know the goal was good.

So, with two seasons gone and two close calls, I went back to training for the 1972/73 season with a real vigour. The thought probably spurred me on too much. I was working maybe a little too hard and did some damage to my leg. I felt the strain in my thigh during a pre-season fixture against Blackburn Rovers up at Ewood Park but I played on, thinking it was just a question of fitness. Back at Melwood for training on the Monday, though, and it hadn't gone away, so I went into the medical room. In those days, Liverpool, and other clubs, didn't have proper medical staff. There wasn't the same equipment and apparatus. Bob Paisley was the physio and, on more than one occasion, including mine, they paid for it.

Bob, Joe Fagan and I knew there was a problem but we all wanted me to play. It was fiercely competitive at Liverpool and I didn't want to lose my place. It wasn't all on them. The decision was made to give it a good massage; a bad decision as it turned out. They should have just put some heat or ice on it, but no. They massaged a muscle that they shouldn't have massaged and it ballooned out. Bob and Joe were anything but experts. I went out after the massage. I jogged around two laps and it went again. I could see it getting bigger and bigger and I could feel my whole thigh getting tighter. It was a bad pull, and it was never given the time to properly recover that year with a constant rush to get me back on the field for both our league and UEFA Cup campaigns.

You see, it was one thing to play in the First Division and another to play at Liverpool. When you played at Liverpool, you were in European competition every year. You were playing Saturday, Wednesday, Saturday, Wednesday; it was a real slog. There was no time off. Plus there was all the travel and there was no rotation. They won the championship one year and only used fourteen players. If Shanks couldn't rely on you, then you began to drift from his thoughts. All the players from that time will have a story about how Shanks ignored them if they had an injury. You'd be blanked, like you didn't exist. I'm not sure why he did it. It certainly made everyone terrified of being unfit, and maybe that was the point. Maybe it was just his way of managing his expectations. He didn't want to be wondering whether you could play or not and then be let down. Maybe it was just easier for him to forget about you, and if that meant the players did everything possible to make sure that didn't happen, then so much the better.

Wales were playing Poland during the time I had this injury, and I think the staff at Liverpool suspected that I was maybe easing off, trying not to play for the club beforehand so that I could play for my country. However, it was genuinely another spell when I couldn't figure out what was going on with my leg. I went into the medical room with my problem and Joe Fagan put me on the treatment table, with the electrodes from this machine sending pulses through the muscle of my thigh, and he said he's just going up to see Peter Robinson, the club secretary, for a few moments.

Now, with these machines, once it's on you, it's on you. You're strapped in, and I had to sit there until Joe returned. So, Joe went out the door, and I'm on the table listening when I hear Shanks outside shouting, 'I'll tell you what, Joe. He'll play for us before he plays for Wales! If he's not fit for us, then he's not going.' Ten minutes later, Joe came back in and I have to tell him I'm not happy about this conversation with Shankly I've just overheard. 'Shanks?' he says, 'I've not seen him.' Now, whether that trick worked or it didn't, or whether you think it was clever or not of Bill Shankly as a way of getting a message to me, you can decide for yourself, but that's what he was about.

Kevin tells a story about a mystery knee problem he once picked up and how Bob and Joe set about sorting it out. They started to interrogate him about all sorts of things. Did he live in an attic with a lot of stairs? Was he walking up hills? Was he going horse-riding? They even asked him if he had been skiing! In Liverpool? Then the Boot Room boys suddenly decided it was Kevin's new car, a green Capri. They went out and virtually stripped the lot down to nuts and bolts, lifting the carpets, testing the stiffness of the pedals. They almost took it completely to bits before deciding that it was one of the pedals that was too stiff. They told him to leave the car for a few days and catch the bus instead. I don't know if it made a difference but the injury went away as quickly as it had appeared.

Shanks would be on at Bob and Joe if anyone had recurring problems. The two of them kept detailed notes on injuries in the famous Anfield Boot Room where all the decisions were made. In there, they had warm-up routines, training sessions and a complete log of all the injuries they'd come across so that they would know how best to work with each one. It was part of the recipe. It was coaching at a level beyond what was going on elsewhere at the time. Ian St John went to see Shanks once saying that he wanted to go on a coaching course and Shanks tried to put him off.

'Oh, no, son! What do you want to go to one of those things for?'

Eventually, he could see that he wouldn't be able to change his player's mind, so reluctantly he gave him his blessing with the words, 'Alright, Ian, but don't tell them anything about what we do here.'

When you were coming back from an injury, you'd always be subjected to one of the Boot Room's infamous weekly five-a-side games. Shanks was in goal, Bob Paisley, Reuben Bennett and Ronnie Moran played in the middle and Roy Evans was up front. They'd play against the apprentices at the club, but if you were coming back from injury you'd get roped in to play with the coaches so that they could have a look at you. They weren't games you wanted to be involved in and they were as meanly contested a fixture as you'll ever see. They'd go on and on until Shanks decided that the Boot Room team were winning. So, you can see why I was as keen as they were to make sure I was back playing regularly with the first team again, but I couldn't seem to shake off this problem with my thigh in that 72/73 year. Between Bill, Bob and Joe, I don't think anyone was too pleased to see me around that time. It was a pity because it was a big year for Liverpool, as the team won its first major honours since 1966. I played 22 of the league games that year, which was enough for me to pick up a league winner's medal, but I'd not been involved in the final months of the run-in at all. I watched frustrated from the stands as Liverpool sealed the title with a goalless draw at home to Leicester. It was something of a hollow victory for me even though I finished as Liverpool's joint top scorer alongside Keegan with thirteen league goals, which was as many as I scored the season before from 29 appearances.

I'd been getting trouble from my Achilles tendon as a result of my body trying to cope with my ongoing thigh injury. I was in and out of the team, scoring plenty when I was fit, but it was a frustrating time; two steps forward and one step back. We'd been going well in the UEFA Cup, though, and I played throughout the competition up until the semi-final stage where we were drawn against the holders, Tottenham. We played Spurs six times that season – twice in the league, twice in the League Cup, including a replay, and over a two-legged UEFA semi too – and these were games I very much looked forward to. I always had a little extra incentive to do well against the north Londoners, of course. What's more, my old Wales colleague Mike England played there at centre-back, although there was no camaraderie when we faced each other on the field.

I had to miss those April 1973 UEFA Cup semis through injury. We went through 2–2 on away goals thanks to a second-half strike from Steve Heighway at White Hart Lane and I was desperate not to miss the final as I had the league run-in. I'd played in all the other previous rounds against Eintracht Frankfurt, AEK Athens, Dynamo Berlin and Dynamo Dresden. I'd been to Greece and had my passport stamped in Germany more times than I care to remember. I'd scored four European goals and set up plenty more and I was determined not to miss out on this trophy too now that this Liverpool team had finally found its feet.

There were twelve days to get fit between that league-winning draw with Leicester and the two-legged final against Borussia Mönchengladbach – who were one of the top German sides of that day – but I'd played no football for six weeks and there were no reserve games left to get me match-fit, even though I was in no pain by that stage. I could tell Shanks wanted me to play against a team which featured the likes of Herbert Wimmer, Dietmar Danner, Günter Netzer, Berti Vogts and Jupp Heynckes – a team that made it to five European finals in that era. But I wasn't so sure that Bob and Joe were on my side.

When it came to the day of the home fixture, I was left out in favour of a more defensive line-up, with Keegan and Heighway as the only two forwards. The Germans had indicated in the build-up that they were going to attack, which turned out not to be the case, and they'd kidded us into a choosing an XI that they could contain without too much bother, with Netzer as a sweeper instead of his usual place at the heart of midfield. Then the heavens opened so spectacularly on Merseyside that the game was called off after 27 minutes. The pitch became a bog. The ball barely moved a yard when it was kicked and the referee decided that the match had to be replayed the following night.

The next morning, I plucked up the courage and went in to see Shanks. I told him he'd been tricked by the Germans and asked him, 'Who picks the team around here, you or Fagan and Paisley?' He didn't much like that and he blew his top. I told him I was very, very disappointed and, by the time I got home, I was convinced that that would be the end of my days at Liverpool. But the phone rang and it was Bill.

'Hello, son. Are you not in your bed yet?' he asked. It was an evening game and players were supposed to be resting during the day.

'No, boss, I've only just got home,' I replied.

'Well, get to your bed. There is a good chance you will be playing tonight.' He now knew he had at least one footballer ready to give everything.

He was true to his word and, that evening in the dressing room, I replaced a shocked Brian Hall, and I justified the change. A German backline lacking height and not expecting the switch were no match for me in the air and, although I didn't score myself, our first two goals came from my knock-downs to Kevin and the last was direct from a corner which I'd won. Three-up and we were in the best of positions for the away leg in Germany, which we fought hard to lose by just two goals from Heynckes. Gladbach were irresistible in the first 45 minutes, playing the kind of football that would see their side win the same competition in 1975 and 1979, but we rallied, finished the stronger team and became the first English side to win both the league and a European trophy in the same season.

I could feel my Achilles tendon throbbing against my sock as I stood on the pitch after the final whistle along with Shanks, the rest of the team and hundreds of ecstatic Liverpool supporters. The manager came up and, putting his arm around me, said, 'Well done, son. Christ, well done.' It was unusual behaviour from him. You'd normally find him somewhere quiet at those moments. I don't think it was about our selection row. I think he could see the pain I was in and he knew that I'd given it my all in the face of it, in both in this match and the previous one. I think he accepted me after that, and my doubts disappeared. Someone asked Shanks about the change, Toshack for Hall, in the press conference after that first leg and he said he'd seen a weakness in the German defence – but if I hadn't gone into his office that day, I'm sure he wouldn't have played me.

Come pre-season of 1973/74, my Achilles had calmed down but the original issue with my left thigh was causing me trouble once more. The extra strain with Wales's 1974 World Cup qualifying campaign meant I was in and out of the Liverpool side like a yo-yo, and things finally came to a head in the early months of 1974 when I was sent off to see the club specialist, a surgeon by the name of Mr Lyall Thomson. He examined me, told me to stay off the pitch for two weeks, to do any fitness training I had to do in the swimming pool where the muscle wouldn't have to take any impact, and that I should then see a big improvement. But when I got back to Liverpool, Bob told me I'd be playing with the reserves a few days later. He said he'd spoken to Mr Thomson and that he thought it would be a good idea, in light of them trying to get me fit for the FA Cup tie the following weekend with Ipswich. That seemed fair enough until I happened to see Mr Thomson the next day when I'd given Emlyn Hughes a lift over to the hospital to see him about his knee. The doctor asked me how I was getting on down at the pool and whether

I was getting enough rest, and suddenly it became clear that getting me in the reserves had been a plan hatched by the staff at Anfield and nothing to do with medical advice. I was furious. I handed in a transfer request which Shanks duly ripped up. I didn't play against Ipswich, or for the next three weeks, but found myself back in the team with the only goal in our 1–0 away win against Bristol City in the following round as Liverpool made its way to the FA Cup Final. I was hardly speaking to Bob any more but I was playing well, so there was little we needed to talk about.

We were second in the league but Leeds ran away with it in the end. We had a good run but there were too many draws in the last crucial months for us to mount a serious challenge. I was in and out of the team all season with just nineteen league appearances and five goals to show for it. We only had a short run in the European Cup too. We beat Jeunesse Esch from Luxembourg by two goals in the first round after an embarrassing draw at their stadium, and then we faced a fantastic Red Star Belgrade team which defeated us 2–1 in both legs, including Liverpool's first loss at Anfield in Europe since Ferencváros managed it in the Fairs Cup of 1967. As a matter of fact, that Red Star victory is the only time Liverpool lost at home in the European Cup at any time in the twentieth century. The Yugoslavs were known to be very technical but that side had ability in every position. They played the ball out to feet from every corner of the pitch, with the man in the No. 3 shirt that day, Vladislav Bogićević, running the show from a deep-lying playmaker position. He was cool and casual as he drifted round. He had a terrific left foot and he knocked audacious little first-time chips over a line of players to his teammates' feet just as easily as he would a simple sideways pass. He was one of the best players I'd seen; always made it look like he had enough time and space to do whatever he wanted. We spent a lot of that tie chasing the ball about. It was such a profound defeat that it caused a major inquest in the Boot Room into how a new Liverpool needed to learn to play both domestically and on the Continent. This was Bill Shankly's last European game in charge, though, and it was only under Bob Paisley that these ideas came to fruition. Red Star themselves went out to the Atlético Madrid team who only lost the final that year to Bayern Munich in a replay, but it didn't matter. The point had been made.

Instead, it was the FA Cup of 1974 where Liverpool succeeded in what was to be Shanks's last big win. We'd nearly gone out to Doncaster Rovers in the third round after the Yorkshire side, who were eighty league places below Liverpool down in the Fourth Division, pulled off a surprising 2–2 draw at Anfield. We needed a replay at Belle Vue to get by them, just as we did with Carlisle after they managed a similar feat, earning a goalless draw on our patch. I wasn't involved in the first tie but my goal in our 2–0 victory in an icy January game up at Brunton Park certainly helped matters, even if I couldn't manage a contribution for the home game. The boys then made it past Bobby Robson's Ipswich Town while I was out injured thanks to Brian Hall and Kevin Keegan, but it was one from me that saw us through the quarters as we beat Bristol City 1–0 at Ashton Gate after Kevin broke through on the left and found me from deep with the outside of his right foot.

Our semi-final against Leicester City was a tougher encounter than the final itself. We played Leicester at Old Trafford and we absolutely battered them; played them off the park, but we just couldn't get the goal and it finished 0–0. Peter Shilton played between the sticks, with Leicester all in white that day, and he was fantastic. That was Saturday afternoon; Sunday off. We came into work on Monday with our heads down, knowing that we'd got to play again on Wednesday: the replay at Villa Park.

After something like that, you come in on Monday and it's in the back of your mind that you've missed the boat, and that Leicester must be thinking that they can't play as bad as that again, that we've let them off the hook. So, we were all a bit apprehensive of Shanks when he called us into the dressing room.

'Well, boys,' he said, 'the rules say that we've got to go back to Villa Park on Wednesday and play against Leicester City again. Bob, have you seen that George Foreman? Have you seen him, Bob?'

Bob nodded. 'Have you seen the size of his arms, boys?'

We were all looking at each other without a clue of what Shanks was on about.

'Have you seen him?' he continued. 'I'm telling you, boys, have you seen George? His arms, I'm telling you, they're like that,' and he motioned like he was trying to put his hands around the trunk of a tree.

'Now, you imagine you're fighting George Foreman. Ding – Round One. George comes out, gets you against the ropes and it's bang, bang, bang. Down you go. Seconds out – end of Round One. You stagger back to your corner. You're sitting down. Have you seen him, Bob? Have you seen George Foreman? Have you seen his arms?'

'Aye, aye. I have, boss,' replied Bob. 'He's a big boy.'

'Seconds out – Round Two. George comes steaming into you. Bang, down you go; seven, eight, up you get. George is standing over you there. Now, you imagine, boys, that this goes on for three rounds and then the lights go out and somebody says you've got to come back on Wednesday and fight George all over again! Well, that's how Leicester City are feeling right now.'

All of a sudden we couldn't wait until Wednesday when we could give Leicester more of the same. Shanks had probably been thinking all day Sunday about how he was going to turn it around for us and it worked. Shilton had to watch as three went by him that day from Hall, Keegan and myself; 3–1.

The FA Cup final against Newcastle at Wembley was a one-sided affair, despite plenty of crowing in the papers beforehand by their prolific No. 9, Malcolm Macdonald, who'd picked up two goals in their semi against Burnley. We beat the Magpies 3–0, with the BBC's David Coleman commentating that Newcastle's defence had been 'stripped naked by Liverpool'. It was a good win. In the build-up, though, I could feel my thigh playing up as the match drew near. I made it through the game but spent ten days in hospital from the Monday on a course of cortisone injections to manage the pain. Any professional athlete knows the importance of sacrifice in achieving their goals, and to lie there along with my FA Cup winner's medal made it all worthwhile. Shanks came into the hospital to see me. I never should have played that game and I think he knew it. I was lucky to get away with it because the morning before the final, I felt something go but I didn't want to tell anybody. I was frightened to death. How the hell I got through that ninety minutes, I'll never know. My muscle was out and I think Shanks started to realise that they'd been pushing me too hard, and I think he felt a little bit of guilt.

That 1974 FA Cup win marked Bill Shankly's last competitive game in charge. His final act as a manager was to sign Ray Kennedy from Arsenal, a man who was supposed to replace me up front, but it's unclear how much of it was his doing, given that it happened on the same day as he resigned. We were all devastated. Even speaking about it with him subsequently, I'm not sure he ever really told me the true reasons behind his decision.

3
Bob's Liverpool

THE YEAR 1974 WAS A BIG ONE FOR ME. IT HAD EVERYTHING. IN THE summer, it was the best of times as I picked up my FA Cup winner's medal at Wembley with Liverpool for the first time in my career, which is the dream of every young boy. We had narrowly missed out to Arsenal at the end of my first season at Anfield in 1971 after Charlie George's famous goal. So, this was something special. It also marked the end of Shanks's time in charge of the team. It was a shock to us all when he announced his retirement at the beginning of the following pre-season. It was also a worry to me as one of his favourites, particularly as I knew I didn't have Bob Paisley's full confidence.

Nobody seems to be that clear on why Shanks chose to call it a day. For a man that was so vocal about what he felt, he kept his cards close to his chest on this one. There wasn't an awful lot said at that 12 July 1974 press conference. What I remember most is seeing that boy in black-and-white on the TV when the news people stopped him on the streets and asked him if he'd heard that Shankly had retired.

'Bill Shankly?' came his stunned reply. 'Mr Bill Shankly? You're having me on…'

Shanks later wrote how tired he'd been after that cup final in 1974. He'd sat down exhausted in the dressing room while he left the players and the fans enjoying the moment on the pitch and in the stands at Wembley. All he'd wanted was a cup of tea, and he feared somewhere inside that he didn't have the energy for the job any more. He'd been in charge of the club for fifteen years and devoted virtually his every waking moment to Liverpool. It had been a Second Division team when he'd taken over in 1959 and he'd brought the club up, turned Melwood into a proper training ground, formed a backroom team that would go on to guide the club to glory for more than another decade after he'd gone. He'd built two great teams who together had won three league titles, two FA Cups and a UEFA Cup as well. Like Bob said, he was a boxer at heart and he wanted to go out as a champion rather than ingloriously fade away.

Shanks couldn't get away from the game, though. It was his life. It was who he was, and by the time the season started again, he'd turn up at training down at Melwood quite a bit and it got up Bob's nose. It wasn't doing him any favours. How was Bob supposed to feel like he was in charge with Shanks there all the time? It wasn't fair on him. Bob hadn't wanted the job to begin with. He'd gone round to see Shanks over the summer and tried unsuccessfully to persuade him to change his mind. I don't think he wanted the kind of attention that Shanks created for himself as boss. He knew he didn't have the kind of personality to do things that way and maybe he thought that you had to have that to be a football manager. He was always comfortable letting Shanks have the limelight if he could be an important voice in coaching and managing the team in the background. Without Shanks, he didn't have that protection and he was forced to find his own way. Bob was a big horse-racing man and he described his first few months in charge a bit like a horse going round the ralls not really sure of what it was doing.

For me, the change in management meant an added problem. Bob had never warmed to me. It was nothing personal. You get your favourites and I knew I wasn't one of Bob's. I was a Shanks boy and maybe part of a style of play that Bob didn't prefer. That might have been OK but it was all compounded by the injury to my left thigh, which meant he knew that there'd be spells where I wouldn't be able to play. Even before he called me into his office, not long after he'd taken over, I knew I had a lot to do to win Bob over.

Bob explained that he hadn't wanted the job, that he had no axe to grind, but that – as the new marquee signing – Ray Kennedy would be his first choice to partner Keegan. As it turned out, Kevin picked up a six-week ban along with Billy Bremner in the Charity Shield in August 1974. The two came to blows at Wembley in what was the first game in charge for both Bob Paisley and for Brian Clough in his ill-fated spell at Leeds. Johnny Giles had already been booked for punching Kevin and it didn't take much for Bremner to push him over the edge. It was the first time the Charity Shield had been televised and not the best advert for the game, so the FA came down hard on the players, meaning Liverpool were without one of its best strikers for the first eleven games of the new season.

That might have been my opportunity to prove Bob wrong but I came down with a mystery virus which made my ankle and knee swell up, and I was unable to walk for three days while it passed. Instead, Ray Kennedy struck up a partnership with Phil Boersma and, for a while, I was out of the picture with the two destroying defences the land over, with eight wins out of those eleven games, including Liverpool's biggest ever in their Cup Winners' Cup home leg against Norwegian team Strømsgodset IF. Fittingly, Liverpool put eleven past them with no reply. Of the ten outfield players, it was only Brian Hall who didn't score.

I didn't get a look-in over the next two months and, with Liverpool already out of both the Cup Winners' Cup and the League Cup by the time I returned, I couldn't see many opportunities for myself as the fourth-choice striker. So, reluctantly, I went to see Bob and together we hammered out a way for me to leave Anfield.

I accepted a move to Leicester City, who offered £160,000 for my services. I discussed terms with the manager, Jimmy Bloomfield, in the boot room at Swansea after a game playing for Wales on 20 November 1974. We got the forms done before the Friday deadline that week, which meant I was clear to make my debut for the Foxes against Manchester City the following day – subject to a medical. In those days, they only examined your ankles and your knees, just your joints, but I told them to have a look at this thigh of mine. I told them because I knew that there was something not quite right with it. I'd had problems with it before and it wasn't going away. I'd had cortisone injections in it to enable me to play in all sorts of big European games. I was getting trouble with it every six to eight weeks. It had dragged me down.

I didn't have to draw their attention to it. Part of me said it because I've always been a pretty sincere bloke anyway. I've never tried to cheat anybody – if you feel there's something wrong with you in a situation like that, I think you're obliged to tell people – but part of me didn't want that transfer to happen either. I was a bit confused. I didn't know the extent of the injury, how much I could control it, and I thought that this was the opportunity for me to get it out in the open.

It was at Leicester's team hotel in Manchester on the morning of the game when the deal fell apart. I was that close to making the move; just hours from kick-off. Jimmy Bloomfield came into my room with his pyjamas still on and told me that something had come up in the medical. A few days later and the move was off.

They'd found a calcification of the muscle of my left thigh and it wasn't a risk that the club could take with the kind of money involved – as much as I was disappointed, part of me was a little bit relieved. So, back to Liverpool I went, not really knowing what was going to happen from there.

Mr Thomson, the specialist, put me through an extensive examination, X-rayed my leg once again and explained to Bob and to me that this calcification was not going to go away. If I didn't train too hard, I'd probably be able to play for another two years, but that was it. That's a very frightening thing to be told when you're 25. You've built your entire life around football. You have a family depending on you. We weren't earning huge amounts of money in those days, certainly not enough to retire on when you're finished, and football didn't have an afterlife of TV punditry like it does now. This was it. I was supposed to be enjoying my best days on the field and here I was in limbo with a club that didn't want me – and couldn't sell me either.

Sue and I had just had our third child, Craig, younger brother to Sally, who was two, and our eldest Cameron, who was nearly four. So, that was a very worrying period for me. If I had to catalogue the times over the years when I had doubts about myself, 1974 was when I had to dig deepest.

Like I said, though, the reality is that an injury, like all big life events, is not necessarily a negative. It's one of those events that you're only able to make sense of with the benefit of time. It's a disruptive force and it very much depends on the player as to how that affects them. I couldn't know it back then but it was undoubtedly the most significant event in my career. If it hadn't have happened, it's likely that I wouldn't have achieved what I have in management today.

It was fortunate that I still had twenty months of a contract left. If I'd only had six months there, God knows what would have happened to me, but I had that leeway and that time to prove that I could still be an important player for Liverpool.

I'd left for Leicester under a cloud with Bob Paisley. I wasn't 100 per cent happy with how I'd been treated, so I took things at my own pace – one step at a time – to see what I could do to heal the scar. I did specialised fitness training alone because there were regular training exercises that I just couldn't manage. I kept the short, sharp stuff going and worked on my finishing, but otherwise all the fitness was on my own down at the swimming pool. I used to get down there three times a week on top of the training at Melwood and exercise my legs in the water; plus I had to have plenty of ice on my thigh before and after games. It's not a lot of fun, especially when you're away from the squad or watching the rest of the boys just warming up as usual, but it was a sacrifice that I willingly made to be able to play on a Saturday, and I'd do it all again.

Things had to change on the pitch too. The minute I failed that medical at Leicester, I started thinking differently about football. I had to. I had to start thinking for myself; how could I get about the field and still be in the right place at the right time without breaking my neck to get there? I watched what was going on around me more in training. I thought more about what Bob was trying to get everyone to do, not just myself. I gradually got back on speaking terms with Bob and talked more and more to him about the matches – what had gone right and wrong, how the other team had tried to adapt – and I looked more closely at the other players playing with me and what they could do for me. It was when I first began thinking like a manager and not just like a player.

I hadn't thought about coaching since I'd been put off the idea as an eighteen-year-old at Cardiff City. Bobby Ferguson, one of the Cardiff City players, was running a course where you could earn your FA preliminary coaching badge over a course of twelve Thursday nights. He was already qualified. So, three of us from the squad used to go down to Llanrumney High School, sit in the gym hall once a week and learn what they thought you were supposed to know. There was myself, a player called Brian Harris, who was close to finishing his career at around 35 years of age, and big John Charles, who was hanging up his boots too. Even at eighteen, I knew that this was something I wanted. It was maybe not normally something an eighteen-year-old, just breaking into the game, would do, but I was like that.

At the end of the course, you had to sit two exams – one theory and one practical. There were probably about fifteen or sixteen of us in the room – some school teachers, some amateur players, there was a fair old mix. For the first part, you had to sit down and do a theory exam on the laws of the game and then you just had to do the practical – attack against defence, or defend in depth or attack in width – so you'd use the other people on the course with you to do it. It was quite funny to see these ordinary folk moving us professionals around a makeshift field.

I passed the practical exam and failed the laws of the game. They put tricky things in there, questions like 'If somebody shoots at goal, the ball rebounds off the post and hits a supporter who is not where he is supposed to be and goes in, is it a goal?' They were questions you would have to be a referee to answer. That was OK because you could go back and take the laws of the game exam again. So I did, and I got my preliminary badge. Big John failed the lot. I don't think he could even fill the form in to start off with. That left such a deep impression on me that it put me off coaching and coaching badges for life. Then when I went to Liverpool, none of them had a coaching badge there: Paisley, Shankly, Fagan – not one between them.

That John Charles, a master of the game, could be told he didn't know enough about football to pass some practical was a joke. The greatest player I'd ever seen, the greatest player Wales had ever produced, and he wasn't going to be allowed to coach because he hadn't passed this? Well, if that's the way it is then coaching was not something I wanted a part of. It scarred me for life and I've always felt that somebody who's been there and done that – who's played at Liverpool and then at Bayern Munich in midweek and then Old Trafford at the weekend – must have a better idea about what's needed in management than someone who's never played at that level but happens to know all the ins and outs of those exam questions. Shanks used to say, 'Coaching is done by people who never could play the game, to help people who never will be able to.'

That FA preliminary badge is the only badge I ever got. It was only when I sustained my injury up at Liverpool that I came back to the idea of coaching and paid more attention to the possibilities of a future career. Back on the field, I learned that if I concentrated and I watched what was going on, and I read the game, I could still be in place to score the goals and make my assists. You see a lot of people making last-ditch efforts to arrive on time, but you can be a lot more economical than that if you have to. Bob Paisley helped me a lot in this aspect. Bob was a great thinker. He didn't always explain things particularly well but you got to learn what he meant and, with his help, I learned to move my way around the field. Sometimes you've got to kid the opposition a little bit. You let them think they're getting the better of you, or let them think they've got you under control, and then you strike, and you move them round at the right time. It's not something you see an awful lot of these days, unselfish movement. Most of the movement you see from a player is to receive the ball and score the goal themselves. There's less thought about taking players out of position so that others can go into the space that the first player has created.

I changed my game enough that I was able to work my way around the field and still stay on the pitch for ninety minutes despite the physical problem that I had. There was no point in me chasing lost causes on a football field. It might have looked at times like I was lazy, but I couldn't see the point in racing after them if it meant I was no good to the team for the next two games. What I also realised is that I was playing with very good players, and that started me thinking in a managerial kind of way about other aspects of the game. I began working out everyone else's game a lot more instead of just managing mine.

I was like the policeman in a road directing the traffic around me; you go there, you cross there. I was able to do that as a centre-forward. I never had to rely on pace, so my game was never about forty-yard sprints, and quick bursts over shorter distances were still well within me. We all know our teammates and what they're good at, and maybe what they're not so good at, but I studied them in detail until I understood what they were going to do on the pitch before they did. I knew, in a bit of a selfish way, perhaps, that I had to use them to help get the best out of me. I remember thinking, 'Listen, John, if you can't play with Kevin Keegan and Heighway, even on one leg, then there's something wrong with you.'

The fact that my injury was now out in the open at Liverpool also made it a lot easier. They knew then that I wasn't kidding or swinging the lead – there was a real problem there. Now we all knew what to do about it. Until then, we'd been running blind. Instead of thinking, 'Toshack is inconsistent – he only plays well for a month and then drops off,' suddenly the real reason was out and I think there was an intake of breath at Liverpool and they realised that they'd made a mistake, and that they were partly to blame. I think it would have been harsh to think it, but maybe they felt they owed me a bit.

So 1974 proved to be a very difficult but also a very important year for me. There's definitely a before and after that Leicester transfer business as far as my career goes. It's probably my most pivotal moment. It changed me as a player and set me on a path to management. Later on, it enabled me to spot injuries. When you're a manager you have your own players to look after, and what Bob did with me, and my own experience that I had, enabled me to understand what a player could do and what he couldn't do within an injury; how much he could give you. There's no better way of finding things out, or knowing how to cope with a managerial situation, than through your own experiences. When I speak with physios and doctors, I know what I'm talking about. If you've been a player, you tend to have picked up these injuries yourself – you know how best to recover. You've got to have an advantage over somebody who's never experienced these things.

What I have to admit, though, is that there are people who have been successful without having had much of a playing career, and good luck to them, but if I was a chairman or president of a football club, and if I had my money in it, and had a choice to make on which manager to hire next, I'd definitely have that question of playing experience at the front of my mind. That doesn't mean that everyone who has played the game is going to be a good manager. A lot of them haven't got a clue. They've played the game, they've done it, but they're not intelligent enough to put that into practice or maybe they never had to think too much for themselves on the field. If you've been through it all yourself, you are aware of exactly what you can and can't push your players to do. I don't think the player has ever gone out of me. I think I learned to give a struggling player the benefit of the doubt. In that way, I've been very different to Bill Shankly. There are players who will try to pull the wool over your eyes a bit but you have to accept that that's going to happen from time to time.

It was hard to come back to the dressing room at Liverpool after I'd had one foot out the door, feeling persona non grata, but the Anfield squad were really supportive of me and there were even letters from fans, which made a big difference. You'd be surprised what that can do for a player's morale, especially when they're having to train separately at the pool for most of the week.

By December 1974, Kevin was back from his suspension, but he and Kennedy weren't hitting it off up front and the team had gone six without a win, plus the two losses that had dumped Liverpool out of Europe and the League Cup – defeats to Ferencváros on away goals and a 1–0 loss to Middlesbrough at Anfield. This was Bob's first season in charge and Liverpool hadn't failed to qualify for Europe for the last eleven consecutive seasons. The side had been underperforming and you could sense that he needed some results, so I could see a way of working myself back in. I asked to play with the reserves to show what I could do, and scored twice in a 3–0 win at Bury, and then another two in a four-goal win against Manchester United. I knew my career and my livelihood were on the line and it pushed me on until I finally got my chance against Luton at Anfield in the First Division on 14 December. I'll never forget the reception I got from the Kop that day. It'd been four months since I'd walked out in front of them, and the sound was incredible. A big cheer went up to see me back. Sometimes you forget what you're working for when you're spending that time alone coming back from a bad injury. One moment like that and it all comes flooding back. You remember why you put yourself through it. I was lucky enough to repay that welcome with a goal as we came out 2–0 winners and the dream team of Toshack, Keegan and Heighway were back all the way up until the end of the season.

By the last game of the campaign, we'd made it into the UEFA Cup and I finished Liverpool's top scorer with 12 in the 21 league games I'd played. We'd just missed out to Dave Mackay's Derby for the title by a single result. We needed a win in the penultimate game against Middlesbrough away to be in with a chance. I had an international on the Wednesday before and Bob had made it clear to me that if I played for Wales against Hungary, he wouldn't pick me for the Saturday game. Of course, I wanted to play both. I didn't want to let either my club or my country down and I hoped that Bob might change his mind. He didn't. I scored in that game in the old Népstadion in Budapest, which helped Wales qualify for the 1976 European Championship playoffs, but I couldn't do much as Liverpool lost at Ayresome Park to a single Alan Foggon goal. It seemed stubborn of Bob at the time but, again, now that I've been on the other side of things, I know that you have to stick to your guns.

It was the following year, the 75/76 season, that was my best ever in a Liverpool shirt. I scored 23 goals in 49 matches, including three hat-tricks, as Liverpool completed another league and UEFA Cup double. I was desperate to win the league, as I hadn't felt I'd deserved that medal from 1973. There was a real battle on between us and Dave Sexton's QPR, who had a team including Stan Bowles, Phil Parkes, Gerry Francis and Frank McLintock. They'd beaten us at Loftus Road at the beginning of the season 2–0 and gone ten games unbeaten. By the halfway mark in December, they were leading the table and averaging more than two goals per game, comfortably more than anyone else in the division, but we were just behind them and on the same points. It had been a tricky start for Liverpool with only three wins from the first seven, but we'd clicked into the right gear by the end of September 1975 and lost only once in the league for the next five months.

There was a sticky moment in the winter of that year when there was something of an injury crisis. Midfielder Peter Cormack was ruled out for the season after his knee gave way in a game against Manchester City in December. He had been told his cartilage was badly cracked and he knew one day it'd go and leave him sidelined for a while. This was that day and while he was recovering from the injury, in a moment you'd have to credit more to genius than a lucky guess, Bob got Ray Kennedy to fill in at left-midfield and it worked a dream. It sounds tough, but Cormack never played for the club again. That's just the way things were at Liverpool; the way they are at any top club.

Kennedy had never quite worked as a striker on Merseyside. When I played with Kevin, we kept it moving and flowing. Ray was more of a 'get hold of it, stop and think about it' kind of player, which wasn't the same. He had very good vision though, predicted the movement of the game very well and so his positioning was very clever too. He could hang on to the ball. He could find the forwards with little passes and on top of all that he knew how to appear at the edge of the box for that strong striker's left foot of his that he always had. He could play anywhere across the midfield, really, but he made that left-sided position his own from then on. It was a masterstroke from Bob and maybe the final piece for Paisley in turning Shanks's second team into a creation of his own, playing the kind of football that he wanted, and that would win Liverpool all that silverware in the years to come.

We only lost two more times that season, hitting plenty of big scores including 4-0 victories against Tottenham and West Ham, a 5-3 against Stoke and a huge 3-0 away win at Manchester City which set us up for a showdown at Molineux for our final game. Sexton's QPR had been just in front for most of the way with a run of results every bit as good as ours, including an incredible twelve wins out of thirteen to finish the season off. They'd slipped up with their last away game of the season at Carrow Road, though, losing 3-2 to a newly promoted and hungry Norwich City, who were one of only two teams to have got a win at Anfield in all competitions all season.

QPR had already finished their run of games, as could happen in years gone by. Sexton had to sit and look on with 59 points to our 58 and hope we didn't get the win we needed to be sure of taking the title. The stadium was packed that May 1976 day, not only with expectant Liverpool fans but the Wolves fans who needed their team to take the points too if they were to avoid relegation. There must have been ten or fifteen thousand who'd made their way down the M6 to stand in the away end. It was like the whole Kop had been transplanted and squeezed in as best they could. It had to be seen to be believed. As one of the Molineux faithful later noted, the South Bank of the stadium was overflowing with Scousers, who seemed to be all over the structure as well as on the terraces, while the Wolves fans were squeezed in shoulder to shoulder at the other end. Phil Thompson had opened a stadium door to the outside for more fans to sneak in during Bob's team talk and they were up on the roof, on the floodlights and all sorts.

We went a goal down within the first fifteen minutes, and Wolves hung on all the way to the 77th, before Tommy Smith knocked one into the box for me to flick on to Kevin. I had my back to goal and I could see my strike partner making the run long before the ball had reached me. We both knew where it was going and the back of the net was the answer when Kevin tucked it home from five yards at the far post. Then I got one of my own when Kennedy gave me the ball. I controlled it, turned and put it through the keeper's legs. A lot of people used that one to describe how I was more than just an aerial threat. It was a good goal but, in truth, not a great finish. I always think it was fortunate because, normally, it's very difficult to put a ball through the goalkeeper's legs. Nobody really tries to do it on purpose, but you do see it quite often these days because of the way goalkeepers now come out and leave their legs open. All the same, it was still a good one for me, receiving it with my back to goal like that. It was well struck but maybe not well placed.

Ray Kennedy finally put the game well out of reach for Wolves, turning his man and chipping one into the roof of the net from a tight angle in the last minute to properly seal the title for Liverpool. The packed terrace behind the goal didn't even wait for the whistle. They spilled out onto the pitch, swarming all around us the moment our third went in. It was a fantastic feeling but I knew where I wanted to be. I pushed my way straight to the offices of the stadium and got on the phone to my parents and to my wife, Sue. I think it was my proudest moment as a player. All the way back to Liverpool, the motorway was a procession of red and white, beeping horns, fans waving to us out of their car windows while we were alongside them in the coach. It was a very special thing but the icing on the cake that year was the UEFA Cup and our semi-final match-up with the Barcelona of the Cruyff and Neeskens era. I've seen a few of that team since – Marcial, Migueli and Pere Valenti Mora, who was the goalkeeper.

With their Dutch stars, Barça were a big club – as big as it got. Heading over there and walking out onto the field at the Camp Nou ... it was without a doubt the finest stadium I'd ever played in. All in white, we played the Catalans off the park that evening and we were well practised in Europe by that stage. That defeat to Red Star Belgrade in 1973 had born a new style of play which had won us the league under Bob and had seen us cruise past the rest of the competition in the rounds leading up to this in the UEFA Cup. Bob had moved Phil Thompson and Emlyn Hughes into defence. They were midfield players who dropped into centre-half, so we got more control and we played out a lot more from the back than we had done with Tommy Smith and Larry Lloyd in those positions as we'd played for years before. Tommy went to right-back for a spell until Phil Neal was signed but it was the end of the line for Lloyd.

Thompson and Hughes gave Liverpool a completely different dimension defensively. When they picked up the ball, we passed our way through midfield and into attack in a completely different manner to the way the Shankly Liverpool sides had. That was an innovation from Bob Paisley. Liverpool used it at home and in Europe. Eventually, after Thompson and Hughes came Lawrenson and Hansen – Lawrenson was a midfielder originally when he was signed by Liverpool and he went into a centre-back position with Alan Hansen, who was another footballing centre-half. Between those two pairs, they went for nearly fifteen years.

That Liverpool style of play was different to anything we'd done before. That came from Shanks and particularly Bob studying European opposition and seeing the way that they played, and it was Bob that introduced it. All the teams in England in those days had a big central defender and maybe someone playing alongside him, or just two big stopper centre-halves. Thompson and Hughes were both very intelligent players and a lot of attackers had difficulties getting the ball. They ran around so much when we had it that they didn't have too much strength left for themselves and, when they did make runs, Thompson and Hughes were very clever at pushing up and catching them offside – something that the classic centre-backs of previous years didn't do too much at all. I can remember when we beat Southampton in the Charity Shield match at Wembley in August 1976 – the year I got the only goal – Mick Channon spent most of the time running offside.

With that switch, Bob changed the whole way of playing. Everything was much more direct under Shanks. We got the ball and we got it forward. Under Bob it was about patience; passing the ball and waiting for our opportunities. To begin with, we strikers would make runs and then be surprised when the ball didn't come, but we got the idea. Bob's way was more sophisiticated and it made him successful in Europe. Bob was a lot more thoughtful. As a player, you don't always feel like playing but with Shanks giving the team talk, you were always ready to go no matter what. With Bob it was different. We had our own ambitions that drove us on. We knew what we were capable of and what we wanted to achieve and Bob had his own ways of getting us going which didn't rely on fire and brimstone. And there was always Ronnie Moran too. Ronnie was important for getting us motivated. He was always up and at you. There was no messing around with Ronnie. We were more than ready when we walked out for that first-leg semi-final at the Camp Nou on 30 March 1976.

We took our time that day, just as we'd learned. Thompson, Hughes and everybody else were good at snuffing out their attacks and our approach play was superb. It was all about keeping it tight and controlled, making sure not to lose our heads and the tie at the same time. Despite all we'd practised doing with the ball, though, in the end it was some route-one stuff that won the first leg: Ray Clemence on to Kevin, and then Kevin on to me to smash in. It was one of those moments as a player which gives you some perspective – you realise how far you've come and what you've achieved. The local fans weren't as impressed by our dominating the game and they jeered and whistled and rained their seat cushions down on their team to show their displeasure. It could have been worse. They could have lost by more. We were fantastic that day.

Barcelona gave it a good go in the return at Anfield in front of a packed house of more than 55,000 fans. It was a hard, battling kind of game, with neither team wanting to give too much away. Phil Thompson put us 2–0 up in the tie when he was there to finish after a Tommy Smith free-kick had bounced around the box off both Kevin and me. Two minutes later, though, and Barça winger Carlos Rexach had it in the net after Cruyff had finally managed to express himself with a run down the left and a cross to find his teammate, who silenced the Liverpool crowd. From then on, though, it was really only the Barcelona goalkeeper, Pedro Mora, who kept his team in it. It was a real contest between me and the Catalan defence in the air and Mora had to punch anything that came his way; in the end, that's the way the score stayed, 1–1 on the night with Liverpool through to a second UEFA Cup Final, where we'd be facing Club Brugge over two legs (a team we'd meet again in the final of the European Cup in 1978, a fixture that I was to play no part in).

The UEFA Cup was harder to win back then than the European Cup for the simple reason that only one team, the champions, went into the latter. But in the UEFA Cup, the second, third and fourth-placed teams from the top leagues all got a go, and very often the team that has won the league the previous year is not the best in their country anymore midway through the following campaign. And there was an extra round in the UEFA Cup and a two-legged final, so it was twelve games to get through instead of just nine.

I remember having a headache with the away-goals rule that year too. We seemed to scrape through each round after a brush with the dangers it can bring. We drew 0–0 in East Germany against Dynamo Dresden in the fourth round and it felt like it was a good result, especially when we were winning 2–0 at home. Dresden got one back to make it 2–1 and all of a sudden we were on the brink. It was a similar story with Hibs in the first round. We'd lost the first leg 1–0 away at Easter Road. I scored a hat-trick back at Anfield to make it 3–1 on the night, but at 3–2 on aggregate if they'd scored again, we'd have gone out. It plays tricks with your mind. You're on the pitch doing the sums in your head while you're trying to concentrate on the game. It was hard for the coaches too. You'd look over and you could see them scratching their heads. Sometimes, I think it's better just to tell everyone to forget about it while you're out there, but ultimately all these little things matter.

I was lucky enough to win two UEFA Cup medals in my time at Liverpool but in very different ways. For one final I'd been fancied by our manager, and in the other I hadn't. Both of them would end up getting it wrong. I had a very good season in 1975/76 and Bob knew the kind of damage I could do to European opposition. We'd seen it in the semi-finals and I'd scored five other goals in our UEFA Cup run that season, including that hat-trick at Anfield against Hibernian and plenty of assists throughout. Unfortunately, the Belgians were only too aware of my threat as well, and as soon as the whistle went for the first game at Anfield, the Brugge defence came straight up. Big Georges Leekens was playing for them and he brought them right out to the halfway line, which nullified my game. We came in for half-time 0–2 down. Bob said, 'John, off you go,' and Jimmy Case came on. Kennedy, Stevie, Kevin and now Jimmy would all attack the Belgians in exactly the opposite way. Out they went for the second half.

I was obviously not very happy. I got straight into the shower, got changed, went out into the car park and got into my car. Off I went. By the time I got to the Mons restaurant up by the crossroads in Walton that leads towards Anfield, I was listening to the radio and I heard: 'Liverpool attacking now; Keegan, Heighway; ball to Kennedy, goal! Two-one! Liverpool have pulled one back!'

I carried on driving. 'Sixty-one minutes gone; Heighway brings the ball; Neal, pass to Keegan, who turns, Kennedy, and Case! Two-two!'

I got to the next roundabout, turned all the way round and went back. I had just come through the gates at Anfield and it was, 'Sixty-fourth minute; Heighway; penalty! Keegan takes the kick and sends the keeper the wrong way! Liverpool have scored! Three goals in five minutes! Liverpool three, Brugge two!'

I got straight out the car, back into the ground and, when the players filed into the dresssing room, celebrating, there I was waiting for them in my shirt and tie like I'd never left. They all came in until Bob walked past me and stopped.

'I thought you might be on your way home by now, son,' he said.

'Actually, I was, but I had the radio on and I thought it'd be better if I came back,' I replied, and so he said with a smile: 'That's the best decision you made all night, son.' Talk about knowing your players.

Bob started me in the second game away from home when we drew 1–1 to win the trophy. Again, I came off after 65 minutes, this time for David Fairclough, but the only goals scored had been one for each side early on in the game, which was enough for Liverpool to lift that big vase.

The next season started well, with mine the only goal in Liverpool's win in the 1976 Charity Shield against Southampton, but looking back, with 68 games in the calendar, perhaps it was inevitable it should end in injury and frustration the way it did after so much time on the field in the twelve months before.

That 1976/77 season was arguably Liverpool's finest, which made it all the harder that I didn't get to play my part as I'd wanted. We had a run at the biggest treble there is, that of the league, the European Cup and the FA Cup. It was Manchester United that proved the fly in the ointment at Wembley after Liverpool took the First Division by a point from their neighbours Manchester City.

To begin with I was involved in things, despite yet another new signing to cause competition among the forwards. It was a club record fee of £200,000 that persuaded Bobby Robson and Ipswich Town to part with striker David Johnson. All the same, I was in from the start along with Kevin and it was all looking pretty rosy, one or two early defeats aside. I was doing well and scoring goals until our European Cup game against Belfast team Crusaders, when my old Achilles injury started flaring up. I had to take a break for four games while Liverpool beat Tottenham but lost to Newcastle. I was back in time for the Merseyside derby and scored as we brushed off Everton 3–1 in October, but that lay-off was something of a warning of what was to come. Just two weeks later I got a bad concussion in a win up at Filbert Street against Leicester City, who needed a win to go top. I scored the only goal of the game but took a hell of a thump, which got even worse the following month against QPR when I received another whack to my head. I'd never quite got over the first concussion and it had me in and out of the team. I felt a lot slower in everything I did and I'd pull up in training feeling dizzy and unwell, not able to continue. Eventually, I went to see a specialist, who had me take a few weeks out.

By the end of January 1977, I was back fit again and Liverpool were flying high at the top of the table and going well in the cups. I had a month of games with no losses and four goals in five before the first part of Liverpool's famous European Cup showdown with Saint-Étienne on 2 March.

Liverpool had played in European competition for a total of twelve season ever since the early Shankly days. Despite our two good wins in the UEFA Cup, though, it was the prize of the bigger competition that had evaded us. The closest the club had come had been in a semi-final appearance in 1965 when Roger Hunt, Ian St John and all of the first great Liverpool side had fallen to Helenio Herrera's Internazionale, playing their famous Catenaccio style on the way to winning their second European Cup in a row. With teams like this and the Puskás–Di Stéfano–Gento Real Madrid side, it was always going to be difficult in the 1960s, but now, with Bob's cannier style of play and the confidence of trophies behind us, we were ready to stop old foes Bayern Munich, another great team of the day, in their search for a fourth consecutive title.

Saint-Étienne from southern France had become a powerhouse in French football in the late 1960s, winning four league titles and two cups in the second half of the decade, and after a change of management in the early 70s they won two league and cup doubles on the trot in 1974 and 1975. They had to settle for just the league title the following year but had made it all the way to European Cup Final in 1976, where they lost 1–0 to that star-studded Bayern Munich who were considered the best in the world.

Saint-Étienne were famous for their giant Argentine centre-half, Osvaldo Piazza. The two of us had been trading little remarks in the press as the big men of our sides, but there was a respect between us. I played against a lot of tough centre-backs in those European games, and with Wales at international level. When you're up against the best players the others have got, that kind of tittle-tattle in the build-up is often the way it is. I took a bit of that into press conferences as a manager later in life.

It was always like that between me and Southampton defender John McGrath whenever we played them in the league. He was one of the hardest, toughest centre-backs I have ever come up against. He'd put his foot in and he'd kick. They were always difficult battles with him. I remember playing against him once, receiving the pass and, just as I'd controlled and turned to go away, he came sliding in and whacked me up in the air. The referee came straight over, blew for a free-kick, booked him and said to him, 'John, you were late there, son.'

'Sorry, ref,' said McGrath, 'I got there as quick as I could,' which, although I was on the deck struggling, I had a little chuckle about.

Just like McGrath and the others, I knew about Piazza. He was a real giant of a fellow. He was probably as tall as I was, but really solid, even broader. I never had any concerns about any defenders once I was settled at Liverpool, no matter how big or strong they were. Everybody could be beaten, just as I was capable of having a bad game, but I never worried about who I'd be facing.

Piazza was very, very strong in the air. He liked contact. It was one of those situations where I had to be a little bit unselfish in my work. I had to make him aware of me, but at the same time move him around so that Kevin and Stevie could exploit other things. I was never comfortable moving out to the flanks, but if my opposite number wasn't comfortable with it either, then that was OK. The other option was to bring my defender deeper into the field and underneath stuff so that our other forwards could go in behind us. Sometimes, they didn't come with me into those places, and then that was OK too, because I was happy to pick the ball up and go at them instead. We maybe didn't think about it at the time but when I look back, we must have been a really good side; very hard to stop. Things were very different tactically back then but the people at Liverpool were really ahead of their time. They signed players like pieces of a jigsaw puzzle. They knew exactly what they were looking for. The lot of them were experts at all aspects of the job: Geoff Twentyman who scouted us; Shanks who signed us; the way they trained us; how they never overburdened us with tactics. When I look at that Liverpool team and the thinking we were exposed to, it surprises me that more of us didn't make a big success in management. From my era, it was only really Kevin and me that made a success of it. Later, it was Souness and Dalglish who could best use what Bob and the Boot Room boys had showed them, but that's a small number considering all those players that worked for so long at Liverpool during those years.

I had a tough battle with Piazza in that first leg and he and his side did well enough to walk out 1–0 winners at the Stade Geoffrey-Guichard in France. He hobbled off towards the end, though, and was never fit in time for that famous second leg back at Anfield. Kevin levelled the tie early on from a corner when his cross drifted straight in, beating the Saint-Étienne keeper at his far post. It was then one hell of a game, with both teams having some very good chances, including a free header of mine that I really should have buried. Instead, it was their talented midfielder, Dominique Bathenay, who'd scored the only goal in France, that levelled it with a beauty from distance, one that swerved well clear of Ray Clemence. It was the noisiest night you could imagine inside the ground, but Bathenay silenced the Kop with that one.

I got to play my part a few moments later, though, when I took the ball down in the box, off my bad thigh as well, for Ray Kennedy to level it at 2–2 overall. However, Saint-Étienne would still go through on away goals unless we could do something about it. Enter supersub Davey Fairclough to write his name into the history books. He later said that when Kennedy sent him through on goal, all he said to himself was, 'Keep it down, keep it low and get it on target,' which is exactly what he did.

Davey and I were such very different types of player; polar opposites. I would take the brunt of the opposition's force for 65 minutes and then I'd go off, and they'd relax a bit with the change. But Fairclough was a completely different kettle of fish. One minute they're receiving balls with Toshack there, back to goal, having to get up for and win headers. All of a sudden it's somebody coming at them quick with the ball on the deck. I had to come off for him to come on, but he was the man to get us to the semis when he tucked it under the Saint-Étienne keeper with six minutes to go to make it 3–1 on the night and 3–2 in the tie, with Liverpool through to a semi-final with FC Zürich.

Unfortunately, my injuries had got the better of me once again just when this biggest of seasons was reaching its home straight. It was the recurrence of my old Achilles problem and there was no choice but to operate on it. I was out for the rest of the campaign and, with the lads coasting through the semis 6–1 on aggregate, it was a bitter disappointment to miss the European Cup final itself.

Bob was desperate to give me time to get fit for the showpiece against Borussia Mönchengladbach, given how effective I'd been against them in the UEFA Cup back in 1973, but I had to pull out from the squad and instead watched from the stands on a fabulous night in Rome as my good friend Emlyn Hughes lifted the trophy. I picked up a medal because I'd played enough of the games, but you get the feeling that somebody who hasn't played at all in the build-up, but plays in the final and wins, is more deserving of a medal than somebody who plays nine or ten games but misses the big one. A final is all about what happens on that day, nothing else. I wasn't going to do a Muhammad Ali and throw my medal into the Mersey, but ask any player who's missed a final and they'll tell you the same.

That Saint-Étienne quarter-final at Anfield also marked the last ever minutes of the Toshack–Keegan partnership, with Kevin heading off to Hamburg the following year. Together we'd been responsible for nearly two hundred Liverpool goals. Kevin had had another terrific year in 1976/77. He'd finished top scorer with twenty over the season, topping it off with a fantastic performance in Liverpool's first ever European Cup final. I'd tried to get fit for that game and for the FA Cup final four days earlier. I'd got myself back into the reserves, like before, and pushed through agony in the training sessions at Melwood just prior, but it was obvious to everyone that it would never be. Of the eight games in that FA Cup run, I'd only been fit for the two wins at home to Carlisle and Oldham in January and February 1977.

I spent until the following October recovering from the operation on my tendon that followed, with the surgeon Mr Thomson watching over me. Kenny Dalglish had been signed to replace Kevin and was already going great guns. I took him over to meet Shanks before the 1977/78 season began. Bill opened the door to us and when the two began talking I could barely understand a word they were saying to each other until Shanks rolled out one of his famous lines that a few of Liverpool's Scottish players had heard before. 'Kenny, here's some advice – don't overeat and don't lose your accent.' It might sound silly to some but I know what he meant. I've always made sure I've never lost mine.

I played alongside Kenny for a few games, but I never got going that year. It was a different kind of thing for me without Kevin. Kevin was so important to me. I had six years playing with him. Kenny was the opposite to him in many ways. Kevin was a lively type of player; his game was about movement. He never stopped running all the time; he was moving, running; here, there; dropping off; left, right. He was everywhere, dynamic. Kenny was 100 per cent brains. I don't say that in detriment to Kevin in any way at all. Kenny with his back to goal was one of the best players I've ever seen. He knew how to shield a ball and he'd turn and strike into the net from positions where you wouldn't think anything was on at all. They were completely different players and, of course, Rushy was different to me. The Dalglish/Rush combination turned out to be probably even more effective than Keegan and Toshack.

My last game in Liverpool red was a 1–1 draw against Bristol City at home in November 1977. I didn't score. While Kevin was at the club, even a bit-part Toshack was too important to lose, but it was another time of change at Anfield. The team and the style had moved on under Bob. They were playing a different type of football and I knew it was going to be very difficult for me to hang around and get in the side. It was the beginning of the third great team that Bill and Bob had produced, the team of Souness and Hansen, and the Rush and Dalglish partnership that scored even more goals than Kevin and me. When you look at Liverpool over the years, it's an amazing thing. Roger Hunt and Ian St John, Toshack and Keegan, Rush and Dalglish; you go from a situation where you think you're never going to replace these and it just gets better and better and better. That says a lot for the judgements of people at Liverpool.

I went to Bob's office to talk about finding me a move. Both Norwich and Newcastle had been enquiring about my availability and the boss didn't want to stand in my way if I wished to look elsewhere. I had no mind to sit around and wind up the remaining eighteen months of my contract at Liverpool but I didn't particularly want to go to those clubs either, no disrespect intended. I think I just wanted a real change and I had a feeling that the level of physicality of some of the football on the Continent might be kinder to my condition. I agreed a move with Anderlecht but, just as with Leicester City four years earlier, the results of my medical scuppered that too.

By the time the injury with my thigh muscle became too much of an issue for me, and for Liverpool, I might have only been 29, but I decided a different direction could be the answer. I was ready for a crack at being a manager myself. It was Fourth Division Swansea City that gave me the chance and, although I had to cope with something of a step down at the time, I don't think it turned out too badly.

4
Swansea, Oh, Swansea!!

WHAT HAPPENED AT SWANSEA WAS ROY OF THE ROVERS STUFF.

There were quite a few player-managers in the Football League in 1978, around the time my days at Liverpool were coming to an end, and for me it was the best of both worlds because, despite my thigh problem, I still felt I had more to give as a player.

The fact that Swansea were in the Fourth Division had its positives but it also had its negatives. The positives were that the squad looked up to me as a player, so as a novice manager I could get away with a little bit more and make some mistakes without them rounding on me. The negatives? The group were nowhere near as technically gifted as the players I'd trained and played with before, and so my patience had to improve.

Originally, I had harboured ambitions of returning to Cardiff City – in the Second Division at the time – before I went to Swansea. I had meetings with the chairman and vice-chairman, Bob Grogan and Tony Clemo, and they seemed keen on the idea of appointing me as a player/coach initially, especially given I was available on a free transfer.

Jimmy Andrews was the manager, though, and he voiced concerns about me not having any coaching qualifications, saying that good players don't necessarily go on to make good managers, which, even though true, left me feeling quite humiliated. I'd attended the meeting thinking I had something to offer, but I was treated like some work-experience kid and like they'd be doing me a favour. The reality might have been that Jimmy was frightened for his job – quite correctly, as it turned out, when he was sacked six months later. Having a player from a top club come along, especially a local lad, he might have felt that it was the first step towards getting rid of him.

Still, that's not the way I saw it. I was hurt. I'd offered myself for virtually nothing. I could still play. I'd had eight years at Liverpool. I was a Welsh international. Maybe they had their reasons, but I was very disappointed and there was a lot of resentment. The more I think about, I went to Swansea on the rebound. I knew I had something to offer and I knew Swansea were the arch-enemy. The rivalry didn't matter. It meant coming home to Wales. More than anything, though, it was a job opportunity and one to get into full management – not just a coaching position – while still being able to rely on some of my ability as a player, particularly as the Swans were right down in the Fourth Division.

It had been a tough few years for Swansea. The club had had to apply for re-election to the Football League after finishing 22nd out of 24 in 1975 – it was a vote they only narrowly won. John Charles stepped down as youth coach at the club during the summer but he'd left a legacy in the shape of Robbie James, Alan Curtis and Wyndham Evans – three young players who proved key to what happened during my time at the Vetch – who established themselves over the 1975/76 season, under manager Harry Griffiths, with Swansea finishing in eleventh place in the Fourth Division. The team managed a record haul of 92 goals in 76/77, while I was still at Liverpool, but couldn't snatch promotion even though they beat the team who finished in first place, Cambridge United, home and away that year.

Despite the slow and steady progression, Harry Griffiths, who himself was only 46 at the time, was of the opinion that the club needed a younger man in charge with more enthusiasm and the energy to take on all the aspects that the role demanded. Three men had already declined the position by the time the first half of the 1977/78 season was up: Chelsea's former manager Eddie McCreadie, Bill McGarry from Newcastle and Colin Addison, who had just performed the Great Escape with nearby Newport County when they avoided their own Football League re-election on the last day of the season. I hadn't been aware that Swansea had been looking for a new manager until I attended a sports exhibition a day or two after my meeting at Cardiff. I was approached by the chairman, Malcolm Struel, in what seemed like a chance encounter, though perhaps it had been something very much on his agenda. Either way, what appeared to be a casual talk turned into something more serious. I played my last game for Liverpool that Saturday in a reserves fixture at Old Trafford, and four days later I was in charge at the Vetch Field. The Monday before, I'd gone over to Rochdale to take a look at the team I was inheriting. I went with Emlyn Hughes, who'd been my roommate for the eight seasons I'd been at Liverpool. He wasn't everyone's cup of tea but I'd always got on well with him. We were close. His passing away after a long illness in 2004 was a big blow. He was godfather to my daughter, Sally.

It took us an age to find the ground which was only supposed to be a short hop. Rochdale were the 92nd team in the Football League at the time – right at the bottom of it all – and they took the points off Swansea with a 2–1 win that day. I'll never forget what Emlyn said to me as he laughed in the car all the way home. I can still see his face now. 'Toshy, what have you done? This morning, you were a player in the squad of the European champions at Liverpool, and now you're the manager of the team that's just been beaten by the worst side in the Football League. What have you done, Toshy? What have you done?'

There's a lot to be said for starting at the bottom as a manager. You're obviously not surrounded by so many people if you go into a Fourth Division club as you would be if you went in at the top. I think it gives you the opportunity to learn all aspects of the job, to virtually run the whole operation and get a good all-round knowledge of management. So, later on, when you are working with specialists from various areas at the top level, you know how best to work with them because you've done a bit of their jobs yourself. I got involved in all aspects of the club at Swansea – medical, financial; all aspects. It was a terrific grounding for me and something that's not really available even at lower levels these days. That's gone now. You have to go beyond the Football League.

I don't altogether agree with these players that finish at 34 or 35 years of age and go straight into the hot seat at a top-division club. I believe that you should start low and you should learn your trade, sit in a patched-up office and watch and sign your own players. It's not about some old-fashioned notion of earning your dues. It's about not trying to run before you can walk. There are too many managers that fall by the wayside because they're thrown in at the deep end. At smaller clubs, you get a hands-on experience of all the different facets of football because there often aren't those people or those structures in place to do it all for you. Plus, you get to do it all without so much of the pressure. That way, when you do climb the ladder, you know how to get the best out of everyone around you and you know a bit more about your own game.

I took over at Swansea on St David's Day, 1 March 1978. It was more like a village than a town back then and there seemed to be a buzz in the air at my appointment. Harry Griffiths had decided he'd done what he could with the team but he'd stayed on as my assistant to ease me into the role. It's a good time to begin at any club with about three months left of the season. There's enough time to get a feel for your squad and what they can do without having to worry about getting the club into any real trouble that they're not already in. You can go for it a bit, and you begin to get a good idea of who or what you need to try to bring in over the summer.

There was a core of local lads in the squad and in the first few weeks I went into the dressing room and told them that they'd be playing in the top division in five or six years. I don't think they believed me. Harry, God bless him, used to say, 'Send them out to play here, down at the Vetch, and you can sit in the stands with a cigar in your mouth. Once they cross that Severn Bridge, though, they get homesick.' It had been a decent start from Harry and the team that 1977/78 season. Swansea City were seventh in the league with thirteen wins from thirty played when I arrived.

My first game was against the league leaders, Watford, managed by Graham Taylor, who would later take the Hornets to the First Division himself, and an FA Cup final. It wasn't your average Fourth Division affair. With Elton John as chairman, they were taking the league at a canter. It was a wet Friday evening but 15,000 showed up at the Vetch and, despite the pudding of a pitch, we managed three goals apiece, including one from myself. Two games later, we picked up our first win, 3–1 at home to Stockport County, thanks in part to the poor floodlighting at the Vetch which meant part of the ground cast a shadow over one of the goals. Their keeper didn't get the best view of the free-kick when I jumped up to head in our first. Alan Curtis and Robbie James made sure of the result and neither we nor the supporters ever looked back.

In those first three months, everything was just geared to winning games and getting out of that league, and it was great to watch. We were in a decent position when I took over with sixteen games to go. I knew that if I put myself in up front alongside what Harry had told me was already a good attacking line-up with local boys Alan Curtis, Robbie James and Jeremy Charles – Mel Charles's son – that we'd have too much for most teams. Curtis was a nippy little forward with quick feet whom I knew from the Welsh set-up. James was a very gifted attacking midfielder who could play anywhere across the line, really, and Charles was an eighteen-year-old centre-forward; very much like myself in many ways. Swansea didn't know what sort of a manager they would be getting in me, but they did know they were getting an international-class centre-forward, which wasn't normal for a Fourth Division side – but I didn't find it any easier to score goals than I had at Liverpool. No, in fact, I would say it was probably even harder, if anything. Physically, I couldn't quite manage what I used to be able to do but, more than anything, it was because I was a mark, a big target who the opposition centre-backs wanted to stop at all costs. I drew a lot more focus and attention than I ever did with Keegan next to me, but then that took all the heat away from those younger Swansea forwards and it gave them the space they needed to score goals, grow in confidence and become the players that they did. We scored a bucketful between us and registered a lot of big scores. Curtis bagged 33 goals, Robbie James got 16 and I picked up half a dozen myself. We went on a run of eight wins out of nine games including an 8–0 smashing of Hartlepool, which is still a club record. Now up into the promotion spots, we stuttered for a moment, losing two on the bounce away from home, which dropped us down into fourth needing two wins from our last two games to have a hope – two games that saw crowds of around the 15,000 mark. In fact, in just those last seven home games of the season alone, the gates had almost tripled, and those crowds were well rewarded when we went up to the Third Division by beating Halifax Town 2–0 at home on the very last day of the season.

At half-time at the Vetch, that afternoon, there was still no score and I was lucky to see a free-kick of mine deflected off the wall and into the goal. It was Alan Curtis who made sure of the matter with four minutes to go. Our celebrations were muted though, what with the death of Harry Griffiths just four days before on the morning of our penultimate game against Scunthorpe. Harry and I had been talking in the medical room at the Vetch as the physios were treating our veteran midfielder Les Chappell and he just keeled over in front of me, almost out of nothing. I was stunned. I just didn't know what was happening until our scout, Ray Lloyd, bent down to try and help resuscitate him. It was all so surreal. One minute we're discussing getting Les involved on the coaching side and the next Harry's hit the deck. The club doctor was there and had seen to him immediately. We called an ambulance but Harry died before he got to the hospital. He'd suffered a massive heart attack at just 47 years of age.

It was a very difficult time. Harry was a household name at Swansea. He was Swansea all his life; played 422 times for them. He did everything at the club.

He was so pleased for me to go there and help. I made it quite clear that I wanted him to stay on, that I felt he was part of the furniture at the football club and that he'd be very important to me.

It was a horrible thing to have to tell the players when they arrived before the match that evening. We were all so shaken. Harry had brought a lot of them through as kids. He'd played at the club for fifteen years. He'd been the manager there for the last three. I don't think I've ever had a more difficult moment in a dressing room. We were all so low. After a lot of discussion, we made the decision to play the match, which we won 3–1, not that it made us feel any better. I had difficulty sleeping for weeks.

To gain promotion was a fitting tribute to the man. It was his team, really. I'd only showed up and guided them through the end. Later I spoke to Harry's wife Gwen. Apparently, the stress had been too much for him until I showed up and he was so pleased that he could take more of a back seat. 'You know something,' he told her, 'Tosh is going to do well here.' I'm glad I did.

I really began to learn about management the following season in the Third Division. I had to organise pre-season training, pre-season friendly matches, signing players and think about what we needed as a club to push things forward. After hitting that first promotion summer in 1978, we started to lay down new rules. There was something of a drinking culture at Swansea at the time – a 'work hard, play hard' kind of mentality, which was not completely out of the ordinary for the day but wasn't the kind of attitude towards fitness that was going to get the best out of the team. So, we had a few words about that and I made sure I'd reward the team for good results. I took them up to watch a Merseyside derby at Goodison Park, we went for a few training sessions with Liverpool at Melwood so that the lads could meet Bob and the team and see how things were done at the top level. We even had our pictures taken with Red Rum one day. That kind of thing.

For training, we began to arrange pre-season in a proper way, not just play Welsh League teams which weren't of a high enough standard. We'd go down to Torquay and play three matches over four days. We prepared well for our Welsh Cup campaign, which could get us into European football and would be a big plus for everybody. The club shop smartened itself up, we got better sponsorship; it was a big response from everyone there from the chairman to the ground staff and we made a huge turnaround.

Once we'd made it into the Third Division, I knew we'd need a more sophisticated approach, so I began to put myself in at sweeper to see what was going on. I started to realise that I could see things a bit better from centre-back, but in a back four I'd get caught out so I put myself in as the spare man and pushed the full-backs forward to make up for it.

I remember one classic FA Cup tie in 1980 against Terry Venables' Crystal Palace, who were known as the team of the 80s because of their young age and the prediction that they'd be playing together for the next decade. They'd played their way up from the Third Division to the top flight. We drew 2–2 at Swansea and I played centre-forward that day. In the return, at Palace, I played sweeper and we finished 3–3 and then, finally, we beat them 2–1 on supposedly neutral ground at Ninian Park. That day I was back at striker again. It was a useful switch to be able to make for team balance, from a managerial point of view and for the odd tactical edge.

Looking back, the freedom to play in defence or attack was a big bonus. I saw my job as being on the field and guiding the other players out there in the right direction. I knew I'd take a lot of buffeting and attention from opposing players but, in return, I knew that the other Swansea players would have a lot more room to move than if I wasn't there, and that all helped get the best out of Curtis, James and Charles, who all became fully fledged Welsh internationals themselves. When I felt it was necessary, or thought I could give something to the team, I played. Other times, I'd be on the bench, as the one substitute you were allowed in those days, and then go on and make an impact, even if it was only a psychological one sometimes.

The role of my assistant was very important. To begin with it was Terry Medwin, who played for Swansea in the first part of his career before becoming part of the double-winning side at Tottenham Hotspur in 1961. Then Tommy Smith took over after I brought him down from Liverpool and, right at the end, Les Chappell and Doug Livermore had the job. Sometimes they might give me a nudge but I tended to work out for myself when it was time to come on. I didn't always introduce myself. There was never a question of ego getting in the way. What you feel is a greater sense of responsibility both as the sub and as the manager. There's a bit more pressure. In that sense, it's not quite the same as putting someone else on. If you're saying that you think you can make the difference, then you really have to do it.

For that second season, our time in the Third Division in 1978/79, I'd brought in Ian Callaghan on a free from Liverpool along with Tommy Smith, who'd just been out in America for the summer for a short loan spell with the Los Angeles Aztecs. The chairman had given me £65,000 to spend on players. So, knowing that I wasn't going to play all the games myself, I picked up another ex-Anfield lad in the shape of Alan Waddle, who Bill Shankly had signed when I was having injury problems. That meant I could play Charles in a deeper role and it left me change to buy a lad called Geoff Crudgington from Crewe Alexandra to play in goal, who turned out to be key. Waddle and Crudgington cost £25,000 and £30,000 respectively and I told the chairman to save the remaining £10,000 in case we needed strengthening in the winter. That seems ridiculous now. Few managers these days could afford to put the club first like that. The precarious nature of football management means that you've got to spend everything you're given and ask for more.

Attendances were up where they had been for the crunch games at the end of the previous campaign. For our opening home league fixture, 17,000 squeezed in to watch us take down Lincoln City 3–0. Season-ticket sales were through the roof at the Vetch too and we picked up where we left off as we tore our way up the division, with plenty of scalps on the journey including knocking Spurs out of the League Cup in a replay at White Hart Lane. Tommy Smith had given their new signing, Osvaldo Ardiles, his version of a welcome with a tackle that made the back-page headlines in the national papers. 'Welcome to English football,' Tommy had told him as the Argentine lay there on the pitch at the Vetch wondering what had just hit him during the first encounter in August 1978. Ardiles didn't come back on for the second half and the game ended 2–2. We had gone two-up but Spurs pegged us back with goals from Hoddle and Gerry Armstrong. The return in north London was a super game for us just one week later in September. I'd noticed in the first match that Spurs were vulnerable in the air, so I made sure we had a big side that day with our teenage centre-half, Nigel Stevenson, pushed up to play in midfield, myself in defence and Jeremy Charles and Alan Waddle up front. There were five or six of us over six foot but we weren't all about playing long balls. Of course, we made our advantage work for us at set pieces but otherwise it was just making sure that we got control of the game in the first place. When you're playing against a midfield of Ricky Villa, Glenn Hoddle and Ardiles, you don't want them seeing too much of the ball. We were the better side. We went through as 3–1 winners and it was a huge result for our new Swansea. That will go down, for me, as one of the most important victories, never mind cups and trophies. To beat that Tottenham team, who were all the rage at the time, over two matches; people really sat up and took notice of what we were doing then.

Things were looking good for our second promotion challenge too. We were undefeated in our first seven which took us to the top of the table, and included a memorable 4–4 draw at home to Rotherham after the visitors had gone 4–1 up with twenty minutes to go. It was a pair each from Curtis and Charles that won the point. Then came a dark moment up at Carlisle on a Monday night in September where we lost our second game on the bounce, and I could feel us starting to slip. We had gone up to Chester on the Saturday to play the two away matches in three days with a day's stop-over in Liverpool. Alan Curtis picked up a pelvic problem that kept him out for three months, Robbie joined him on the injury list and Tommy Smith got himself a straight red and that was all in the first game. Then, on the Monday at Carlisle, Nigel Stevenson, who had been developing fantastically, got his marching orders too after a crazy decision from the referee resulting in a penalty that never should have been. We lost both games 2–0. It was my first sense of that despair that can creep up on you as a manager; when everything goes against you and your plans are shattered by events beyond your control. I felt like my world was caving in, and then the phone rang.

'Hello, son,' came the rasping voice over the line. 'You've had a bloody miserable few days, eh?' It was Shanks. I was lucky enough to have Bill coaching me as a player but to have him on my side when I was learning to be a manager was even better. We would talk every few weeks. He was always watching and always seemed to call when I most needed it. Sometimes he'd come and meet the team if we were playing up north, and I know the young players got a lot out of it when he talked to them individually.

After another near miss away to Chesterfield, which saw us slip to third, we regrouped back at the Vetch and went for another nine league games with only one loss. That took us up to December 1978, a month which saw us strengthen again with two new additions thanks to the money from the increased gate receipts. One was another of my Liverpool teammates, Phil Boersma, who joined us from Luton for £35,000. What with Alan Waddle firing on all cylinders, that meant I felt we had enough in the tank for any opposition, even if the likes of Curtis or Charles had to miss the odd game. Yet it took the signing of Aston Villa's captain and Wales international, Leighton Phillips, for a club record of £70,000, to stop us conceding so many in the first place.

Those senior pros were important characters to have around. Tommy Smith wasn't very mobile any more but the young players listened to what he said. These older players knew how to win. They knew what it took to achive through a long season and it rubbed off.

We emerged after a tricky winter in sixth place in the division but, between our young Welsh players and our seasoned pros from Anfield and elsewhere, we pushed on up the table, losing only twice in our final nineteen games. By the end of my second season, there we were competing for promotion back up to the Second Division for the first time in sixteen years.

Tommy Smith had to miss the last five games with injury but Alan Waddle had been doing the business. He never really got it going at Anfield but he was working a dream at Swansea. The six-foot-three Willy Waddle, as the lads knew him, was top scorer that year, topping if off with a hat-trick in our win against Southend, which was followed by a draw at Plymouth Argyle in our penultimate fixture. That set us up for a game at home to Chesterfield on the very last day needing victory to secure our passage to the Second Division.

We went one-down direct from a corner and it was Alan Waddle who levelled it for us just before half-time. With twenty minutes to go, we still needed a goal. I looked at the clock over at the top of the North Stand. Tommy Smith leaned over to me in the dugout and said, 'Well, it's now or never,' and I knew what he meant. On I went. Five minutes from time, we won a free-kick over on the left side of the penalty area and Danny Bartley stood over the ball. Anyone could have scored our goal that day. We had such a lot of talent with Curtis, Waddle, Robbie James and Jeremy Charles, but when that ball floated over I realised it was me that was going to get it. I rose high and unmarked and put away what was probably my most important ever goal for Swansea, and landed to the sound of 23,000 Jacks at the Vetch going mad.

I remember scoring the goal then running off the field and going into the dressing room. There were people falling everywhere, everyone jumping up and down, and the BBC were there too. I just said to the cameras that I didn't know what all the fuss was all about. As far as I was concerned, that's exactly what I was there to do. At Liverpool, winning like that was just something we expected. We felt like failures if we didn't. That's what Shanks had taught us. That determination that the man had driven into us had made us all believe that anything was possible. When I went on with twenty minutes to go, that was what I went on for – to win. I was struggling with injury, and I couldn't play much more than that, particularly in a high-tension game, but I could get on there and make a difference when it counted, and I was grateful for that.

A few days after that Chesterfield victory came a call that was truly one of the most satisfying in my life. Off the back of our performances, Mike Smith, the Welsh team manager, rang and said, 'We've got the home internationals next week. I've got Robbie James and Curt, will you come and play?'

I thought my international career was over. But it wasn't. We played Scotland at Cardiff. Robbie James, Curtis and Toshack up front – promotion-winning Swansea lads – playing a Scotland side featuring Kenny Dalglish, Graeme Souness and Alan Hansen – three ex-teammates of mine still at Liverpool. I scored a hat-trick that day – one with the left, one with the right and one with the head; 3–0. There I was at full-time with the match ball in one hand and Kenny's shirt in the other. I was made up. I'd failed a medical five years before. Two specialists had told me I'd had twelve months left to play. Winning trophies is a big deal in football but those are the real moments that people on the outside don't always understand.

Once Swansea moved out of the Third Division, my job became more demanding and I didn't want to play so much. The sweeper system had worked with Leighton Phillips in his pomp, but by the age of 31 he'd lost a yard or two of pace. What's more, I was beginning to struggle injury-wise and, while we scored a few over the following season, we shipped a lot more. It became something of a managerial lesson for me that football is primarily about players and not systems. There's no point in trying to squeeze people into a formation just because it's worked for you in the past.

On top of that, we lost Alan Curtis to Leeds United over the summer for a club record £350,000. I'd tried to persuade him to stay but he wanted to test himself at the highest level, as any top player would. At the same time, Tommy Smith had done as much as he could and Phil Boersma's career was over after one of the worst injuries I've ever seen, just eighteen appearances into his Swansea career. It was during a big game against our promotion rivals at the time, Swindon Town. You could hear the crack to his ankle all around Swindon's County Ground that day.

I managed to patch things up by signing my cousin, John 'Joshy' Mahoney, who had over a decade of experience under his belt in the First Division with Stoke and then Middlesbrough. He didn't come cheap at £100,000, but he's one of the hardest working professionals I've ever trained with and he was just what we needed in the engine room at Swansea. Tommy Craig was another I brought in, from Aston Villa for £150,000. Then there was Dave Rushbury from Sheffield Wednesday, a left-back for £60,000. In the second half of the campaign I brought in David Giles for £70,000 to add a little zip to the wings and just before the summer we paid out £120,000 for Leighton James, finally bringing the talented winger back home to Swansea after leaving the city as a fifteen-year-old to play in the top tier for Burnley. I'd been chasing Leighton all season since Burnley had come down to play at the Vetch in September. They didn't want to let him go but I wore them down eventually.

Leighton and I had known each other from playing for Wales for years together but it didn't matter whether I was his boss, his countryman or his teammate, we got on with the job at hand. It was the same for the rest of the players, whether they knew me from before or not. Off the field, I was the manager; when I was on the pitch, I was treated the same as everyone else. If I was playing badly, they'd let me know about it just as they would with the rest. The only time I've ever found it difficult to separate my roles of both player and manager came in that season. Most of the time, it's a clear division. You're on the pitch and your mind is on the job of scoring goals; you're in the dugout and you're thinking about how the team needs to work to get the better of the opposition. At that time, though, Alan Waddle wasn't happy with his contract. He'd had a belter in our previous promotion season, bagging 23 goals from 50 matches, but he refused to re-sign until the club met his demands. I wasn't convinced of his ability further up the leagues, though. It's a strange feeling to be playing alongside someone but be having a running battle with them about contractual matters off the field. You spend a bit too much time watching how they play and you start to question the motives behind the choices they make. There was quite a stalemate for a while but, in the end, we reached an agreement for another two years.

New Year's Day 1980 brought the first meeting of Cardiff and Swansea for fifteen years and, of course, there was something special in this one for me given my connection with the Bluebirds and their rejection of me as a coach. It felt good to come out 2–1 winners in front of 21,000 at the Vetch, even better to score one of those goals and fantastic to finish in twelfth above fifteenth-placed Cardiff at the end of the season, even if we did lose the return 1–0 at Ninian Park.

All in all, it made for the classic season of transition, but I was pleased to consolidate our position with a mid-table finish in Division Two and I felt we had enough to give it a better push the next time around. That year also saw some big ambition from Swansea as our chairman, Malcolm Struel, unveiled the plans for a new two-tiered East Stand behind the goal where there'd previously just been a bank of terraced earth. It was all the more ambitious financially speaking given we'd had to spend a fair bit on upgrades to the ground to comply with new regulations in the Safety of Sports Ground Act.

Our second season at that level did not begin as successfully as the history books might suggest, with only three wins from our first nine including an opening-day 2–1 loss to the Watford team that seemed to be following us on every step of our adventure. We managed a memorable 1–1 draw at home to Arsenal in the League Cup but couldn't do to them in the replay what we'd managed to against Tottenham before. We were a little soft at the back and didn't quite have the thrust up-top to make up for it. We bought a pair of fantastic Yugoslavian players, Ante Rajković and Džemal 'Jimmy' Hadžiabdić, the latter of whom ended up player of the season by a long way, but it was ultimately four local boys who tipped the balance. You can work with players with skill and experience but sometimes there's a drive that you only achieve with an irrepressible desire to win. Wyndham Evans, Nigel Stevenson and Dudley Lewis were three Jacks that had been with us when I took over. The first was approaching his testimonial, the second the club had wanted to sell before I arrived, and the third was a youth-team player. When you've been on a losing streak, it's players like this, playing for their club and willing to die for the cause, that'll pull you through. It's important never to overlook those characters in your squad. It's not a quality you can buy in later.

In December 1980 came the return of one Alan Curtis. He'd not had the best of luck in his eighteen months with Leeds. He'd been hampered by injury after a collision with Peter Shilton and an early change in manager from Jimmy Adamson to Allan Clarke meant there wasn't a lot of room in the club's plans for him. Leeds were in some financial trouble and we managed to get Curt back for £175,000 – half of what we'd sold him for. The news was so good that we smashed four past Newcastle at home on the same day it was announced. As disappointed as Curt was at his time away, he was glad to be home and picked up exactly where he'd left off with three goals in his first four appearances, including the winning penalty on his return as we took revenge for that opening-day result and beat Watford 1–0 at the Vetch just before Christmas. The feel-good factor would only last to the turn of the year, though. A famous 3–3 away-day clash with Cardiff on 27 December 1980 was our last point for two months, which meant we crashed from second to a lowly ninth, with our hopes of a dream promotion to the First Division not looking so good. It had started with a 5–0 thumping from top-tier Middlesbrough in the FA Cup at home and coincided with the opening of the East Stand for our visit from league leaders West Ham, who ran out comfortable 3–1 winners. We had to suffer losses to Cambridge United, Queens Park Rangers, Notts County and Sheffield Wednesday before we could shake off our mood but, whatever the results, the squad was in good balance, and we had the fire in our bellies to finish this job off that we'd started three years ago in the Fourth Division.

We went on the kind of late run that you need to achieve things in football and lost just once in the last twelve games. With two left to play, we had clawed our way to fourth and had to take on a very good Luton Town, under David Pleat, looking for a promotion of their own just behind us in fifth. It's possibly one of the hardest fought and most important draws we ever got at the Vetch. It was two teams both going at it hammer and tongs for the win. We went two goals up thanks to Tommy Craig and Leighton James but Luton reeled us in thanks to the talented Ricky Hill, who turned the tide for the Hatters. Luton had the ball in the net for their third late in the game only for it to be flagged offside. It finished 2–2 and that point meant that we needed a win at Preston to finish third and pip Blackburn to the prize on goal difference.

There was plenty to play for for Preston North End themselves. They needed the points to avoid relegation, so it was a winner-takes-all affair up at Deepdale with an atmosphere to match. Ten thousand fans had travelled up from Swansea. There's nothing better to get you fired up for a game than that. We'd been preparing and resting quietly on our own in the team hotel near Burnley but to come out to a moving sea of black and white scarves singing your names at the biggest moment in their club's history is something else. I'd love to have played in front of that crowd. To get a winner on a day like that would be something special.

In the build-up, I had to make what's been without a doubt the hardest selection decision of my life. Nothing since has come close. Preston were not a good side. They didn't have much that I thought would bother us at the back, but any team is capable of digging in on a day like that when all they need is a point at home to survive. So, my only concern was having enough going forward to break through.

For that reason, I knew I was going to play Jeremy Charles with Alan Curtis up front and Leighton James in the attack too. Robbie James was too much of a threat to leave out, so I pushed him back into a deeper midfield role from where I knew he could come forward. The question was over who I'd have to partner him. Do I play John Mahoney or Tommy Craig? Tommy Craig, cultured, left-footed Scottish international; John Mahoney, todoterreno as they say in Spain, all-terrain, Welsh international, wins balls, my cousin?

As I say, football management is about decisions. You've got to make them but that doesn't mean they always have to be instant, and this is one that took a few days to cook. There were two ways of looking at it and a game is ninety minutes. Maybe John could have given us a balance and I could have put Tommy on later in the game but, I thought, if I've got Charles, Curt and James there, Tommy Craig is better at giving them the balls that they need than John is. So, Josh might give me the balance and more control but, if they're not getting the service, then there's no point. It was shit or bust, so to speak.

When I told John, he was so disappointed that he broke down in tears, and I must say it took me a few moments before I could go into the team meeting with him afterwards. John Mahoney is one of the best professionals I've ever played with without a shadow of a doubt. Apart from being a bit more skilful than he was given credit for, he's remembered primarily for his 100 per cent endeavour as a midfielder, but John had a lot more than that and, as someone I'd played the game with from when we were kids on the street, I was sorry to have to leave him out of this one. In the end, of course, my decision was justified but that doesn't mean we wouldn't have won if I'd played John instead. That's one of those funny things about managerial decisions – sometimes both options can be winners and sometimes both are losers. You can never really know how much of your control is illusion.

Our first goal was a classic piece of Leighton James beating his man on the left wing, inside the area and then floating a beauty around the last defender and into the top-right corner past a helpless keeper. The second was from Tommy Craig after some good work from Neil Robinson on the right, and that left us two up at half-time.

Preston rallied and got one back from close range following a cross, and then it was a case of all hands to the pump as we fought to keep them out. Finally, though, we got a break when Alan Curtis ran his way up the right wing, cut inside and drew the Preston players to him. It was across to Robbie James and on again to leave Jeremy Charles the pleasure of hammering it home unmarked to unleash some of the best celebrations I've ever seen inside a football stadium.

We were out on the pitch for ten or fifteen minutes with the fans after the final whistle. I thought I'd waved goodbye to moments like that when I'd left Liverpool but that was one of those days in football that you dream about. I'd hate to think about what it would have been like had we not got the result.

A few weeks later, I took a trip up to Anfield. I needed reinforcements if we were to succeed at the top level, and I had an idea that defender Colin Irwin would be surplus to requirements up on Merseyside. The season had finished, Liverpool had just topped it off by winning their third European Cup and I sat in the famous Boot Room waiting to speak to Bob. On the face of it, the Boot Room was a small space, no more than a few metres square with all the boots hung up on the walls and kit all over the place, but it became the nerve centre where they'd discuss the team, the tactics, the opposition; a lot of the big Liverpool plans were laid down there. Shanks was in there sometimes but he had his office. Mostly it was Ronnie Moran, Joe Fagan, Reuben Bennett, Roy Evans and Bob, who would go in there with his carpet slippers on. They had their little fridge in the corner with a bottle of whisky, a few cans of Heineken and a bottle of water. These days the opposition managers go up to the boardroom for a bottle of wine but, back then, the Boot Room was the sacred place. If you'd been invited there as a manager, you'd been invited to Buckingham Palace to meet the Queen.

The Boot Room wasn't somewhere you went as a Liverpool player but now, as manager of Swansea, I walked in there to a big welcome from Joe, Roy and Ronnie. 'Aye! Come in, son. You've done well, son, the bugger.'

'Aye, you've done well. Have a beer, son, have a Heineken.'

'He's done bloody well, aye, Roy! Fourth to the First – easier to say it, not so easy to do it. So, what do you want?'

'Well,' I say, 'I've got a team now that's in the Welsh Cup, the European Cup Winners' Cup from winning the Welsh Cup last year, the League Cup, the FA Cup and the First Division now.'

With that, Bob walked in.

'Alright, son! Aye, Joe, done bloody well, he has! Fourth to the First, the bugger! Who do you want, then?'

So, I repeated to him, 'I was just saying, we're in five comps and I think I've only got about five players who can play at the level.'

'Bloody hell,' Bob comes back, quick as a whip, 'that's three more than we've got! Bloody hell, Joe, we're going to have to watch out for Swansea next year! Bloody McDermott and Johnson, thinking they can play First Division football . . .'

I felt so small. I wanted to disappear behind the cabinet but that was typical of Liverpool and the way they always kept your feet on the ground. The day after we won the championship one year, Ronnie Moran came into the training ground with all the medals in a box going, 'Here, here you go. One for you, one for you. Take them home, have a look at them, put them away and then get back here on the twenty-fourth. You'll get nothing for them when next season comes around.' If you build your successes up too much then you're putting them on a higher pedestal for the next time. Ronnie's death in 2017 was a real blow to all true Liverpudlians. What a servant to the club.

Liverpool agreed to let me take Colin Irwin to replace Leighton Phillips at the heart of the Swansea defence for a club record £350,000. I picked up the Wales No. 1, Dai Davies, to play in goal for our first season in the big league and I got some more top-level experience with the £125,000 signing of Bob Latchford up front from Everton, a man who'd been top scorer for the Mersey Blues every season he'd been at the club; a steal even at thirty years old, as far as I was concerned.

It was a special sunny day at the Vetch on 29 August 1981; a historic occasion for Swansea City's first ever match in the top flight. Everybody could sense it and there was a real carnival atmosphere inside the ground, with 24,000 fans crammed inside to witness the fruition of all our hard work. It was beautiful. Everything was perfect and it just couldn't have gone any better.

The match was of particular significance to Alan Curtis as we'd been paired with Leeds United. He had no hard feelings over his time away in West Yorkshire but any player will tell you that you want a good game against your old club, especially in Curt's circumstances where he'd not really had a chance to show the best of what he could do. According to Alan, his hands were shaking before the game he was so nervous. He went to the toilet about a hundred times before we could get out onto the field.

Now, this was not the Leeds side I'd had all those battles with during my time at Liverpool in the 70s. Don Revie had left in 1974. The team had been rebuilt to afford it enough success to reach the European Cup Final in 1975 but, after a series of managers who were not really given enough time, Leeds were very much in decline. Nonetheless, this was a side that still regularly finished in the top ten and certainly nobody was expecting what happened to them that day. Swansea City had been waiting 67 years to play First Division football and I'd been in charge for 146 games trying to make it happen. With the sun shining in Swansea, though, and all the hunger we had after the journey we'd been on to get here, perhaps the writing was always on the wall.

It was a very attacking side we put out, with five international-quality forwards in there with our full-backs pushing up with them. Between Alan Curtis, Jeremy Charles, Bob Latchford, Leighton James and Robbie James, there were 500 professional goals. And between that team and the Swansea fans packed in the Vetch to the rafters, we destroyed Leeds that day. It was Jeremy Charles who started things off after just five minutes when he found Alan Curtis's low cross at the back post. Leeds looked like they might spoil the party when they equalised in front of their fans with a Derek Parlane header before half-time, but it was all over within ten minutes of the restart with debutant Bob Latchford picking up a hat-trick with goals on the 46th, 50th and 55th minutes – the first two with his feet and the third with his head. It was a fabulous little spell but it was all upstaged by the last goal, an incredible solo effort from Curtis in the 70th minute. He picked up wide on the right with a ball from Ante Rajković and attacked Trevor Cherry, backpedalling as fast as he could in the Leeds defence, as Curt moved inside to the corner of the penalty area. He sold Cherry down the river with a perfectly executed little drop of his shoulder and smashed the ball into the top corner with his right for one of the best goals in Curt's career. While he famously wheeled away towards the Swansea fans in sheer joy, I turned to Allan Clarke with a grin, gave him a huge thumbs up and shouted, 'Cheers, mate!' It might not have been the most sporting gesture ever but it certainly felt very good.

It had everything, that opening day – a debut hat-trick for Latchford, a goal for Curtis, a goal for another of our young Swans and a big first win for Swansea. You couldn't have scripted it better. In fact, it proved to be a resounding start to a huge season which very nearly saw us go all the way. We won seven of our first ten, including victories over Arsenal and FA Cup holders Tottenham, with only two losses in what was the first season of three points for a win. That saw Swansea at the top of the table in September 1981, which led Shanks to offer some of the most effusive praise I'd ever heard. I found it quite embarrassing at the time but I'm not so coy when I remember it now. He said: 'What he has done is the greatest thing to have happened in the history of football; to take a team from the Fourth Division to the top of the First Division. It's easy to say it, but it's a lot bloody harder to do it, I can tell you.'

And I just thought, why are people so surprised? The idea of coming here was to do this. But I've realised in the years since that it's not as straightforward as that.

Bill Shankly had been in and around what we were doing at Swansea City since the start. He loved the company of my players and had been a constant help to me in my transition to management. He was there at Preston before the game making sure the players were ready and he was the first person I saw in the dressing room afterwards. When all around him were celebrating and drinking champagne, he stood there with a cup of tea in his hand reflecting on it all. It was the most remarkable achievement since the war, he told me. So, it was a terrible tragedy that he died on 29 September 1981, just four days before my return to Anfield as a manager. The first time he'd brought me there as a player and now he'd helped me get there as a manager, but he never lived to see it.

When we lined up on the pitch in front of the Kop for his minute's silence, I took off my Swansea tracksuit to reveal a Liverpool shirt with my No. 10 on the back. It was meant as a sign of respect of what he and the club had done for me. Some of the Swansea supporters didn't understand it at the time. I hope they do now.

The game ended in a 2–2 draw after we'd been 2–0 up, which was a pity, but we did best my old team in the return at the Vetch in February. We pushed on through the season picking up scalp after scalp, including a fabulous 2–0 home win over Manchester United where we unveiled our new £160,000 signing from Liverpool, my old teammate Ray Kennedy. It was the Welsh lads that did the damage that day, though, with one each from Curtis and Robbie James.

The Vetch Field had become a very difficult little ground for other teams. No one liked coming to us with the stands full of singing and the Swansea fans right on top of the players. I heard someone once say that the crowd had pulled us up by our bootlaces in the season before and they were at it again that year against the biggest teams in the country. Up until the end of March 1982, it was only Brian Clough's Nottingham Forest that managed to come away with all three points, and even that was only a late win from a dubious penalty decision. So, there we were on 20 March 1982 after a 1–0 away win at Wolves with twelve games to go and in pole position in the league. We hadn't been out of the top six all season. It was ridiculous to think that Swansea could emerge from the Fourth Division and win the First Division championship.

Liverpool, meanwhile, had suffered something of a slump. Bob had been in charge there for seven years and after three European Cups, four league titles and the rest, the thinking was that he'd lost his appetite for the game. Swansea's chairman, Malcolm Struel, knew that if ever the Liverpool job came up, I'd want to talk to my old club. The call came at about that time and I met Peter Robinson and John Smith, the men in charge at Anfield, at the Clifton Hotel in Southport. Bob had recommended me for the job. It was felt that Bob would finish out the season and that I'd take over the following year.

I went back to Mr Struel. We talked about a successor at Swansea. Larry Lloyd – an ex-Liverpool colleague of mine – was doing well at Wigan at the time. I'd mentioned him, and then it all just blew up in my face. Liverpool went on an unbelievable run, unbeaten for sixteen games, with only two of those draws, and Swansea couldn't hold on. We lost our next two games – both home games, Ipswich Town and West Ham – and dropped down to fourth. April saw us lose just once in five encounters but Liverpool had already run away with it. By May, they had a nine-point gap on us and a game in hand. We knew we weren't going to catch them, our heads went down and we ended up losing five out of the last six games and finishing in a disappointing sixth position. Liverpool won the league title in the penultimate game of the season. Bob decided to stay on and I was left out in the cold.

I don't think it was any kind of ploy by Liverpool to upset Swansea's title tilt. I think it was all genuine. It was just circumstance, but it definitely did something to upset my focus in that final run-in. I think Bob had been so successful that it was generally regarded that the minute things went wrong, he was going to get up and leave. Maybe, people thought, he didn't have the stomach to fight and turn it around, which is understandable when you've won championships and European Cups and everything else there is to win. Things weren't going well and it's easy to see why someone would have had enough.

Peter Robinson was very aware of what was happening. Bob turning it around was a big, big blow to me. When I went down to Swansea, if I'm honest, the idea that I had was that one day I would do a good enough job down there to go back to Liverpool. That was my plan. It took a lot of the enthusiasm that I had for the Swansea job away. I don't think that helped at all with what happened the next season at the Vetch. Maybe I should have finished at Swansea there and then. It wasn't a very nice feeling to have mentioned it to the people there for it all to go up in smoke. I lost a lot of affection for Liverpool after that.

For our second season in the First Division, pretty much anything that could have gone wrong went wrong. There were one or two key issues that hit both me personally and the club hard. We had a shocking run of luck with injuries. We had four or five first-team players who needed operations. Colin Irwin had to pack the game in with a bad knee injury, as did John Mahoney after breaking his leg in three places. Robinson, Charles, Alan Curtis and Robbie all went under the knife, which meant long spells on the sidelines, and Jimmy Hadžiabdić had to finish the season early in March too.

There were financial issues as well. With a recession taking grip, season-ticket sales were down by half and the gate receipts were low. Where crowds of 15,000 and more had been turning up for most games, now it was down to more like 7,000 on average. Swansea's not a big place and there's always the rugby to contend with when it comes to pulling in the crowds. With Neath, Swansea, Llanelli and Aberavon there's a lot of competition for a Saturday afternoon match. There wasn't much for our fans to get behind and perhaps it's understandable that they chose to watch something else instead.

The club had borrowed and spent a lot of money which was now not possible even to be paid off at the rate we were managing before. Swansea City had to admit that it was £2 million in the red in January 1983. Of course, that also meant there were no funds available to bring in new players and replace those we'd lost. Even if we could have afforded it, we were given a transfer ban from issues of payment during our deals to bring in Ray Kennedy and Colin Irwin. At one point, we only had twelve players in the squad. We had been competing in five different competitions that season – 65 games by the time summer came – and those hours on the pitch took their toll.

We didn't have the numbers to be playing midweek games but we had European commitments in the Cup Winners' Cup after we'd won the Welsh Cup the previous season. We'd already gone two rounds by the middle of September by beating Sporting Braga and Maltese Cup winners, Sliema Wanderers, the latter of whom we tonked 12–0 at home; a shame only 5,000 supporters turned up to see what is still Swansea's biggest ever win. It was the return of Ossie Ardiles with PSG in October that knocked us out of that one. There was no Tommy Smith to put him off this time and the Parisians ran out comfortable winners in both legs. Of course, it was famously Fergie's Aberdeen that lifted the trophy in the competition that year.

Our league form was shocking. Things were OK for the first two or three but then we lost four on the belt and seemed to lose another two for every other draw or win we could muster. By the halfway mark, we were in nineteenth, just above the relegation places in what was a 22-team division back then. Things got worse in January when I was banned from the touchline for four months. The ban hit us hard. I'd been charged with bringing the game into disrepute after a penalty against us had to be retaken when our keeper had saved it fair and square. The following one went in and we lost the game by one goal. I appealed the ban but the punishment came back worse. It went to a panel at the Welsh FA and whether there were some people who wanted to see Swansea brought down a peg or two or whether they wanted to make a strong example of Welsh values in an English division, I don't know, but they came down on us like a ton of bricks.

It's very difficult to manage from up in the stands. That's when your assistants become more important. It wasn't so bad at the Vetch, where you were almost in the dugout when you were in the stands anyway, but away from home I didn't have that contact with the players and my team that I'd wanted. It wasn't a nice feeling as well and it came at a very difficult time. Results nosedived.

We had first-teamers out, young lads in to replace them and not enough experienced heads to show them what to do. Some of those that there were weren't performing as I wanted either, not that there was much I could do about it from the stands. Ray Kennedy had been the club's marquee signing. He was won of the most decorated players in the game when he arrived from Liverpool. Now his touch and his work rate seemed to have deserted him and even the newspaper reporters noticed it. Everybody thought he'd lost interest. I was so incensed with his behaviour, what with everything else that was going on, that I stripped him of the captaincy, banned him from playing and transfer-listed him. It's terrible to think of it now but what we were all witnessing was a very early onset of Parkinson's disease, something he wasn't diagnosed with until 1984, one year after he'd agreed to have his contract at Swansea terminated. When we heard that, we all felt like we should have twigged at the time but Ray trained and he had such a good left foot that his ability maybe kept it hidden.

Ray was one of many on whom we made a big loss. We were forced to sell players for financial reasons for far less than they were worth, but everyone was feeling the pinch and we were never going to get value. In the end, it was a Leighton James-inspired Sunderland – galling that we'd let him go on a free – that beat us to safety and we were relegated back down to the Second Division.

It had been such a big push over the the previous five seasons to take us all the way up to the First Division, and even come close to winning the thing, that everyone was burnt-out for this sixth campaign. The big prize had always been getting to the top of the pile and now, after we had, it was harder to keep everyone motivated given all the different competitions we were involved in too. It's one thing to be part of a Liverpool squad that's used to finding those reserves year after year, to win and win and win again, but it wasn't yet part of the culture of a club like Swansea. Maybe I was a little burnt-out by that stage too what with all the work I'd put into the club beyond what was happening on the pitch. There was only more of that to deal with the more we grew, along with the even bigger task of competing with the best football teams in the country. As a group, we hadn't had to cope with the slumps and strings of bad results that we were now facing. It was a new thing for me as a manager and, of course, it was a very different experience. I tried all sorts of methods, things I would never do again – fining players for minor indiscretions, moving their kit to the reserves' dressing room if they weren't performing, anything I could think of, from the carrot to the stick, to get the fire back in our bellies, but against the financial background of what was going on at the Vetch, it was too much to ask and at times there was a bad atmosphere between me and the players. I became a bit erratic.

When things started to go wrong, I have to admit that I felt a lot more pressure. It was my first job in management and it's a very different experience when results aren't going your way. People close to the club started offering their opinions. I was at my weakest, then, and I allowed them to make decisions for me that two years earlier I wouldn't have allowed. Little decisions within the club, the kinds of things a more experienced manager would never have allowed; things I would never let happen again. I agreed to hire Harry Gregg as my assistant. Harry had been manager at Swansea before Harry Griffiths. Obviously, he was a terrific football man but – and I say this with all due respect for everything that Harry Gregg has ever done in the game – it wasn't the right fit, and I blame myself for that. He was only with me for two months before we had to bring it to an end. Our fate had been more or less sealed by that point anyway. Our fall was every bit as irresistible as our rise had been.

We had just one win in the first ten games in our season back in the Second Division in 1983/84. Malcolm Struel resigned with the club £1.5 million in debt and going deeper into the red by £10,000 every month. There were wage cuts and transfer requests all over the place. Players we wanted to keep, we had to sell, and those we wanted to recoup their transfer fees on had to be let go at woeful losses. Our sense of togetherness that had taken us all this way had finally fallen apart.

On the morning of our game against Blackburn in October 1983, I announced to the players that I was leaving Swansea City by mutual consent. I didn't feel like there was much I could do what with the financial outlook, and my own wage at the club wasn't helping matters either. Doug Livermore took charge and the results got even worse. Doug had been my assistant but there wasn't much he could do either. We'd had to sell Wyndham Evans, Robbie James, Jeremy Charles, Leighton James and Alan Curtis; Colin Irwin and John Mahoney had finished; Bob Latchford and Ante Rajković left in the winter. Our team had been decimated. We had only won two games by Christmas 1983. We were going down as fast as we had come up.

With only one win in seven, Doug Livermore decided that this wasn't a task he could help with either and he handed in his notice. The new chairman, Doug Sharpe, asked me if I'd consider coming back. I thought it was my duty to try and agreed to do so on a much lower wage than before but, even still, on reflection it wasn't the best idea. I even had to get on the pitch myself given the threadbare squad situation. I scored a pretty good goal too in our Boxing Day local derby at Ninian Park. We were already 3–1 down when I broke through with the ball at my feet with about forty yards to goal. When you've not been a player known for your pace and you haven't played a competitive game for a while, that's a lot of distance to cover, but the Cardiff City players backed off enough for me to shape it beyond the keeper's reach. We couldn't get the next goal to really make it count but it did make for some very satisfying symmetry. I played another six times for Swansea before I was sacked in March 1984 with only four wins in fifteen. But that was the last goal I scored for them. It was the last goal I scored for anyone; the last goal of my career scored at exactly the same place as my first – in front of the Grange Town end of Ninian Park.

Les Chappell took over for the remainder of the season. There was nothing he could do with the club fourteen points from safety except be the one behind the wheel as Swansea crashed back to the Third Division ahead of only Cambridge United. Colin Appleton took over the job on a permanent basis in the summer of 1984 but he'd had enough by the winter with the club looking odds-on for a third consecutive relegation. John Bond came in and spared Swansea that particular ignominy until the following season, but the club found itself back in the Fourth Division in the autumn of 1986, nine years after I'd found them there.

The more I look at it now, it just happened too quickly. You just couldn't and wouldn't want to stop it. You can't say, 'No, I don't want to go up this year.' In football, you've got to take it when it comes but, with all the success that was happening on the field, the club just couldn't keep up with it off the field. I've always been a little uneasy about everything that happened when it got tough, but it was the first time I'd been through anything like that.

I was a young man with no experience of management other than what I'd seen as a player. Starting at Swansea, in the Fourth Division, like I did, was the perfect way to learn. You can make mistakes at that level without getting punished. It gives you that breathing space to find out how the job works, and then there was the fact that in the those first few seasons, I could always bring myself on to help make up for anything I couldn't get right from the bench. As the team went up, so did my understanding of how to manage a football club, so it meant that we all grew together. There's a lot that's been said about our rise and fall – the finances, the injuries, my relationship with certain players – but in the end, I think it was just the speed that it all happened that did for us. It's very difficult for any club to keep up with anything like that, especially a club that's never hit those heights before and has to grow so quickly in every facet. Finally, gravity caught up with us. We didn't have any fuel left to keep us up there and it all came crashing down.

At Swansea City, I learned how to be the manager that was lucky enough to find success at the very top of the game. As much as the good times in South Wales taught me valuable lessons, what I did wrong when things got difficult became teachings that were just as important; mistakes that I didn't then make in other jobs when they weren't going well.

They were marvellous days down there in South Wales while we were on the up. They were some of the most special times I've ever had in football and it was a super introduction to management.

Of all the things that people talk about — Real Madrid, Liverpool, Sociedad —

what I'm most proud of is what happened at Swansea. From arriving in March 1978 with the team in the Fourth Division, to travelling back on the bus from Stoke City when we became league leaders in October 1981, at the top of the First Division looking down from above on the rest of English football, that's the greatest thing I ever achieved. Swansea City will always stay in my heart.

5
Sporting chance

I'M VERY FOND OF LISBON. I'VE A LOT OF TIME FOR THE PORTUGUESE people and it's a very special city for me. It was my first taste of football abroad and I loved it. I'd been to Portugal regularly for four or five years on the trot on holidays to the Algarve and elsewhere and, when I went over to Lisbon to work for Sporting, I thought it was absolutely fantastic. I had Portuguese lessons, and the climate suited me; I've always been one for a bit of sunshine. With all due respect for countries like Holland and Germany, it's no coincidence I've never worked in those parts of Europe. They don't appeal to me. I like the climate further south. All these jobs I've taken have been in places where I'd go on holiday – France, Turkey, Spain, Morocco, Portugal – and I thought I was on holiday when I arrived in Lisbon.

The Alvalade, as it was, was a huge stadium. I remember Cardiff City playing Sporting in 1964 in the Cup Winners' Cup. I'd seen that game at Ninian Park; the famous green and white hoops, the black shorts. I was so impressed and then here I was. I felt so fortunate.

I hadn't thought about going abroad at all, strangely enough, but at that particular point, after all the disappointment with the way it ended at Swansea, with getting let down over the Liverpool job, it was just what I needed. It was so different, so fresh. I'd never been to Lisbon, even as a player, but I was really up for it; totally ready for this big international capital city, this big club with over 100,000 supporters. I felt like I'd won the lottery.

I'd got a call from a man called Abdul Zubaida about the job not long after I'd finished in South Wales. He was a Mozambique national who was based in London and he'd begun to make a career for himself by connecting European clubs with players from Brazil. Growing up in a former Portuguese colony, it was his knowledge of the language that connected him with all these places including, of course, what was going on in Portugal itself. Sporting were looking for a new boss, he'd put my name forward knowing that they wanted a young coach, they'd had a look and were asking to meet me in London. I'd had an offer from Stoke City that I'd been mulling over but I knew that Sporting was the right opportunity as soon as we were introduced. I signed straight away, no doubts. Maybe other people would have wanted to go to a Rotherham, a Barnsley or a London club, but I don't remember ever being as excited by any job as much as this one.

The experience of Swansea had hit me really hard. I was living in the city. I couldn't escape it even when I'd finished the job. I'd seen the club go right the way through all sorts and there were reminders of what had happened everywhere, even walking down the street. So, to get the opportunity for such a beautiful change of scenery to Lisbon was a key moment for me. Everything I did and saw of Lisbon and of Sporting brought my appetite for coaching right back. It was just what the doctor ordered.

My eyes were wide open and I was taking it all in; looking at my team full of all these players – Rui Jordão, António Oliveira, Manuel Fernandes – some from places like Angola and Mozambique who'd become Portuguese nationals, some from South America. It was such a rich mix of people that I'd never worked with before. Like lots of clubs in Europe, it's not just about football and Sporting is called Sporting Clube de Portugal, not Sporting Lisbon. They are a club for all kinds of athletes. They had a couple of long-distance runners who'd won gold medals at the Olympics called Carlos Lopes and Fernando Mamede. I'd see them every day training in the stadium too and it made me realise me how huge this club stood, how important it was for the city and the local community.

A few weeks after I'd arrived in Lisbon, though, there was a tragic accident. Everything went flat. A famous Portuguese cyclist, Joaquim Agostinho, died in the 1984 Tour of the Algarve. He was a Sporting man and the club was down on its knees. There was a terrible state of mourning too in the whole city and the country. He was a national hero, the fellow, and the funeral was an unbelievable affair. There were thousands and thousands of people lining the streets and it was my duty to be there as the coach of the football team. Standing there, in front of this scene of such terrible sorrow, a huge stadium packed full of grief-stricken faces all looking up to where we were stood, the magnitude of my appointment finally hit me. This was more than just a jolly. It was a huge responsibility. This was their man, their country, their club, and I had a duty to do right by them.

We went to America on a pre-season tour and I remember being in Boston and there was a street of Portuguese restaurants and all the local community came out to greet us. It was like being in Lisbon. There was a club shop for Sporting, for Benfica, Portuguese TV playing in all the bars and restaurants and it hit home again just how big this club was around the world and what I'd taken on. Perhaps I didn't realise how big it was until I got there.

My number two was a lad called Pedro Gomes, who had played for Sporting and the national side and could speak perfect English, and I worked very closely with him. It allowed me to integrate a lot quicker while my Portuguese lessons were coming on and he was a big help in those early days. Ultimately, he took over for a short spell when I left a year later as part of his 35-year coaching career during which he ended up managing just about every club there is in Portugal.

There wasn't any culture shock in terms of the training methods, but I had a bit of learning to do with the African and Portuguese players, understanding how they work differently to British players. I started the job in March and this gave me some breathing space; the time to find my feet, to see what was what and have a bit of tinker before the summer when I would decide what to do.

I never had to get involved in any personnel problems, nor did I have to clear out unwanted players and bring other players in, and that was fine by me. Often, on the Continent, you're virtually there just to coach the team, and that was a good thing after all the work at Swansea, where I felt like I'd had to do everything short of making the tea.

Leaving Sue and the kids back in Swansea was the only hard part. They were backwards and forwards a bit on holidays but, with the children at school in Wales, I couldn't just uproot the whole family and bring them out to Lisbon. It was so precarious. I'd only signed a one-year agreement. If I'd got everyone up and over there and then, five months later, I'd been out of a job, it would have been a mess. So, they spent time out there during holidays and here and there when possible. It wasn't ideal but I had no doubt for a minute that this was the right thing to do. I was so focused on my career, even when I was in the family home, it was the obvious step. None of us thought for a minute that I'd never come back.

Curiously enough, my first game in charge was a home match against Vitória

Guimaraes, managed by Raymond Goethals, the Belgian coach who'd tried to take me from Liverpool to Anderlecht as a player before a scan on the muscle in my thigh scuppered the deal. Football has a way of throwing up these coincidences. We won 2–0 and lost our next against Porto, but we remained unbeaten for the rest of the campaign, which meant we finished the 1983/84 season in third place with plenty of optimism and with everybody looking forward to starting the next campaign. I was fortunate that the supporters took to me early on. Malcolm Allison had been there a few years before and I think it paved the way for me. They saw a little bit of Allison in me and he was extremely popular there after winning the double for Sporting in 1981/82. They loved him for that. He was tall, broad; a little bit like myself in that respect, apart from his trademark fedora and cigars, and he'd come from his assistant-coach work at a very successful Manchester City of the late 60s alongside Joe Mercer, through Galatasaray in Turkey and plenty of clubs in the English divisions too. The Sporting fans knew my history at Liverpool and Swansea and there was a lot of goodwill hoping for the same results that Allison managed.

Benfica, Porto and Sporting is, of course, a huge three-way rivalry and there was particular bad blood at the time between Sporting and Porto. It was like World War Three. When we played in Porto that following season, we had to wait three hours before it was safe to leave the stadium. We had snuck in over the summer and pinched two internationals from Porto – big players who'd just been out in France with the national side to play in Portugal's first ever semi-final at the European Championships. These two midfielders, António Sousa and Jaime Pacheco, had both played their part. Porto would never let this stand without reply, and they certainly didn't. A few days later, during training in July, a young lad called Carlos Xavier, whom I later took to Real Sociedad, came running over shouting, 'Mister, mister! Futre has signed for Porto!' It was revenge for what Sporting had done to them.

Paulo Futre was the great young hope of Sporting. A tricky, left-footed winger, he was eighteen years old and there were plenty of comparisons made between him and Maradona. 'Futre is like a Subbuteo doll,' said his later coach, César Luis Menotti, at Atlético Madrid where Futre eventually spent the best of his years, 'rarely falling, already rising.'

Futre had been part of Sporting's academy since he was nine up until the day he asked the club president, João Rocha, for a pay rise. He was only on the equivalent of around €350 per month. Porto had tapped him up behind the scenes and offered ten times as much plus a house and a car, and Sporting refused to match it. It's hard to say why the club didn't do everything it could to keep this young star, who went on to become Portugal's best player and win trophies in Italy and Spain as well as at home, but things probably got too personal somewhere down the line. Sousa and Pacheco moved back to Porto two years later, so it was a move from Sporting that backfired in the end.

Lots of strange things happened in those days. You can't believe what it was like 35 years ago in Portugal. The movement between African players – Mozambicans and Angolans – into Portugal; false passports; everyone turned their heads the other way to make it happen so long as they were good players. There was nowhere near the control of today. During the last three months of the 1983/84 season when I first arrived, people were pushing me to play Futre but I hadn't seen an awful lot of him. I was aware he was coming through but I'd not had much to do with him in the previous months. I said, 'No, I've got Jordão, Oliveira, Lito; all these other players here with the experience I need.' I arrived late in the season, so I'd only had a few games to assess what was going on and I was looking at the players. I thought, OK, Futre, he's useful, he's young, but I need to look at these other players first. And then, all of a sudden, he was gone before I had a chance to fit him back in. There was a lot of money involved and, in those days, the word of the coach went for nothing. I never had a say in any of it. The first thing I knew about it was when Carlos Xavier came and told me. It was a blow to the club, obviously, but not necessarily to my plans. There was a rumour that I'd wanted to send Futre out on loan. I don't really remember that but I do know that the ability Futre had was not something you could easily buy or find again. I've got my ideas of how I like my players to behave and, from the sound of things, Futre and I may not have got on that famously had he stayed anyway, but that's one we'll never know for sure.

I never really had a preferred way to set up the team while I was there but I knew I wanted to attack, particularly with the full-backs; I offered them a lot of freedom to get forward. It might have left us open to the odd counter-attack but Sporting, of course, are always going to be one of the strongest sides in the division and I knew we had the talent to outscore most of our opposition. Generally, I played a back four. The goalkeeper was Vítor Damas, the Portuguese number two, who was something of a rarity for a keeper at under six foot, but a decent standard.

I had two young full-backs around 21 years old in Xavier and Mário Jorge who were like a pair of brothers together, two young jack-the-lads. I had a super player at centre-back called Pedro Venâncio, who spent ten years at the club, and alongside him was the great Oceano, who was born in Cape Verde and picked up more than fifty caps for Portugal. I took him over to play in San Sebastián along with Xavier before he returned to Sporting. That was my four.

I had a midfield player called Virgílio, who I used as a sweeper every now and then, which worked especially well the two times we played Porto that year. The defence there took to the use of a sweeper a lot easier than the British players I'd used it with. A lad called Lito from Angola played wide on the right, and then there was the trio of Jordão, Oliveira and Manuel Fernandes. They were like Messi, Suarez and Neymar. They really were fantastic players. They were great on the field together, they played and they passed, but off the pitch they did not get on well at all. Oliveira and Jordão didn't even speak to each other. Manuel Fernandes, who was the captain, had to be their go-between, but it was frequent in those days that there'd be players in any squad that wouldn't get on with each other. Tommy Smith and Emlyn Hughes was the classic example. I was a big mate of Emlyn's, God bless him; we had a sports business together for a while, but I liked Tommy as well. So, I was the one there that acted as the intermediary between the two of them. I can understand why Emlyn got people's backs up and I could appreciate that Tommy did as well, but they were still both great professionals and two players I would certainly rather have on my side than not. I felt a lot happier when they were both on the pitch with me. I think the bad feeling all stemmed from some jealousy involved when Shankly took the captaincy off Tommy and gave it to Emlyn. I've no idea what sparked it between Jordão and Oliveira, and I had no intention of getting in the middle of it.

Oliveira was a terrific passer. He played behind Jordão and Fernandes, who were the strikers and generally the goalscorers. That Sporting side was my first taste of working with a whole side full of foreign players – where, in fact, I was the foreigner. When I look back on it now, they were not the most disciplined bunch, but at the time I just thought that was the way it was there. It was only later that I had the confidence to go into these places and lay out my ideas from top to bottom. You've got to feel your way in a little bit sometimes. All managers have to win players over. It doesn't matter who you are and what you've done. I was probably just another manager to them. They'd had two or three managers already the year

I arrived. They used to – and sometimes still do, in Portugal – go through managers pretty quickly and, with the language barrier, you don't have much time to find things out.

If you go to work in a foreign country, you owe it to the people who've employed you, who've chosen you to work in their club, to know as much as you can about the club and their culture. You can't just get in at half-past nine in the morning, work for an hour and a half, and then clear off. You've got to mix in a little bit and see what makes the club tick; go to the supporters' meetings. When you're out and about in the town, you need to go around and meet and see lots of people. You've got to integrate and I didn't have any difficulty doing that. Never have.

I lived in the city, staying in a hotel not far from the ground. I was happy there. But Sporting is a big club. It was difficult as well; the mentality, the supporters voicing their opinions – it could be hostile. I remember going out to talk to the supporters after one game. The club director had advised me to go out the back door of the stadium but there was no way I was doing that. I went out and I confronted them about their criticisms. It had crossed my mind that if I had gone out the other way, they would have put it out in the press that Toshack went through the back door and I'd have been in all sorts of trouble. Not many of them spoke English and my Portuguese wasn't great. But we talked and eventually everything was fine.

I wouldn't say I did well. I didn't win anything at Sporting. We finished runners-up in the league in 1984/85. We got knocked out of the cup. I wouldn't count that as a successful season for the club. It was a successful season for me, personally, because I'd broken the ice, if you like. I'd gone to another country, I'd learned a new language and I'd proved to myself that I could work abroad but, in terms of success, well, Porto were a cracking side. They were the best and we had to compete with them. Under Artur Jorge, they were one of the best – if not the best – Portuguese club sides of all time. They won the European Cup in 1986/87 for the first time in Porto's history. They called him Rei Artur – King Artur – after that. They beat a very respectable Bayern Munich 2–1 in the final having been a goal down right up until the 78th minute when their star striker, an Algerian called Rabah Madjer, scored a famous backheeled goal. The winner was volleyed home only a few minutes later by the substitiute Juary.

We had two draws in our games against them but they were always up at the top of the table, always in the lead. We only lost one match while I was in charge that year – away from home to a team from the north called Penafiel in the Vinho Verde region, where the white wine comes from. It was an early game after a mid-week UEFA Cup tie in France, where we'd had to go to extra time to win our tie against Auxerre. We'd played for two hours, come back from France, gone up the country and we were a bit rusty, lost the match and that was it. That cost us the championship, which is ridiculous. How can you only lose one match and not win the league? It was still two points for a win in Portugal but Porto only dropped five points all season – and two of them were to us! Otherwise, they lost one, drew one and won the rest. Sadly, we didn't go much further in the UEFA Cup either, going out in the next round on penalties to Dinamo Minsk.

I ended up leaving before the last two games, by which time Porto had already taken the title. The chairman at Sporting made it clear that my contract was not going to be renewed the following season. They wanted to try someone different and we agreed that there was no point in me staying any longer.

I've got fond memories of Sporting, though. I was very happy there. I felt I'd done as well as I possibly could. Porto were a better team. You're never allowed to say that, although you might think it and everybody might know it. So, under the circumstances, I was happy with the job I'd done, bearing in mind it was the first time I'd worked aboard, the language difficulties and that I didn't know anybody. I've been back there a few times and been very well received. I managed Real Madrid twice and people in Portugal are very well aware of what's going in Spanish football, so they're always pleased to talk.

Pedro Gomes took charge for the remaining couple of fixtures and I went back to Wales, but I consider it a successful spell for me: firstly, because I lasted the year, which wasn't always easy in that environment, and secondly, it gave me a taste of working abroad and it didn't scare me off. It opened the door to the rest of my life. It was the beginning of an eye-opening experience, coming to these places. It really broadened my cultural horizons.

Within a month of being back home, I had a call from somebody about the job at Real Sociedad. It seems that our loss at Penafiel hadn't been totally for nothing. It so happened that one of the directors had been on business in Auxerre at the time of that European tie and had seen the match. Auxerre were a very decent side, and this Sociedad director had watched us knock them out of the tournament. They had the famous French coach Guy Roux – one of the most famous in the history of French football. He was renowned for bringing young players through and they had a few good foreign players as well. They had Andrzej Szarmach and Paweł Janas, both part of Poland's golden generation; Joël Bats – the French national keeper – Jean-Marc Ferreri, a European Championship-winning midfielder with France in 1984; and Basile Boli, the big centre-back who went on to win the Champions League with Marseille. They were a very well-respected side.

When it came for Real Sociedad to look for a new young foreign coach, they looked at the stuff I'd done at Liverpool, what I'd done at Swansea and the fact that I'd worked at Sporting as well. Unbeknown to me, my time in Lisbon and that game in Auxerre had opened the door, and my big break was to come with the Basques.

6
Basqueing in glory

YOU LOOK AT THE COACHES AND PLAYERS IN THE PREMIER LEAGUE now, you look at the English national team, and it's frightening how far behind the British are tactically. It gives me no pleasure but I was saying these things twenty years ago, and it's still true today.

British coaches were fashionable in 1985 when I was appointed the first foreign manager of Real Sociedad since Harry Lowe in the 1930s. My eyes were open to that responsibility coming into the job. My experience at Sporting had helped me realise that before I arrived this time. I was aware, politically, that there had been a current of opinion against the decision to bring in a non-Basque for the job; not so much within the club but within the city. The Basque region was a complicated place for foreigners to work. It was a lot more delicate back then, yet another reason why the board at Sociedad needed things to go well. It was a big decision for them. The president, Iñaki Alkiza, had placed a lot of faith in me and I understood the situation. I knew I had a job on to win the people over first before I'd ever get a chance to do so on the football field, and I knew that it would be a matter of my players and myself showing discipline and being professional and, ultimately, getting results.

They'd given me the opportunity partly because they'd looked at what I'd done at Swansea and the type of club that it is, and how I'd brought through young players and shown what I could do on limited resources, which is how it had to be at Real Sociedad, a club who, at the time, only fielded Basque players. Possibly a bigger influence on my appointment, though, was Terry Venables. Terry had become the first really successful British manager in Spain. He was considered ahead of his time, tactically speaking, back in England and we'd had some good battles between my Swansea and his Crystal Palace and Queens Park Rangers sides. Each of us would learn from what the other had been trying do with his team on the previous encounter and we'd adapt our approaches for the next head-to-head. Those were some of the games that had brought the best out of me as a manager and I was looking forward to locking horns with him again.

Terry had gone to Barcelona after a vote of confidence from Bobby Robson to the board there in the same year as I'd gone to Lisbon, and he'd won La Liga at a canter in his first attempt, despite having to sell Diego Maradona before the start of the season. Terry had them playing a classic 4-4-2, but they had very good defenders and he got the side pressing higher with fewer men to beat once they won the ball back. It worked, and other clubs wanted to see what a British manager could do for them. Later, my success at Sociedad paved the way for Howard Kendall to move to Athletic Bilbao down the road. Jock Wallace went to Seville and Ron Atkinson moved to Atlético Madrid along with Colin Addison, who himself had brought Celta Vigo up from the second division at the first time of asking, not long after I'd begun at Sociedad.

For my part, I was very happy to be in such a beautiful city with a big challenge ahead of me. I'd had my year of getting used to life abroad. I was ready for it. I'd been to San Sebastián with Liverpool on our way to winning the 1976 UEFA Cup. We'd stayed in the Hotel Londres on the seafront of the famous La Concha Beach and all of us remarked what a super place the city was. The goalkeeper who had played that night, Luis Arconada, was still at the club in 1985, now captain of the team and Spain's first choice No. 1. He'd been a core part of the Real Sociedad side that had won back-to-back championships in 1981 and 1982 packed with well-known Spanish internationals, himself included, but the average age of that team had gone up beyond 28 and they hadn't kept the youth system rolling down below – a system that this Basque-only club needed just to survive, let alone succeed. They had become satisfied with their success and had started to go downhill in the years following. So, I knew there was a big job on and that I had to set about starting to bring young players through. What's more, I'd been told that the team had become very defensive and boring to watch. That older side had been built on counter-attacking but they'd lost their edge, leaving a fairly stodgy spectacle which was turning crowds away from the old Atotxa stadium. Everything had stagnated. Not only did I need new personnel but also a team who played with more ambition.

It was very similar, in many ways, to the state of affairs when I took over Wales twenty years later. The president here had used a phrase – *la vaca no vale para mas* – the cow has run out of milk – but, at the same time, the club wanted to stay faithful to the players who had won them those titles. The coaches were ex-players for Sociedad, many ex-teammates too, which made the loyalty even stronger, and maybe they didn't have what it took to let go with the past and work with younger players too. It was always going to be easier for an outsider to dismantle what had been so successful and build again.

I was very, very aware of being a foreigner. The Basques have a reputation for being closed to outsiders. It takes a while to bring them out. I quickly moved out of my hotel room at the Costa Vasca, where I'd been living for the first three months, and into an apartment overlooking La Concha, the stretch of beach around which San Sebastián sits. I wanted to make sure I was living in the city and not holing myself up in an expensive suite with no roots, appearing to all like I was ready to leave when things got difficult.

When David Moyes was manager here he spent his whole year living in his quarters at the Maria Cristina, the most expensive hotel in the city. I don't think the Basques found that very respectful. He made noises about going for walks every night and having Spanish lessons twice a week, but he didn't endear himself to the locals in any real sense. Some people can adapt to foreign climes and some can't. In fairness to Moyes, I was 36 when I got stuck in at Real Sociedad. He was 51. That's a big difference in terms of the energy you've got and your willingness to take new things on board. This is one of the better clubs to work at. The Basques have had their problems over the years, but these are good people and they got it wrong with David Moyes. I just think it was a big mistake for both him and the club. It took Moyes a while to work out how to move on from that. He didn't do any favours for the reputation of British managers in Spain.

Sometimes, for a manager, it's just one club that suits them. Sometimes it's going in at the right time that makes things go well for them. If you look at Moyes, with his work at Manchester United, Real Sociedad and then Sunderland, he's a classic case. That said, I don't think he was as successful at Everton as a lot of people think he was. Everton is a big club. Always has been. For me, Everton should always be up there with Liverpool.

To be manager of Everton for ten years and only qualify for Europe four times, for me, that's not a success. It's by no means a disaster, but it's certainly not a success. In fact, his immediate successor, Roberto Martínez, got more points in his first season than Moyes managed in any of his. If his relationship with Bill Kenwright hadn't been so good, maybe he wouldn't have been at Everton as long as he was.

A lot of these managers, when they go abroad, they take an entourage of four or five people with them. Moyes took Billy McKinlay, whom he'd managed at Preston, as his assistant to Real Sociedad. I've never done that. With the exception of my spell at Macedonia, I've always gone wherever I've gone on my own. Then, if they want to get rid of me, they only have to get rid of me, not have four or five others to get rid of and have to pay them up. All the places I've been, wherever I've travelled, wherever I've gone, it's always been a philosophy of mine to have the people working with me who know the club inside out. That way, you get to learn all the idiosyncrasies of the club from somebody who knows the place, and in return I teach these people what I know myself, so it's a two-way thing. You go in the door on your own, you get given assistants, sit down with them and go through your method of work every day so that you all know how to train.

A lot of people will tell you that you've got to be careful, you've got to have your own man on your side. There's a lot of people in Spain who use the phrase *hacer la cama* – that they make the bed for you; they go behind your back and stitch you up. I trust everybody until they let me down – I can't be looking over my shoulder all the time. Besides, at the end of the day, good results benefit everybody. It's never bothered me that the president would talk to my coaches or go behind my back because they'd be throwing stones at their own greenhouse if they did. If you can't trust the people who you're working with, then you're in the wrong job anyway.

My number two at Real Sociedad that first time was Marco Antonio Boronat, another of the team that I'd faced as a player during that UEFA Cup tie with Liverpool in 1975. He'd been assistant to the previous manager, Alberto Ormaetxea, during the league-winning years and he had plenty to offer me in his knowledge of the players and the club. I worked closely with Marco and with the second- and youth-team coaches. We chose the best six young players at the club to come and train Tuesday, Wednesday and Thursday with the first team. Then they'd go back on the Friday and play their ninety minutes at the lower level at the weekend. This meant that when the time did come for them to move up, they knew the senior players better, they'd have trained at a higher tempo and I'd know them better than I would have if I was just watching a bit of their game at the weekend.

I've often heard coaches complaining because they've only got 25 pros in the squad and they want more, and I'm not just talking about the clubs in European competition who have to play twice a week. It's crazy. I'd always have twenty players in my first-team pool and then make up the numbers from the younger group. It's better for the club, it's better for the players and then better for the managers. I don't understand why these coaches can't see it.

Initially, it was difficult for me to adapt to the club's strict cantera system – quarry, as it means in Spanish – the Basque-only youth policy. Normally, if you need a full-back, then you go and buy a full-back, but that's not how it worked here. There were also players that I thought were not good enough for this level, but they were the best I had at the time, and I had little choice but to work with them. It was a terribly frustrating job at times but, ultimately, very rewarding. The first year was very much about me getting to know both the club and the league. I'd worked in Portugal but not in Spain, of course. The football was of a higher level, the league a step up and playing Real Madrid and Barcelona was huge. We didn't start badly, but we didn't set the league on fire either. We were in around sixth place and pushing up. We went to the Bernabéu for my first time and lost 1–0 to a Hugo Sánchez penalty. By the time we played them at home in the last game of the season, we beat Madrid 5–3. They'd already won the championship with a game to go and perhaps they arrived in San Sebastián still a little bit in the throes of recovering from the celebrations, but it was a good win for us nonetheless.

The big result in that first season was our win at the Camp Nou against Terry Venables' Barcelona. They'd outplayed us at the Atotxa at the beginning of the campaign and ran riot to the tune of a 5–1 scoreline, because our young goalkeeper had had a bit of a nightmare. In my very first league game in charge of Real Sociedad, my captain had got injured at home against Celta Vigo; Arconada, a legend in Spanish football, captain of the national team, captain of Real Sociedad, gets injured in my very first game and was out all season! Some people say I've been a lucky manager, but that's the worst start anyone could have had.

Arconada was the governor. I had two good centre-backs in front of him, Alberto Górriz and Agustín Gajate; good professionals but very quiet. Arconada did all the organising. His replacement was a twenty-year-old called Agustín Elduayen who, obviously, didn't have the years to be a great talker. Ten games later Elduayen was struck down with appendicitis and so he was out for the rest of the season too. That left me with the third-choice Basque goalie, who was José

González. So, apart from Arconada being difficult to replace anyway, I could see a serious communication problem at the heart of my defence. Fortunately, the vice-captain, Juan Antonio Larrañaga, a holding midfielder, was a strong enough personality to bring the defence together. So, I put him in behind the centre-backs and in front of the young goalkeepers in a version of the sweeper system from Swansea which later became known in Spain as Sistema Toshack – Toshack's System – and it started to work very well for us.

That Barça win was one of the first games we played with that system. That victory gave me, and a lot of people at Real Sociedad, a lot of confidence. They'd had two or three barren years, so this first season of mine certainly wasn't any worse than what had gone on before. Given all the problems – the injuries, getting some fresh faces in, me getting acclimatised – people were pretty pleased with what had come to pass in that first twelve months.

I think the most significant moment of that season, the one that really set the tempo for what was to come, was an incident when we got knocked out of the Copa del Rey in the third round by Real Oviedo. Oviedo were a second-division side who eventually went through after a terrible mistake from our reserve goalkeeper, Elduayen, just two minutes from time in the return leg at the Atotxa, but it was away at their place along the northern coast of Spain over in Asturias where we really lost it. We offered nothing that night. They'd thoroughly deserved their 2–1 advantage and none of my players seemed to care. We went back to the hotel in Oviedo to stay the night and sleep before travelling back by coach the following day. It was about a six-hour drive. We were just finishing dinner and the team doctor, Dr Etci Vardy, who'd been at the club as long as anyone could remember, finished his food, turned to me and said, 'What time do we leave in the morning, mister?'

'Four o'clock in the morning,' I said, nice and loud so that the whole table could hear me, 'everyone downstairs at four a.m. We leave at four-fifteen.'

They all looked across at each other, but nobody said a word and off they went to get what little rest they could. Bearing in mind that this had been an evening game, that wasn't much rest at all. A few hours later, sure enough, they all filed out to the coach with the sky still pitch-black and the sounds of the crickets all around us, rubbing their eyes, faces glum.

The news of what was going on had got back to the press in San Sebastián by the time we got to the training ground, at 10 a.m., ready to start our morning session. The local media were making a big deal of this. They were furious and I could see I had a problem here.

When I came off the bus, all the TV cameras, all the microphones and everything, were pointed at me and all the angry questions came flying. 'Who does this coach think he his, getting our boys up at four a.m.? This is totally out of order.'

I replied, 'Well, I always learned that, as soon as you finish one game, you started preparing for the next game.'

And they said, 'Yes, but four-fifteen in the morning?'

Then I thought of our journey driving through the streets of Oviedo in the small hours of the morning. Oviedo's a big mining area and we passed all the miners on their way to work; the tired looks of their faces matching those of my players on the coach.

'Yes,' I replied, 'four-fifteen in the morning. There are a lot of people in San Sebastián, who pay for their season tickets, who have to get up at four in the morning and earn a living: the fisherman out there on their boats in the Bay of Biscay trying to catch enough to feed their families, the dock workers at the port moving all that cargo all day long.'

And that's one of the most significant things I've ever said because all of a sudden, the media realised that I was right, and the people of the town, who were reading and watching and listening to the coverage, they realised it too. They remembered that they pay their money to watch these players, that these players had it lucky; that they didn't know they were born; that maybe they had been too protective of these players. Why should they get off lightly for a poor performance against a second-division team? That was a key moment for me. We went two years without losing a cup tie after that. Having never been in a final before, we made it to two in a row. As we went through the rounds of those cup runs, I could see the looks on the players' faces and I knew there were little whispers between them – if we don't win today, then we're going to be up at four o'clock in the morning. Not all the most significant managerial decisions are made on the pitch.

I can't say that I had it all planned out back in that hotel in Oviedo but, when the team doctor had asked me that question, I was aware that I wanted to give them a kick. All football fans, when it goes wrong, they often blame the players for not caring. Perversely, at local teams like Sociedad, that happens even more and, without knowing it, this business had tapped right into that feeling. The strange thing was, the following day, one of the Sociedad directors – a lovely fella, nicknamed Patxi San Sebastián – came over to my house with a bottle of Rioja and said, 'Mister, don't worry, we never do well in the cup competitions over here. Real Sociedad, we haven't got a good record in them.'

I said, 'Sorry, Patxi, but I like cup competitions and I wasn't very happy at all.'

He died playing Basque pelota, the outdoor squash-like game, a few months later. He never saw the team lift the cup in 1987 and I remember saying that Patxi would be happy. I looked up to the heavens after the final whistle that day and said, 'There you are, Patxi. I told you.'

That second year at the club, the 86/87 season, was similar in the league to the first. We were always mid-table but looking upwards. If we ever dropped below that, and we were looking over our shoulders, strangely enough, the players always put in a little extra and won but, when it came to making that step up to the top six, we just couldn't quite do it. I used to wonder whether it was ambition that they were lacking. Could they only do it when the wolf was at the door because I couldn't bring in any players to put pressure on them when they began to get comfortable? It was difficult to threaten them as I wanted to. There might have been a bit of relaxation there. If the first-team players looked over their shoulders, there were only young lads behind them and they knew there was no danger to their place. Sometimes you need to be pushed in order to perform. You look at the big teams now with their huge squads; it's not just about having enough footballers to cover injuries and the fatigue of playing twice a week. It's about making sure everyone at the club stays on their toes. That's how you win championships and European Cups. When I was at Liverpool, they signed a new striker every summer. I had to fight them off every year and that certainly kept me performing.

When it came to the Copa del Rey, of course, there was a definite cause for motivation for everyone on the pitch. We went into the competition at the second round and won a series of 1–0 wins away at a host of lower league opposition grounds around the country, from other Basque sides to one over in Mallorca too. They were good wins but it was the semi-finals where things got serious and we were drawn against our neighbours and old rivals at Athletic Bilbao.

We drew the first game of the double-header at the Atotxa 0–0 and everything looked grim. Bilbao had been cagey, knowing that we were set up to hit them on the counter-attack, and they didn't throw too much forward. However, we'd had a man sent off in the second half and I was delighted with the result. Everyone in San Sebastián was very downbeat, but I told the press and the players that

I thought it was the moment that Bilbao lost the tie. We'd battled hard, we were strong and they didn't have an away goal. Bilbao went away with nothing. We won a draw from a disadvantaged position and it turned people's perception from negative into positive. I'm not sure I should have felt positive, but you've got to find something in a situation like that. You can't say that you've missed a chance there and concede that you're out. It's the kind of thing I learned from Bill Shankly. They're the tricks he'd use to keep us motivated. That's part of the psychology of the game.

It was a similarly tight affair over at the San Mamés, but our chins were up and we nicked it to win 1–0 with a headed goal from a corner by José María Bakero, who was playing up front on his own. Bakero was only five-foot-eight but he was very good in the air and scored a lot of headed goals. He had a good spring to him. He was a wide player by trade but I'd moved him into a striker's position because he was quick and could sit on the shoulder of the last defender and do the business very nicely when the moment came. Depending on the sort of encounter, I'd either play him up there alone or I had a young centre-forward I'd moved up from centre-half called Loren. Sometimes I played him as the target with Bakero in behind, and sometimes I'd use the extra man to strengthen the midfield. It was a big, big thing to win like that over there in a Basque derby with a lot at stake, and Bilbao traditionally the more successful side.

We had a marvellous evening on the way back. We stopped in Eibar, which is about halfway between Bilbao and San Sebastián. We'd arranged a sociedad – a men-only place where friends meet and talk and they cook the food themselves. It's a typical Basque tradition. We were there celebrating until three or four in the morning. It was a very special night and to do it against the old enemy and reach the cup final was marvellous; one of the big nights for Sociedad.

Then, there we were: Zaragoza, 27 June 1987, on a roasting-hot day. Our opponents for the final were Atlético Madrid. Luis Aragonés was in charge. He was later to manage the Spanish team to their first major win in the modern era with a victory in Euro 2008, for both the country and for tiki-taka, but on this day, Atléti already had his replacement sitting up in the stands along with the new man's first signing of the summer. César Luis Menotti's appointment was short and not successful in the end, despite the hopes that came with his 1978 World Cup trophy with Argentina and all the domestic spoils he captured later at Barcelona. It was the young player next to him who would later make more of an impact over his six years at the club – during which he would win Copa del Rey trophies himself – my old acquaintance, Paulo Futre, fresh from his European Cup win with Porto. Atlético Madrid were the clear favourites that day, but we had terrific support in a 37,000-capacity stadium that had not long been overhauled as one of the venues for the 1982 World Cup. It was a fantastic match. It ebbed and flowed until it reached 2–2 at full-time; you couldn't ask any more from a cup final.

Now, I was quite comfortable with the idea of penalties because the goalkeeper I had was my captain, the great Spain international Luis Arconada. We practised penalties the day before. Psychologically it's important to do so, although it's a very different thing to do them in an empty training ground than it is in front of 40,000 people. When you practise penalties, it's really for the goalkeeper. They're the most important person in a shootout. Everyone always thinks about the penalty-takers, and it's good to get the idea into their minds that they're prepared for the occasion, but it's very important for the goalkeeper; for their technique, for their reflexes, to make sure they're sharp.

It wasn't a case of attempting to play for penalties. I wasn't so confident that I told everyone to sit back and wait. Like I say, this was a very hot day. By half-time in extra time both sets of players were on their knees in that 37-degree heat. There was no chance of anyone scoring in open play and we could all see which way this was going. We only needed to take four each in the end. My players converted the lot. Atléti missed one of theirs and Arconada saved their last to take the win. For another team, on another occasion, perhaps, the goalkeeper would have been the hero, but we were all heroes for San Sebastián that day.

Travelling back on the coach was one of the most memorable days of my career. Going through the Basque Country, seeing all the villages and all the people waving in the streets, and getting back to San Sebastián with the city a sea of people; I'd never seen anything like it. Everyone, everywhere, was so pleased. These lads who'd done it were from all the towns and villages in the Basque Country – Deba, Zarautz, Getaria, Fuenterrabía, all sorts. They used to bring their own supporters to games. There were groups who knew the family of this player or another; it was very much a family thing. They all came out in each village to celebrate with us. They had their radios on to find out where the coach was and when it would be coming through. It's normally a two and a half-hour journey back from Zaragoza but we slowed right down as soon as we got to Pamplona. It must have taken another two hours from there alone. It was marvellous. We got back to the city and took the cup up to a platform at the top of the town hall, the Ayuntamiento, as they call it. Standing up there, the Concha Beach, which stretches right out from there across the town, was absolutely packed with supporters looking up to us. It was a sea of blue and white stripes; flags waving, scarves swinging in the air. I'd been lucky with all the years of winning trophies as a player and a manager but this was something really, really special. That, for me, pushed out any doubts that anyone might have had about my appointment – even the most hardened of Basques. At that moment, I became one of them.

The cup was a real turning point. It was the catapult for what we did the following year. It gave the whole club and the whole town a lift. The younger players started to believe that they could play at this level and the Basque-only system, which had always felt restrictive, we all now had faith in. The downside was that we had to lose players that were deeply set into the club's fabric, otherwise the system wouldn't develop. There had to be space for those young players to grow into and, only a week after that final, I had a decision to make about the future of one of the side's star players, our speedy forward Roberto Ufarte. Roberto had been part of the side who'd won back-to-back championships in 1981 and '82. He scored one of the goals in Zaragoza and it was Atlético Madrid who had made a good offer for his services. I had a few young lads coming through and Roberto had picked up a couple of injuries. He'd just lost a little of that wonderful acceleration of his. He had been so quick off the mark. He made his debut when he was seventeen and had been playing for La Real for eleven or twelve years. Bakero and Txiki Begiristain were pushing him for the same positions. They were excellent and I felt like I couldn't hold them back because of Roberto. It was a decision that a lot of people were against and it was a pity it had to be made right after the final. It was a big surprise to the players and everyone else.

It would have been easy for me to tell the president to keep him there but I felt it was the time to push these young ones. I knew that Roberto could go. Sometimes you just get this sense. You see things in training every day and it begins to seep through. It may feel like gut instinct but these intuitions are often a lot more informed than we think, and you have to trust them when you get them. The way I wanted to move the team on, I couldn't really see a place for him. I had another player there called Jesús Zamora, another famous Spanish international who got the winning goal the year they won the first championship in Gijón. He was older still than Ufarte but he was a different kind of player and he could still do a job for the team. I wasn't sure that Roberto could.

In the end, Roberto only played another two seasons before a knee injury got the better of him, but he came back to Real Sociedad to work as my assistant and has done so since during my time in Casablanca. At that moment, though, this was a big story and this transfer pushed things back against me again; but I felt like with what we'd won I'd earned enough credit to make that call. So, the board went ahead on my advice. They were quite happy to say it was my decision, because they didn't want to take the criticism themselves. That's something I've never been frightened of. As I said before, you've got to make decisions in this job, popular or not.

I'd been here two years but it had been two steps forward and one step back all the time. Finally, I had a good group of youngsters, and I had the belief and the silverware to prove it. We started the third season flying. Arconada was in goal, we had the same system we'd been using successfully before and it became very difficult to score goals against us. We were a well-balanced side with experience and young lads coming through. We went to the San Mamés again and played Bilbao off the park. We won 4–1. We were super that evening; one of the best performances I can remember. We had a big home win against Barcelona and found ourselves right up there in second place by the halfway point in the season. We reached the second round in the Cup Winners' Cup too before getting knocked out on the away-goals rule when we couldn't find the target against Dinamo Minsk, but it was all part of the learning process for this generation of players. The Copa del Rey, though, we had previous with, and we wanted a second straight win just like those league championships of the generation before.

When we won the cup that day in 1987, we'd had a pretty straightforward run through with a couple of second-division sides all the way up to the semis. In 1988, the following season, we got to the final once more; only this time, the journey was a lot tougher. We'd gone in at the round of 32, which meant fewer games, but it was top sides virtually all the way. We had to beat a very good Sporting Gijón in the last sixteen and then it was Atlético Madrid, this time under Menotti and featuring both Futre and Ufarte, in the quarters. We lost the first leg at the Vicente Calderón 2–1, picking up our vital goal at the end, and then turned it around 3–1 back at the Atotxa.

Then it was Real Madrid in the semis. We won the first leg – a very tight game – 1–0 with an early goal from Bakero. It was a good result but everyone knew we'd be up against it playing this free-scoring side of Hugo Sánchez, Emilio Butragueño and friends. They were out in front at the top of the league and very confident in their abilities, but perhaps a little too confident. Our best weapon away against a side like Madrid was always going to be a counter-attack and they knew it. What made most sense for them was to play a nice, balanced game at the Bernabéu, so I needed to make sure that a nice balanced game was not what they played. I needed to get under their skin and make them a little more reckless in their pursuit of the tie, so I went out into the press before that second leg and said that these Madrid players weren't anywhere near as good as they thought they were, and that we weren't just coming to defend our 1–0 lead.

People had said not to poke Madrid in public, and maybe it was a coincidence, but I think that just opened the door for us. They kept it tight until half-time but the Madrid coach, Leo Beenhakker, threw the lot at us in the second 45 minutes and we just countered again and again and again. By the time we were done, it was 4–0. That was definitely the game that got Real Madrid noticing me. With every goal, they'd come flying at us even harder and, before they knew what had happened, they'd thrown away the tie. All the goals had come inside the same fifteen minutes.

The final was at the end of March and back at the Bernabéu as the chosen neutral ground. So, when we lost that day to Barcelona, having bested Real Madrid, Atlético Madrid and Gijón, it was completely different to the year before when we'd got to the semi-final without facing a first-division team. We maybe had more merit getting that far this time than even winning the year before. We beat Bilbao in the semis in 1987, which was obviously a big one, and faced Atlético Madrid in the final, but we never had to deal with a Barcelona or a Real Madrid. This second time, we'd done enough to win the cup even before we walked out at that final, but the odds were stacked against us. What we didn't know at the time was that three of our team had already agreed to sign for Barça before the game – Bakero, Begiristain and Rekarte.

Barcelona had been struggling. There was a lot of talk about how they needed to improve the next season. They finished a lowly sixth in the league and, if they hadn't won this final, they wouldn't have qualified for Europe for one of the first years in their history. Luis Aragonés had suceeded Terry Venables as Barcelona manager and there had been big problems at the Camp Nou that year. There was a lot of controversy involving the board, the players and the managers, and the final itself was a poor game. The only goal was a sloppy one and it came from a set piece when their centre-back, José Alexanko, managed to push it in.

In my mind, though, there was a dark cloud hanging over that game. Now, I don't think for one minute that those three players in our team who had already agreed to sign for our opponents at the end of the season went out thinking that they were going to throw the game. I don't think, by any stretch of the imagination, that that happened. But, I don't care what you say, if you've got your heart set on Barcelona, and you know that Barcelona aren't going to qualify for European competition unless they win the match, then there has to be a part of your mind that's aware of that fact. Unless you're actually in that situation yourself, you'll never know. I could never say that these players thought that during this game. Maybe saying it was 14 vs 8 is a bit harsh but, at the same time, you have to wonder what was going through the minds of the eight as well. It's a situation that should never have happened.

Everything was kept very quiet about those transfers from our point of view. There was a lot of speculation but nothing came out until the end of the season. I wasn't aware of the situation, but I was aware that we had become a threat to Barcelona and Real Madrid, and history showed that, when this kind of thing happens, these two go in and they make teams like us weaker by taking our players. It's a lot different now because you can have more foreign players in the league and they can pick and choose from wherever they want. In those days, of course, Real Sociedad only played with Basque players and Barcelona and Real Madrid could only sign three foreigners. So, they had to have the best Spanish players, and that meant our lads too. There was a lot of bad feeling about it, especially after all we'd overcome in that cup run. It was a blow and it left a bad taste.

We finished the season second in the league. We always felt that we might have a chance at the title but Madrid were too strong, and I think that the disappointment of the cup put us off a little bit too. Having those three players with their heads already turned for the final third of the season did not help. Rekarte, Bakero and Begiristain went off that summer and began long and successful careers at the Camp Nou; the last two in particular, both of whom went on to become a core part of Johan Cruyff's Dream Team which won the club's first European Cup.

We picked ourselves up. That second place meant that we qualified for the UEFA Cup. This was before the days of the Champions League and only the winners went off to the European Cup. We were pleased to get another crack at a continental trophy and we did very well. We made it all the way to the quarter-finals, beating some very good sides on the way – Dukla Prague, my old friends at Sporting and then Cologne in the last sixteen, who were managed by Christoph Daum in his first managerial appointment, before he won the Bundesliga with Stuttgart. In the first leg, at Atotxa, it absolutely chucked it down, as is its want in the wintertime in San Sebastián. Daum stood there on the sidelines in a long raincoat shouting out his orders while I took shelter in the dugout. It was a big, shiny, double-breasted, dark-green thing that covered him from head to toe.

'Smart coat, that,' I nodded to him as he walked back to his seat.

'If you beat us, I will give you one,' he replied in perfect German-inflected English.

We knocked them out after a 2–2 draw in Cologne and, good to his word, Daum came into the dressing room and presented me with one. Very smart thing; buttons all over the place. I wore it lots. I still have it somewhere. Sadly, it was Daum's soon-to-be team, Stuttgart, that did for us in the following round on penalties. This time Arconada couldn't bail us out, with two of our Basque boys missing from the spot. Stuttgart made it all the way to the final but it was Maradona's Napoli that lifted the UEFA Cup that year.

We struggled a bit in the league in 1988/89 and finished mid-table. It was difficult because I couldn't bring in the quality of replacements that I'd have liked. We started the season with a squad of twenty players, ten of whom had virtually no first-division experience, and that was that. Any problems have to be solved as best you can. It so happened that all my best defenders were left-sided, but you just have to adapt. We did well to replace the three players that we lost. Without Bakero and Begiristain at Real Sociedad, Loren played more often up front. He scored a dozen or so goals that year; enough for Bilbao to take notice and pay 300 million pesetas to take him along the coast the following summer.

These clubs paid the money required, but the money for me as coach of Real Sociedad was no good because I couldn't use it to bring anyone in. It was good for the club because we moved to a new stadium which was really handy, but when the players at Sociedad realised they could go to Barcelona, play at the top level and earn much bigger wages, that was very attractive for them.

When Real Madrid came knocking at the door in the summer of 1989, it was attractive for me too. I'd given Real Sociedad four years. I'd taken the club to two finals when they'd never been to one before. I'd turned the club around almost to the level they had enjoyed in their early-1980s heyday. They were back in European competition. We won the cup for the first time and I was generally regarded, at the time, as the best coach around. I'd won coach of the year for two years running and there was an opportunity to show what I could do at the very top of the game.

Ramón Mendoza, the president of Real Madrid, had quite a strong affiliation with the Basque Country. He used to go on holiday there a lot, so negotiations weren't as complicated as they might have been. When I'd signed a new contract at the end of my second season at Sociedad, I'd told the president that I wanted a clause put in that I could go if Real Madrid came looking for me. It was only them. That was the only clause. I'd heard rumours back then that an approach might have been on the cards. The San Sebastián locals weren't quite as easy-going about it. Relations between the Basques and Madrid, politically, were not the best. It was a delicate situation that I was in and there were a few unpleasant moments on a personal basis. Some people who'd always supported me turned the other way. They felt that I'd been a traitor, but it was very much a professional decision for me. The players that had gone to Barça certainly got a lot less stick than I did but, though I was very grateful to the people of Sociedad for giving me the opportunity to work in Spain, off I went to Madrid.

When I look back at those years, it was possibly my most successful spell, taking into account everything. It was a very important time. It was coaching in its purest form and very much a blueprint for what I did later with Wales at international level. It was different to what they'd been used to. Sometimes I did things I knew were in their best interests but they couldn't see it because they weren't accustomed to that kind of thing; leaving players out, being critical after games. A lot of coaches only say what they think is correct and they're reluctant to criticise. That's never been my way of doing things. It's not a case of criticising players every week but there comes a time where giving a player a knock on the head to wake him up might not be a bad idea. I've never been frightened to do that. They weren't used to that, and they certainly weren't used to getting up at four o'clock in morning.

By the time my four years in San Sebastián were up, there were only two British managers left in La Liga – me and Colin Addison at Cádiz, and Colin only lasted another year before returning to take over at Hereford United. That there's only been four or five since is a sign of where the British game has gone. We've always been 4–4–2, up and at them, get on to the knockdowns, chase, chase, chase. It's about time we became more sophisticated than that and I hope it's coming. I really do.

7

Real Madrid

REAL MADRID IS A CLUB THAT IS DIFFERENT TO ANYTHING ELSE YOU can imagine. The obsession with the European Cup is well known and, when I arrived at the Bernabéu, in the summer of 1989, it was 23 years since anyone in their colours had lifted the trophy. That obsession was at its peak. There was nothing uncertain about my brief from Ramón Mendoza – to win the European Cup. My predecessor, a Dutchman by the name of Leo Beenhakker, had failed in that task for the past two seasons and, despite picking up the league and cup double, he was handed his papers with no more than the usual thanks.

It was a tricky situation when I went in because I'd criticised the Madrid team in the press on the way to our second Copa del Rey final with Real Sociedad, just to get under their skin before the semi-final tie. I was trying to wind them up, as managers do from time to time, telling them that they lacked consistency and that some of them weren't as good as they thought they were; when we turned them over 4–0 at their own ground, it seemed I'd made a good point. So, a few of the players were looking gingerly at me at our first meeting. But it didn't last long.

I was forty at the time, so I was fairly close to them in age. They knew my history as a player at Liverpool, which they respected. They'd seen the work I'd done at Sociedad and they respected that as well. Maybe some of them felt they had something to prove after my criticism but some had a strange mentality and didn't care. There was a snobbiness about Madrid; *superbio*, as they'd say in Spanish. Perhaps I was looked down on by some of them for coming from a Basque club. Whatever the case, the tensions between the players and myself eased fairly quickly, as they often do once you're in there and working and everyone realises that you're all in it together.

We had a decent pre-season in Galicia but there was no need to familiarise myself with the players. I didn't have to watch them. I knew enough about them. Everyone did. You were only allowed three foreign nationals in total in your squad at the time, which made it very different to the era of Galacticos that came later. Instead, the late 1980s had been dominated by a homegrown group of Spanish players, known as *La Quinta del Buitre* ('Vulture's cohort'), who had come up through the ranks together at Madrid's La Fábrica academy. Four of them were still part of the first team set-up when I arrived – Martín Vázquez, Manolo Sanchís, Míchel and Emilio Butragueño, the twinkle-toed creator and scorer with the nickname of *El Buitre* or 'The Vulture', after whom the group had been named. There's been a lot of rubbish written, then and since, about my relationship with the Quinta, but most of it's not true. Generally, I got on well with them, particularly Butra, Míchel and Martín Vázquez, who would later play for me in La Coruña. Sanchís was not my cup of tea. It was his lack of discipline that lost our tie against Milan in the European Cup that year, which nearly cost me my job. He was a bit of a strange one. He was always sitting there reading the *Financial Times*. No player reads the Financial Times.

Mendoza was like a father to the Quinta. He forgave them for everything, he really did. He used to play little games with them and the rest of the team. He'd come into the dressing room if we had three games in the week, say, and create a bonus system to motivate them. If, for example, we were playing Atlético Madrid at home, then Mönchengladbach on Wednesday away and away again to Real Valladolid the following weekend, he'd say, 'I'll give you all this extra money if you win them all, but you get nothing if you don't.' It did make things a little bit difficult working with those players when they had that relationship with the president, but you let them get on with it, and despite whatever's been printed in the past, I don't believe that the end of my tenure at Madrid had anything to do with the Quinta.

People always talked about the Quinta, but the whole group at that time were special. Bernd Schuster was one of the three foreign players in the team; super passer of the ball, with as many team and individual medals as you could have – he'd made the bold switch to Madrid after eight years at Barcelona. The second import was Oscar Ruggeri, who was a World Cup-winning centre-back from Argentina. He came to Madrid when I arrived. A one-season spell with La Liga minnows Logroñés was enough to show that his Copa Libertadores successes with River Plate were very much translatable to the European game. Strong, experienced, maybe he lacked a bit of pace, but Ruggeri made up for it in his ability to read the game. Then, finally, there was the Mexican forward Hugo Sánchez. Hugo was the star among stars of that Real Madrid team. He has an astonishing record at the club of 164 goals in 207 La Liga appearances, and a total of 208 goals in 283 appearances over the seven years he was there. If there was a No. 9 anywhere that you could rely on to do the business, Hugo was your man.

I had a good relationship with Hugo because he was a little bit like me – he was a foreigner, and was a little bit outside the group of Madrid players despite his importance to the side during the same era as the Quinta. We went to Mexico once during pre-season to Veracruz and I've never seen a player get a reception quite like that. The crowds were incredible. Hugo's success meant everything to people over there. He had to have a stack of autographed photos in his pocket just to be able to make it out of the airport.

Thanks to Hugo and Butra this Madrid side was very dangerous going forward, but it was known that the team had some problems at the back. So, alongside Ruggeri came another new recruit – 21-year-old Fernando Hierro from Valladolid. I'd known that the club was interested in him and that was fine by me. You're not in charge of the buying and selling at Madrid and that suited me. There's enough for a manager to cope with already, as I discovered at Swansea, and I was quite used to working with what was available from my time in San Sebastián but, like I say, I'd seen Hierro playing at Valladolid when I was with Real Sociedad and it was obvious that he had ability.

Ruggeri struggled with a knee problem on and off and, perhaps better than most, I knew how to work with his injury to make sure I got the best out of him. Playing in Logroño, in a small stadium where you've got everybody defending and then counter-attacking when the opportunity comes, is not the same as playing in the Santiago Bernabéu when you're the team that's attacking all the time and the opposition leave one quick little fellow up front who can catch you on the break. It's a completely different game. So, with Ruggeri not as quick as he was and Hierro still learning his trade, having them in a back four meant we would have had problems. Instead, it seemed obvious to me to work with the sweeper system I'd fine-tuned in San Sebastián after I'd first started using it at Swansea.

It's often referred to in Spain as a 3–3–3–1 formation but that's never been the way that I've thought of it. At the heart of the shape is a defensive diamond of four players. It's two centre-backs as usual but assisted by two others – one defensive midfielder, or holding player, in front and a sweeper in behind. The attacking unit is made up of a line of three forwards and then a No. 9 in front of them. Most of the width you get from your wing-backs. It's a very solid way of working but it really depends on who you've got in each position.

In my opinion, it's a system that protected Ruggeri a little bit. I used his experience to its full value and exposed very little of his weakness. It also helped that I had two full-backs who were fantastic, Chendo and Rafael Gordillo; excellent professionals with good positional sense. They could run all day, which very much suited their roles as wide players needing to both attack and defend, often in quick succession. So to begin with, I started with Ruggeri and Hierro as the two markers at the sides of the defensive diamond, Sanchís screening in front in a deep-lying midfield position, with Schuster in behind the markers as sweeper.

We played that way for our first competitive fixture in the Santiago Bernabéu Cup – the traditional Madrid curtain-raiser – against, after all these years, none other than Kenny Dalglish's Liverpool. It was a matter of months after the tragedy of Hillsborough and Liverpool had arrived in Madrid as the FA Cup winners. I remember having dinner with the Liverpool people before the game along with Ronnie Moran, Joe Fagan and Kenny, and I spent quite a bit of time in the tunnel before kick-off speaking with John Aldridge and persuading him to sign for Real Sociedad as their first non-Basque player. He would go on to sign for them days later in a move worth £1 million, and he made a success of himself over two seasons, with 40 goals in 75 appearances. Ian Rush had returned from Juventus and he and Peter Beardsley had become the first-choice strike pair at Anfield, leaving Aldridge to consider his options.

We won the game 2–0, as we did our first home game of the league season, and everything seemed to be moving in the right direction. We then had two tricky little away games, either side of a home fixture to Valencia, against Mallorca and newly promoted Castellón, both of which we drew 0–0 and then, bam, the critics in the press came out saying that the system was too defensive and that Real Madrid can't play like this and all the rest. It's not the system that is most important though, it's the personnel who play within the system which dictate whether it's one for attack or defence. You can play with attacking players in a defensive system and you can play with defensive players in an attacking system. Italian teams had been using a sweeper for years in a very defensive way before I made it successful in Spain. Cruyff very often played the same system at Barcelona but, whereas I had full-backs who went high up the pitch, he had wingers that had to come back. The diamond of four was pretty much the same but whereas I had Chendo and Gordillo, who were full-backs, he had Begiristain and Goikoetxea, who were wingers. Now, I always find that full-backs will get forward more than wingers will get back, so I went maybe for the safer option in that respect, but at either of these clubs you have to be offensive. You know you're going to have more of the ball than the opposition. You'd be a fool if you were going to have defensive plans.

The players were trying to get it to work, certainly at Castellón. We just couldn't find a way through against a team on a tight pitch set up to frustrate us. But then came the game at the Santiago Bernabéu against Valencia, which turned out to be very significant. We played in the same style, the same way, but I'd decided I needed to change around my defensive four. Schuster's passing skills were a bit blunted all the way back at sweeper and I could see they'd be more useful in getting us moving up the pitch. So, I moved Ruggeri from the left marker position to sweeper, I brought Sanchís back from midfield to sit alongside Hierro, where Ruggeri had been, and got Schuster controlling the play from the back of midfield. It was a lot of responsibility for Schuster but it suited him well. If not entirely solid from the off, it was definitely effective.

The system allowed us to form a lot of triangles all across the pitch which, when you're working with players of this calibre, is very hard to defend against. Importantly, it also freed up Hugo Sánchez. It gave him less defending to do and meant he played closer to the box where his qualities would count. We won 6–2, and then the next home games 4–1, 4–0, 5–2, 4–0 and 7–2, and so it went on. It got to the point where the crowd would get bored if we only scored three or less. That shut people up for a while, but only for a while.

We rarely reached the same heights away from home but we still ground out plenty of wins, with the only losses a 3–1 at the Camp Nou and a 2–1 defeat against my old team in San Sebastián. I remember that afternoon before the game at the Atotxa going for a walk along the Concha beach. Normally, I'd be back in the team hotel resting. It was early afternoon, very quiet. No one bothered me. Everyone was eating in the Basque Country. I didn't want to be holed up, stuck in a hotel room like you have to be before away games in that awful way of waiting for the time to pass. It was a town I knew and I felt I didn't have to.

When I got to the ground, I had something of a mixed reception but I just accepted it. I knew what I'd done for Real Sociedad in my four years. I knew the players who we were playing. I knew them all. I'd worked so much with them. I'd never wish them ill, not then nor now, but the experienced ones among them, they really turned it on that day. They were really up for it; the fact that Toshack was the coach of the opposition. They didn't even say hello. It was heads down and on with the battle on one of the muddiest pitches I've ever seen. John Aldridge scored for Sociedad and I began to wonder whether convincing him to join the Basques had been such a good idea.

In Europe, things had started well. It was before the Champions League era and its seeded groups. It was a pure knockout competition at the time, where anyone could be drawn against anyone at any stage in the tournament. We put our first-round opponents, Spora Luxembourg, to the sword by 9–0 on aggregate, and then got the draw that everyone had been looking to avoid. In the previous season, under Leo Beenhakker, the Madrid players had been humiliated by Arrigo Sacchi's AC Milan 6–1 on aggregate, including a 5–0 thrashing at the San Siro with goals from all three of the side's deadly Dutch trio of Frank Rijkaard, Ruud Gullit and Marco van Basten. The Italian team had gone on to win the European Cup that year with a special group of players whose names still trip off the tongue – Paolo Maldini, Franco Baresi, Mauro Tassotti, Alessandro Costacurta, Carlo Ancelotti, Roberto Donadoni – and they were now in search of their second in succession. They had been Beenhakker's undoing and I did not wish them to be mine.

I went over to Italy to watch them play along with my friend Joe Moruzzi from Swansea, who still runs Verdi's cafe in the Mumbles. He was always a big John Charles fan and I spent a lot of time with him when I worked down there. He and John went up to Anfield once to watch as I played for Liverpool against Barcelona, and it was a nice opportunity to catch up with Italian Joe again.

The two of us travelled to Cremona to see Sacchi's team play the local side, Cremonese, who were struggling in Serie A but managed to shut Milan out and snatch a goal themselves despite trademark acrobatics from Van Basten. What I wanted a closer look at was one of Milan's favourite goalscoring moves. They would get Van Basten to run out wide with the ball beyond the left-back, Gullit would close in at the near post dragging players with him and then Rijkaard would make a late break into the box to score almost unmarked when the cross came in.

Back in Madrid, we worked on how to defend that over and over with Schuster, Ruggeri, Hierro and Sanchís. My plan was that when that ball went in behind Gordillo, and Van Basten went wide, Ruggeri would go with him and get tight, Schuster would come across just short as cover, Hierro would go with Gullit to the post and Sanchís's job was to stop Rijkaard getting on the end of the cross. We had two or three of the Madrid reserves playing the parts of those Milan attackers; ball there, cross there; again and again. Sure enough, about ten minutes into the tie at the San Siro it happened. Tassotti passed the ball – beyond where Gordillo was occupied with the Milan midfielder – to Van Basten just outside the box. The Dutchman flicked it out wide towards the corner into the empty space and ran on to it. Ruggeri was with him; Schuster followed them level inside the area in case Van Basten burst through, as planned. The ball came over and Marco Simone, who'd replaced Gullit that day, arrived to find Hierro there already outjumping him. The ball went over the pair of them, Rijkaard raced in and Sanchís was ten yards the wrong side of him. Bang. Goal: 1–0. We ended up losing 2–0 after our goalkeeper, Buyo, took out Van Basten outside the area. The Dutchman put away a penalty that should never have been by the letter of the law, but you'd be hard pressed to say that he didn't deserve it. Two weeks later, we went a goal up at the Bernabéu on the stroke of half-time courtesy of Butra, whom we'd missed in the first leg. Unfortunately, we just couldn't find a way through them in the second 45 minutes, our comeback not exactly aided by Sanchís getting himself sent off after 78 minutes which, combined with his lack of discipline in the earlier game, might partly explain why the two of us never quite saw eye to eye. We won the game 1–0 but we went out of the European Cup, and AC Milan went on to successfully defended the title, a feat not to be repeated for 27 years, when Zinedine Zidane managed it with Madrid in 2017.

With my team out of the European Cup by the end of October 1989, and that 2–1 loss in San Sebastián the Saturday after, it was 'Crisis at Madrid' in the papers once more. Normal service resumed almost straight away though. I felt we'd been unlucky against Milan and the conditions at the Atotxa had been unique. My system of play that the press had branded defensive was working and we scored by the hatful from that moment onwards; 4–0 against Bilbao, 3–2 in Tenerife, 7–2 versus Zaragoza. We went the rest of the season unbeaten in the league, scoring 107 goals – a La Liga record which stood for 21 years. Of those, 38 belonged to Hugo and, quite astonishingly, all of his were scored with a single touch. He never gave the goalkeepers time to set themselves. It was Hugo's best season for Madrid. He was the first player to win the La Liga top scorer's trophy, the Pichichi, with an average of over one goal per game since Ferenc Puskás in 1960, and he picked up the European Golden Boot that year too.

It didn't always go Hugo's way, though. During our home game against Mallorca in February he was having difficulty making his mark. Hierro had put us into the lead but our visitors had equalised just ten minutes later. Mallorca had a terrific goalkeeper by the name of Ezzaki Badou, whom I later came across in Morocco. He was manager of the national team while I was working at Wydad Casablanca. Zaki, as he was known, was a real killer between the sticks and I remember the day he almost battered Hugo as they went for a fifty-fifty. If Hugo hadn't jumped out of the way in time, he'd have been down and out. As it was, the game went on and, with it balanced at 1–1, we got a free-kick from 25 yards out. Hugo put the ball down to take it, walked back and as he ran up he stopped and said to the referee, 'Hey, the wall! They're moving forward,' but the ref, Ángel Calvo Córdova, told him to get on with it. Hugo turned back to take it again, began his run-up, stopped to remonstrate about the same thing and, bam, the ref gave him a yellow card. So, Hugo went back once more, ran up, spotted the wall still playing its tricks, complained to Calvo and the man in black sent him off. Hugo could be like that but it was very difficult to be furious with him because he was such a fantastic footballer. He scored some memorable goals and pulled Madrid out of trouble on a number of occasions.

We'd gone into that game three points ahead of Barça at the top of the table and I was wondering what to do about making sure we maintained our lead when I got the word through that Barcelona were losing 1–0 to Castellón. So, with that, I told Miguel Tendillo, our back-up central defender, to get stripped off. There were fifteen minutes to go and Mallorca were throwing it at us. So, I took off Butragueño, shut everything up and the game finished 1–1. We went four points clear.

Madrid had a club secretary at the time called Manuel Fernández Trigo from La Coruña. He more or less ran the club while Mendoza spent most of his time elsewhere. He was very strict, very stiff and always dressed up in a shirt and jacket with his tie knotted up tight to his neck. Any result that wasn't a rout of the opposition – even if we had won – and he'd call me into his office first thing on a Monday morning and say, '*Que pasa en sabado?*' – What happened on Saturday? – and I'd have to explain myself. It was almost frightening to go in and speak to him. 'Don Ramón will not be happy,' he'd warn me, talking down the length of his nose to where his glasses sat pinching on the end.

After the Mallorca game, Trigo came straight in fuming, shouting, 'How am I going to tell Don Ramón that we drew one-one when you take Butra off and Hugo is sent off as well?'

Mendoza was away on his boat, so I just said, 'Look, Manolo, just tell him that we were three points ahead of Barça before the game and now we're four points clear, and don't tell him anything else.' That seemed to shut him up, or at least he took his fury away from me.

In the end, we won the championship in April at Valladolid with four games to spare. Given it was just two points for a win at the time, it was something of a canter. It was a super night. Mendoza was delighted and he was there afterwards. We stopped at a hotel on the way back and had a big meal and celebration and I remember the president stood up and toasted the championship, but no one seemed to care except for me and him. None of the players seemed that interested. It was the fifth one in succession and it was just like, 'here we go again'. But, of course, the Madrid board had taken me there to win the European Cup. That was the one they had wanted, but that Milan side was fantastic and it had still been a great year at Madrid for me. I'd won the cup with Real Sociedad and now I'd won the championship with Real Madrid.

We went to the town hall after winning the title. Looking at the players, it was a bit like going to the aquarium. You see these deadly sharks in the water and then they fill them up with food until they're stuffed and barely moving. Then some guy can jump in with them and look brave when those bloated creatures have had so much to eat that they don't even want to look at him. If you've been top for five years, you lose the passion for it and I remember going to Mendoza and warning him that this team had passed its peak, that this couldn't go on forever, that it was going to come to an end, and it did the following year. I could see it coming. For one thing, the team needed changing. Hugo had just turned 32 and I remember saying to him, 'I'm not looking forward to being the coach who has to say to you, "I'm sorry, but you can't do it any more."'

The rest of the goal tally in that 89/90 season was spread around the team, but the one other notable haul was the eighteen from Martín Vázquez. Martín was a couple of years younger than most of the Quinta and was a little bit more on the periphery. Of all of them, he had been struggling the most to really establish himself on the field, but he came to life that season. I think playing in that front three behind Hugo really suited him. We worked well together. I asked him to play further up the field and to use the ball much more when he got it. He listened and he thrived.

Vázquez was a very talented player and he'd had a super season, but I can remember Mendoza not offering him quite the same level of favour as he did Míchel, Butragueño and the others. He was a quieter lad, a little bit more introverted and he was probably closer to Hugo than the rest. He'd got a good offer from Torino way back around December time and he signed a pre-contract agreement to join them over the summer. It must have seemed like the right move for both him and the club but he was a big loss for me. He might have felt that he wasn't as appreciated as he should have been. Also, he'd won the Spanish championship a few times and some players want a new challenge. So, he left.

Ruggeri was another who had to be replaced. He was having problems with injuries and we couldn't count on him to be fit any more. Yugoslavia, as they were then, beat Spain 2–1 in the World Cup in Italy that summer. They had a centre-back called Predrag Spasić. Julio Salinas, the Barcelona No. 9, was centre-forward for Spain that day and I remember Alfredo Di Stéfano coming back and telling Mendoza that he'd seen a centre-back who was terrific. Madrid signed Spasić on his say-so and let's just say it was less than successful. This was not a player that was good enough for the club and the people really turned against him. It became very difficult for Spasić to play in the Bernabéu. He was fit and he was strong but his positional sense was not good. He was used to the old Yugoslav defensive regime of man-marking – when the No. 10 goes to the toilet, you follow him into the dressing room and you wait with him and when he comes out of the toilet you follow him back onto the pitch – which was a completely different idea to what I had. It is one thing to mark a man in a man-for-man system, and it is another thing to mark zonally. With regards to having the ball at his feet, well, it became a bit of an embarrassment.

I recommended two players to Mendoza to sign in place of Martín Vázquez and Ruggeri – John Barnes and Des Walker. I had made advances to Peter Robinson and Cloughie about each of them but, a week or so later, Madrid signed Spasić and Gheorghe Hagi, who played in the same positions. They also signed Luis Milla to replace Bernd Schuster, who had just passed thirty, and for whom Madrid had received an offer from city rivals Atlético which was deemed to be good business.

I knew it had been coming because a week or two before, Ramón Fernández, the man who was responsible for making signings, asked what I thought of Milla, whose contract was coming to an end after six years at Barcelona. I asked, 'How many goals does he get?'

'Oh, he doesn't get many goals,' was the reply.

'How many bookings?'

'Oh, he gets eight or nine in a season.'

He might have been a defensive midfielder, but he was a totally different kind of player to Schuster. I told him we had two young lads who were coming through the ranks who could play the positions we needed, Juan José Maqueda and Santi Aragón, who'd had a few good loans and was a better fit for that role than Milla. Why go ruffling the feathers of Barcelona to sign a player who doesn't fit with the philosophy anyway? Of course, it was too late. They'd already signed him by the time we were having the conversation.

I played Milla in a pre-season tournament down in southern Spain, in Cádiz, and he picked up a terrible knee injury that kept him out for ten months. Trigo turned to me at the time and said, 'There you go. Now you've got what you want.'

It was not a nice thing to say. I knew Trigo very well and I had an awful lot of respect for him. He was a terrific employee for Real Madrid but that moment was one of the few times I was ever disappointed with him. He was the wheels that kept that club going for a long time. It was more out of frustration on his part, almost saying that I was right but not quite able to. I said, 'Manolo, nobody wishes that on anybody.'

So, the three that came in were nowhere near proper replacements for the others that went out. It was like chalk and cheese for the lot of them. Hagi had great qualities, there was no doubting that, but he had been the star of the show at Steaua Bucharest and he could be a bit anarchic. He was an itinerant and undisciplined type of footballer and he seemed to just play wherever he wanted. He'd had all sorts of offers before joining Madrid, including advances from Arrigo Sacchi, even after Hagi's Steaua had lost to Milan 4–0 in the 1989 European Cup final, but the Ceauşescu regime had always seen to it that Romania's star would never defect. Of course, that had all ended by 1990 and in Madrid swooped. The culture shock was just too much for Gheorghe, though. He had been used to being the big fish in the little pond and I couldn't rely on him like I could Martín Vázquez.

As for Spasić and Ruggeri, well, you wouldn't get two more opposite players.

Ruggeri had problems fitness-wise, but he was an intelligent player and got by on his intelligence. His reading of the game took him into the right areas of the field. He was very clever, very cute, a typical Argentinian defender. It was an art. Spasić was the opposite. He would win a 100 yards race with anybody but his legs were quicker than his brain. He had a lot of difficulty learning the language. It was just too much for him. I think the asking price for Walker and Barnes was more than Mendoza had wanted and it suited the president to sign Spasić and Hagi, but there was no comparison. Walker's pace for Real Madrid would have been fantastic. At that time, when you were attacking, you needed to have quick defenders waiting to pick up the counters, so that was a problem. And Milla was out straight away from the start. He was a lovely lad, a good professional, but had been brought up at Barcelona's La Masia, which was too different.

I'm not saying that Madrid didn't need to make changes, but I don't think the people that arrived were the right fit. I'd have preferred to give those two young players a try as well. In the end, they both left. Santi Aragón went to Zaragoza and had a decent career there and played for Spain. Juan José Maqueda went to Valencia and later Albacete.

So, I had difficulties starting off with this team for my second season at Madrid, plus most of the players had won five titles on the belt. The third and no less important ingredient was that Barça, under Cruyff, had started to push on. The previous year had been Cruyff's second season in charge at Camp Nou. He'd won nothing in the first twelve months and could have done the same in 1989/90, but his side had beaten mine not just once in the league but also in the final of the Copa del Rey that summer after Hierro went for an early bath after just 45 minutes. The Catalans scored twice in the second half to take the cup 2-0 in Valencia and I do believe that, had Barça not won that game, Cruyff would have been out. They'd have won nothing again and he'd have been on his way. As it was, it gave him the breathing space to adjust his team, to buy Hristo Stoichkov, who became a very important player for them, and have Michael Laudrup and Ronald Koeman settled and get the side playing the kind of football he wanted. They were on the up and Madrid were on the down, and it was Barça's time to dominate. They won the next four championships, and the European Cup in 1992 as well. It was going to be their time and that cup win gave them the boost.

As for Madrid, our opening game of the 1990/91 season was a tight win at the Bernabéu, and 1-0 is not enough if you're Real Madrid playing the likes of

Castellón. Our second match was away to Sevilla, and I told the players before kick-off that they could go out for a drink after the game. It was before the start of our European Cup run, I knew we wouldn't have the free time again for weeks to come and the players needed to get together and let their hair down a little after a lot of fitness work in the build-up to the season. There was a rule that you couldn't go out 48 hours before a game, so when there were two games a week, they never got a break. Unfortunately, we lost 2–0 to Sevilla – who played the last half-hour with ten men, even managing to double their lead – and when my players came back into the hotel at 6 a.m. the following morning, some clever paparazzo was there and snapped a shot of our full-back Gordillo, among others. Now, Gordillo was a Betis boy before he was at Madrid and it was a chance for this Sevilla-leaning paper to make him look silly. They published the picture alongside the headline: 'Real Madrid lose and he goes out to celebrate'. Mendoza called me in a fury, saying he was going to fine Gordillo, and I said I'd given him permission, but there was no changing Mendoza's mind. The following day, I had a meeting with the players and I wrote a cheque for the amount of money that Gordillo had be fined and gave it to him. I think it was about £2,000.

Things got better briefly on the field with a more convincing 3–0 home win against Mallorca the following week. I steered the club successfully through the first two rounds of the European Cup, but our league form deteriorated with some bad losses on the road and a run of draws, including a 1–1 draw at the Atotxa. After a loss away at Valencia in November, I got the bullet. I could see it coming and, as daft as it sounds, I was quite happy. I wasn't comfortable in Madrid. We'd won the championship with a record number of goals and still no one had seemed pleased. I felt I'd achieved something here but it was very stressful. I left on good terms with Mendoza. I think he realised what had happened with the team but the crowd had become impatient and it was time to make a change.

A few weeks later, a fabulous box arrived at my door with a superb bottle of Andalusian white wine inside it, the best wine they do, but it was the casket itself that was almost more impressive. It was a lovely wooden box that opened with a lock – I still have it in my house – and I opened it up and there was a note along with this bottle and it read, 'Good Luck, mister – Gordo.' He never cashed the cheque.

*

8

Return to San Sebastián

REAL SOCIEDAD IS A CLUB WITH A VERY PARTICULAR DNA. IT WAS never a club where you had to work hard to build a team spirit. There was never any issue of work ethic. There were players who, if they hadn't been Basque, wouldn't have played in the Spanish first division. They played for Real Sociedad. They gave everything they had. It was their club, their town, and what the odd player might have lacked in talent, they made up for in feeling and togetherness. That togetherness and sense of pride in every result is an often underestimated strength in football. There are games when it makes the difference between winning and losing, and there's no other way of creating that feeling of belonging. It's about trusting that everyone around you feels exactly the same way as you do and that they're busting their guts just like you are. That spirit very often kept Real Sociedad in the top flight.

I remember, after that third year of my first spell in San Sebastián, when Barça had poached our best players, saying to one of the directors:

'How can we keep doing this? How can we keep pushing players through when other teams come in and take them? How can we keep turning this over when Bakero, Begiristain and Rekarte all move to Barcelona, and Arconada, Zamora and Celayeta all retire?'

And he said, 'There'll always be three teams worse than us in this league.'

'To be honest with you,' I replied, 'That's not really a phrase that motivates me too much.'

But I knew what he was trying to say. The spirit that there is in this club, you won't get anywhere else. The only time Real Sociedad really struggled and went to the wall was when they had ten or eleven foreign players in the squad. It was when Barcelona came in and took those three players in 1988, that prompted everybody to think again and it was only then that everyone could see the benefits of signing foreign players. There was a feeling that it had reached the stage where the club was going to have to do something, and relaxing Real Sociedad's rules was the obvious answer.

I was the manager at Madrid when John Aldridge became the first non-Basque signing the club ever made, and it was on my recommendation too. So, it was a very different situation regarding players when I went back.

I wouldn't say I was happy to leave Madrid, but I wasn't exactly torn up about it either. It's never nice to be dismissed, particularly from such a huge club, but I'd reached the pinnacle of the game, and I'd been pretty pleased with what I'd achieved at the Bernabéu. Mendoza had been very decent about it as well: we sat down, we sorted things out and I left. It was a lot different to the second time I left Real Madrid, which was an ugly, ugly situation.

It was made easier on that first occasion because I knew I could go back to Sociedad. I knew from inside the club that the option was there if I ever wanted it and it was somewhere I felt I really belonged. I had a home there and the idea of going back and starting again really appealed to me after all the madness of Madrid. I had been back to San Sebastián regularly. Even now I have a home up there. It's a part of the world where I feel very comfortable. If people ask me what's my team, obviously, I've an interest still in all of them, but Swansea – because what happened at Swansea was incredible, so they're very close to my heart – and then Real Sociedad are the two special places. I spent sixteen years or so at those two clubs. That's a lot of my career, and a big attachment. I think they both go with my character as well; a bit of an outsider – Welsh, not English; Basque, not Spanish – and the way I've done things tactically and as a manager has always been a little different to the generally accepted ideas of everyone else around me, for better or for worse.

Real Sociedad, like Swansea before it, was a great learning experience for me. My first job as a player-manager, my first major successes; both clubs having to work mostly with limited means and both with a strong emphasis on working with young, local lads; both small towns with passionate support for the clubs. I was aware of that big responsibility that I carried. I was happy to be back at one of those places. I was also happy to be by the sea again. One thing that connects most of the teams I've managed is that they've been by the sea. In Madrid, you're miles away, but you can go to San Sebastián for a swim. It was good to be back on the coast again.

When I'd left Real Sociedad for Madrid, eighteen months earlier, they put my number two in charge – Marco Boronat. He'd been with me for those first four years and he'd played under Alberto Ormaetxea through the good years before, so he was someone that the club knew. They had a decent first year under Marco, qualifying for the UEFA Cup. However, the second season under Marco wasn't going anywhere near as well and they were as happy to take me back as I was to return.

It was just before Christmas in 1990. There was a league rule in those days that meant you couldn't manage two teams in the same division in the same season. So, technically, I went back as general manager, with Javier Expósito officially in charge of the team, but it was me pulling the strings in training. I sat up in the stands of the Atotxa during the games, communicating my instructions using walkie-talkies. It was something I shouldn't have done really. I gave the president advice on what to do over the summer before I started the next season in earnest. The biggest job of all, though, was moving out those first three foreign players in the squad who'd arrived while I'd been gone – all of them English.

John Aldridge had been successful. He'd scored sixteen La Liga goals in his first season and then seventeen in his second. Only Butragueño scored more with nineteen in 1990/91. Aldridge did not quite manage to settle himself in San Sebastián, though. Not everyone welcomed him there with open arms as the first non-Basque player at the club. There was some nasty graffiti and he and his family were not always greeted with the respect that they should have been out in the community. He handed in a transfer request and there was some silly stuff on behalf of the club with them threatening him financially and asking him to pay back £25,000 of his contract. It should never have happened but I think he and the other foreign players were on more money than the club could afford. There were some financial difficulties with the move to the new stadium, the Anoeta, that was happening at the same time and the directors were doing anything they could to balance the books, not that that excuses this particular situation.

For the other two non-Basques, it was more a case of encouraging them to leave. They'd dipped and they weren't worth what they were being paid nor were they really good enough to justify taking up one of those three slots allowed for foreign players in your side. What I was able to do in that period before officially taking over was sort that problem out.

Kevin Richardson and the late Dalian Atkinson were the other two Englishmen in question and they had not hit it off so well on the field. Atkinson had a lot of talent, but he was an undisciplined player. The crowd liked him because he scored super individual goals, but as brilliant as he was in some games, he was conspicuous by his absence in others and we never really saw eye to eye. I'd always thought it right to assimilate myself into the local culture, but I suppose that was always going to be much harder for Dalian. Not only was he foreign but he was also the first black player at the club, and living in a small city comprised almost only of Basques made it understandably difficult for him settle in. He was also a young man without a family of his own, so he was out and about a lot. He drove around a bright-red Porsche and on one occasion he ran through some red lights at four o'clock in the morning and caused an incident. He tried to say it wasn't him but there was only one car like his in the whole of the Basque Country. Plenty of the lads at the club had a lot of time for him, but it just wasn't the best match.

There's a story that he was given a local cheese made from sheep's milk, called an *Idiazabal*, as a gift by some of the fans. It had become a tradition for the foreign strikers. John Aldridge was given a load of steak every time he scored a goal. Later Meho Kodro earned hake for the same. I leave it up to you to decide who got the best deal there. Anyway, Dalian took the cheese with a big thank you from the supporters club – the members of which watched as he got into his car – drove a few hundred metres up the road, then rolled down his window and lobbed out the *Idiazabal*.

The fans gave him the nickname *El Txipiron*, which is a dish of black squid in its own ink. He was asked in the press whether he minded, and he said it was preferable to the kind of things he'd been called back in England, though that may be the primary reason as to why he didn't settle in Sociedad. It can't have been easy for him. He went back to the UK and signed for Aston Villa for £1.6 million where he won the League Cup, very nearly the inaugural Premier League trophy and scored some memorable goals. Regardless of whether the two of us got on well or not, I was shocked to read how he died during that incident with the police, right outside his father's home. A terrible thing.

With Kevin Richardson, I think he could see that he wasn't really quite what we needed in the midfield. He was a good, steady player but he was exactly the type that Real Sociedad are good at producing from their own. He was a good pro but not the best fit. Given the limits on foreigners, it didn't make the most sense to have him on the roster, and I had other ideas of whom I wanted. I let Kevin know that he should keep his eye out for a move and he ended up going in the same deal as Dalian for £450,000 and captained Ron Atkinson's Aston Villa.

So, those three – Aldridge, Richardson and Atkinson – were good, but they weren't my type. We needed something different because Real Sociedad were flirting with the bottom half of the table and that couldn't happen. They went back to England and we brought in three different foreign players that turned out to be extremely positive.

You had to be very careful of the foreign players you picked. You had to understand the place to get the right ones. If you did a history of the top six foreign players to ever play for Real Sociedad, they'd have been signed by me. There was a while here when they just went and signed players without enough care or any sort of plan. They'd have six foreigners sat in the stand watching the game. It was ridiculous. Foreigners, OK, but more than four at Sociedad was too many but, after the club's ruling had changed, they'd lost it completely and the floodgates had opened. Then they had the problem that the parents of the young players going into the club, when they saw that the chances of their lads getting into the first team were gazumped by foreign signings, they didn't have such faith in the system. They looked for better opportunities elsewhere and they signed their boys up at Bilbao and other places instead. So, it had a knock-on effect. That's one of the reasons the club eventually got relegated to the second division.

Iñaki Alkiza was the president who changed the Basque player rule but it was his successor Luis Uranga who really went to town buying foreign players throughout his time in charge during the 90s. When I went back to Real Sociedad for the third spell a decade later in 2001, I had to tell him that he'd gone over the top, that this was not the idea I had when I suggested relaxing the rules to Alkiza back in 1989. I'd been watching it happen from afar while I was working at other clubs. It's easy for coaches to come in and say that what's there is not good enough and that you've got to sign more players. Well, that's not how it's supposed to be at Real Sociedad. You've got to make sure that they are good enough. You've got to work with players to make it happen. That's what the club was based on. Relaxing the rules a little was meant to avoid the situation where an injury means that you don't have any goalkeepers or to make up for a genuine dearth in a given position.

You had to keep the numbers down in the squad to keep the club as it was. When they went and signed ten foreigners I wasn't at the club, but I wrote a letter in the newspaper criticising Miguel Fuentes – a friend of mine who had played for the club for years before taking over as president in 2005 – telling him that this could not go on, and the following year they got relegated. There's nothing positive about signing ten players. How can you have six or seven of them sitting in the stand watching the game and all the while you're not going to produce the young players either? They lost their heads for a couple of years.

Back in the summer of 1991, though, they had the reins on the situation a bit better, and I had a very good idea of two of the non-Basque players that I wanted to shake things up a bit. I'd worked with them both before and as soon as the season finished I went off to Lisbon to see if the president at Sporting would be good enough to let them go, at the right price, of course. Oceano had been almost the first-choice pick of that team since my season there in 1984. Real Sociedad had been conceding far too many goals in La Liga and he was the perfect player to tighten things up from the midfield and make sure we were no pushovers.

Our other problem was with our left-back Mikel Lasa, who had already arranged a transfer. I'd given him his debut at Real Sociedad during my first spell when he was only seventeen and he'd done so well in the last few years that Real Madrid had paid good money for him to replace Gordillo. After a sticky start he did well at the Bernabéu for six years or so. He picked up a few championship medals and a Copa del Rey crown until Roberto Carlos came along and supplanted him. Carlos Xavier at Sporting had always been one of my favourite players and, now that there was an opportunity to bring foreigners to Real Sociedad, he was an obvious choice. He was always a lovely lad, one of the most skilful players I've ever worked with; a very talented player. Discipline-wise, he was maybe not the best. Like a good Portuguese, he liked his food. He was almost always three or four pounds over the weight he should have been, but he was still such a fantastic player on the ball. There was a lot of noise that came out in the press a few years later, while we were still working together in San Sebastián, saying that the two of us had a big falling-out and that I had banned him from the team, but it was a load of nonsense. There was a game in Guimarães, Portugal, where he wasn't doing the business and I took him off after thirty minutes which, of course, is something no player ever wants. Of course, it was a lot worse because it happened in his home country, which was an embarrassment as well as an insult. We did have a few training-ground rows after that but you have those with lots of players and you learn to take that kind of thing with a pinch of salt in this business. We didn't get on for two or three weeks, and then it passed. Otherwise the two of us got on very well and always did. In some ways, that made it more tricky. At that time at Real Sociedad, I had to be careful that the local players didn't see or feel or think that these foreigners were my favourites. That's a sure way to destroy any sense of spirit and togetherness at a club. I always had that at the back of my mind and I think that particular spat between Xavier and me was maybe when I'd been a little harder on him than I'd needed.

Luis Uranga was not very happy about the 200 million pesetas that the deals for Xavier and Oceano were going to cost. It's peanuts these days, of course, about £1 million, but he took a fair bit of persuading and luckily both players were a big hit. They stayed three years before heading back to Sporting once more in a single agreement.

My third foreign signing was Meho Kodro, a striker to replace John Aldridge. He was a Bosnian playing for his hometown club Velež Mostar – a very successful club in the old Yugoslavia which itself was on the verge of collapse. The same Croatian journalist living in London, Borko Krunic, who had put me on to Rajković and Hadžiabdić while I was at Swansea, pointed me his way. Kodro was good in the air but also very technical like many of the players from that region, and his scoring record was very good. It was even better during his four years at Real Sociedad with 73 in 129 La Liga appearances, and all this was at a very delicate time because the war was just beginning. The deal meant he actually got out of Bosnia about a month before all hell broke loose over there. He was very happy to leave. He went back and got his family out just in time too, and the Basque Country became a second home for him, as it had become for me, and he's ended up coaching at Real Sociedad at various levels since. I had Meho working up at the top of the training ground behind closed doors before I signed him. I wanted a good look before I decided. We paid 150 million pesetas for him and eventually sold him to Barcelona for 750 million.

To begin with, though, it didn't feel like those decisions had worked out particularly well when both Kodro and Xavier got injured before the start of the season. We got one point from five games until they were ready to play again. I had to push a few young lads in who were going to take a bit of time to settle, so the results were no particular surprise to me, especially as three of them were against sides that finished in the top six that year. But whether we felt like it at the time or not, we'd hit the jackpot with those three foreign players. We slowly turned it round over the season and eventually finished fifth to qualify for the UEFA Cup. The key was that we still kept it feeling like a local team. In terms of the language, the football, the culture and the positions they played, these three were a better fit and the Basque people took them in. The Basques are good people. They can take a while to warm to outsiders but, once they do, you're theirs for life. That's part of what helps make the club so special. You get team spirit through a sense of cultural identity. The more homegrown players you have in your team, the easier it is to achieve that. They've grown up in the same club as footballers and, as people, they identify a lot more with the values of the city where the team is based. Kodro, Xavier and Oceano had obviously not grown up in San Sebastián but, because of the way the city and the players accepted them as ones of their own, they added to that sense of togetherness too.

After his difficult start, Meho Kodro came back into contention for selection a few weeks later. It hadn't been a good start, neither for him nor Xavier, but we began cranking through the gears as our new Bosnian front man found his shooting boots, his first goal coming against Real Madrid at the Bernabéu. They say you always remember your first and last for a club. Well, Kodro's first that day came from a direct free-kick and his last came alongside another two when he scored a hat-trick in front of our own fans as we took down our eternal rivals Athletic Bilbao 5–0. Both impossible to forget, so he says.

We only lost three times in the second half of the season, with Meho scoring thirteen goals. Not bad from just 24 appearances when you're coming back from an injury and in a new league too. A hake is a very large fish, but he and his family managed to get through all of it without a problem. There were a lot of people in his house at the time because of the war. Even if it was a huge hake, as they often were, they could polish them off in a single meal. The fish in San Sebastián is very good. If nothing else, Kodro certainly learned that.

Fifth was a good position for Real Sociedad that season and, perhaps, to some extent, we overachieved. During that second three years I was at the club, we were generally a top-half team that could finish anywhere between around fifth and thirteenth position, depending on what else was going on around us. The point margins were often very small. The difference looks big but we were of a very consistent standard at that time. Sometimes we got a bit of a lead and were lucky enough to stay ahead of those around us and some years we weren't so consistent and finished mid-table. We fell at the first hurdle in the UEFA Cup in the second year, having worked so hard to achieve it the season before, which was a pity. We went out to Portuguese side Vitória Guimarães 3–2 on aggregate despite a decent comeback in the home leg. We'd lost our goalkeeper, Gonzales, to Valencia over the summer, which didn't help. He was a safe pair of hands and had done a good job of stepping into the breach ever since the irreplaceable Arconada had hung up his gloves. We tried one of the young Basque lads called Javier Yubero for a season but he wasn't up to the same standard. His inconsistencies were one of the many personnel reasons that stopped us from picking up some of the points that the team really should have. The only sides with more goals scored against them that season were in the relegation places, but every now and again that kind of thing becomes a problem at Sociedad. You're just short in one or two positions, but an army only marches as quickly as the slowest man. So, if you can't sign players to fill the gaps, then you're stuck with what you've got. Over the years the Basque Country has had great goalkeepers, but back then there was a bit of a low. Elduayen had gone to Atlético Madrid and it took us until 1993/94 to settle on Alberto as our No. 1. He had also come through the ranks and he grew into the job quite nicely. Not the best at corners and crosses but he did the club proud for a decade until Real signed the Dutch keeper Sander Westerveld from Liverpool.

Of course, 93/94 was always going to be tricky for another major reason and that was the club's move to a new stadium. The Anoeta is a super multi-purpose venue for the city but it's a world apart from the old Atotxa which, like so many other old stadiums, is now blocks of flats. The Atotxa was a tight little ground where the fans were right on top of the players, and suddenly they were twenty metres away at the Anoeta. Home advantage is a big thing in places like the Basque Country and we suffered without that intense atmosphere that had always been a given. Those kinds of issues are part and parcel of moving grounds but they were particularly pronounced for Real Sociedad and particularly so for that first season. The club lost more identity in that process than it did when it decided to sign foreign players, but at the heart of both changes was the same fundamental problem – money.

One of the reasons that Real Sociedad broke its Basque-only policy was the belief – and probably an accurate one – that you can do it but you have to be the only ones. So when you have your neighbour, Athletic Bilbao, doing it too, and they have the financial muscle that you don't, it becomes much, much harder to keep up in the league. You're not only already competing using a limited market of players but you're competing alongside another team that's also targeting that identical limited market but with more money than you. In fact, one of Real Sociedad's big beefs with Athletic Bilbao is the fact that they feel like, in international eyes, and in the eyes of other people in Spain, that their club isn't seen as being as Basque because the Basque flagship is Athletic, but Real Sociedad is as proudly Basque too.

It was very much a transitional time for Real Sociedad during those years, but the directors were aware of that and I still had plenty of support despite the team's average form because I was generally well thought of in San Sebastián. The results were disappointing but it was always one of those places where they had much more patience with what you were trying to achieve, principally because they were used to dealing with coaches having to bring young players through and they knew it took time.

Given everything that was going on, the only time there was pressure on my position was when I chose to put my name forward for the position as Wales manager halfway through the season, at the beginning of 1994. Terry Yorath had failed to win qualification for the World Cup in the US that summer and his contract had not been renewed. I was approached, I got permission from the people of Sociedad to go and work both jobs at the same time and the idea at the start was simply to see how it went, but I realised straight away that to do it properly I'd have to finish at San Sebastián and I wasn't prepared to do that. So, I packed it in as Wales boss after just one game. As it happened, I ended up leaving Real Sociedad anyway. Not everyone at the club and in Donostia, the Basque name for the city of San Sebastián, had been entirely happy about what had happened and it left a bad taste in the mouths of the people who thought that I shouldn't have gone to Wales in the first place. I wasn't getting the results that some believed we should and their patience had evaporated. It was a pretty dark period.

A few months into the 1994/95 season, I sat down with Luis Uranga and we decided that it was in everyone's best interests if I stepped down. It was a difficult way to leave things. After another three years working there the Basque Country had become a big part of my life. It was home. It was in my blood. I'd bought myself a house just along the coast in Zarautz. It's a super place with a lovely beach and a Michelin-starred restaurant. I was very happy there. It's easy to finish a job when you know you've done all you can but if it's your home too, that makes things more difficult and you tend to hang on longer than perhaps you should. What finally made my mind up was that my son, Cameron, had not been going so well back in Wales. He'd been playing professional football for Bristol City, Cardiff and others but had ended up in hospital with some serious health problems on more than one occasion. Eventually, he was diagnosed diabetic and, for Cameron, it meant that he couldn't achieve the kind of fitness levels that he felt he needed to compete at a high level. I felt a long way from my family and it was an opportunity to go back to Wales and refocus on the things that really mattered.

9

'Super Depor'

I'VE NEVER BEEN ONE TO SUFFER FOOLS GLADLY BUT LOOKING BACK now, there are times when I might have been a bit more diplomatic. Generally speaking, it's served me well to stand my own ground in football management, to know how I want things done and to make sure they're done that way. That was the way it worked at Liverpool, both in the attitude of the players and the methods of the managers. I've taken that model and made it my own and done very well with it. I've got more decisions right than I have got wrong, but what I've come to learn is that sometimes getting my ideas over to a team, a president, a club or a group of fans might have required some more patience on my part. That was never a problem at Swansea, Real Sociedad or even Madrid but I might have had a bit more success if I'd been a little less strong-minded at Deportivo de La Coruña.

The root of my troubles there stemmed from the fact that the club president and I had very different ideas on how to get Depor to the top. We didn't see it in March 1995 when I agreed to take over that summer, having spent the previous winter in Wales, but we were a marriage that should never really have been. It's important to see eye to eye with your club chairman or president. If a manager hasn't got that right, then he's doomed from the start.

Augusto César Lendoiro was a Gallego, a Galician, a local to La Coruña. He was president at Deportivo for 25 years until he stepped down in 2014 and, at the time, in 1995, he was recognised as one of the most astute presidents in Spanish football. He'd taken charge of the club in 1988 when it was 600 million pesetas in debt and had been languishing in the Segunda División since the early 70s. Together with coach Arsenio Iglesias – himself a former Deportivo player – Lendoiro had lifted the club into the La Liga Primera where Super Depor, as they were now nicknamed, had become the rising stars of the division and had just won their very first major trophy, the Copa del Rey.

Lendoiro was particularly successful at making very clever signings; good deals on experienced players and some exceptional talents from Brazil too. Apart from the midfielder, Fran, who was like a local hero in Galicia, they never really had anybody come through from the lower ranks, though, which was something I wanted to put right. Even the second-team coach at La Coruña wasn't that interested. Nobody was bothered. The president seemed to say, 'No, we're not interested in that here. We prefer to go out and buy.' So, early on, I described the club's success as a 'castle in the sky' because it didn't seem, to me, to be built on any kind of solid base like the academies and youth structures which were the lifeblood of a club like Real Sociedad. That was one of the many comments during my time there that did more to distance me from the fans than it did to convince the president and directors to change their way of doing things.

Lendoiro had a different idea of what he wanted and he'd managed to sign Bebeto and Mauro Silva, which, in 1992, was an absolute scoop. Both of them had become a core part in the creation of Super Depor and would be part of Brazil's 1994 World Cup-winning team. The two were a contrast; both Brazilian but very different in their mannerisms, in the way that they played the game, in the way that they were; very proud players, exceptional talents. They were players that could win you games out of nothing and you have to be careful with players of that level. I'm fortunate in as much as I've been there and done it myself. The fact that I'd played at the very highest level and won everything that there is to win, that gives you an advantage because top players can be fickle. They'll turn to you one day if they don't agree and say, 'What do you know about it anyway? What have you done?' Players couldn't do that with me, which definitely helped in my managing of them. Sometimes, as well, you needed to be a little more lenient with them and the other players knew that, so it was OK, but Bebeto and Mauro were never ones to take advantage of that kind of thing.

Bebeto was a fantastic goalscorer; in the same league as Hugo Sánchez. Just a terrific finisher, very acrobatic and spectacular; a genius. You wouldn't see him for ten or fifteen minutes, but when the ball went in the penalty area he came alive. I remember one game early on against Albacete, he'd scored in the second minute with one of his trademark scissor-kick volleys but had disappeared after that.

At half-time, I threatened to take him off if he didn't get involved. We ended up winning 5–0. Bebeto scored the lot – that one in the second minute and then the 82nd, 83rd, 86th and 89th. He'd probably have scored them sooner but I imagine he wanted to make me sweat.

A lot of Argentinians and Brazilians go to Spain to work and to play football, of course. On the football field, the stereotype is that the Brazilians are much more easy-going and play the samba tricks and style, while the Argentines are much more disciplined. Bebeto might have been one of the former but Mauro Silva was one of the most disciplined players I have ever worked with. He was a lot more down-to-earth, hard-working; a vital ingredient for any side. It was him and Dunga that were the engine room of that Brazil team while Bebeto and Romario were the fantastic duo up front.

There has always been a break at Christmas time in Spain. We were due to play Real Madrid at home at the Riazor on 20 December in that first season, before returning for an away game at Real Oviedo on 2 January. I wanted to be back in training for a few sessions before then to make sure we were up for the fight, but I knew that I'd get some stick from the foreign lads like Bebeto and Mauro who had to get all the way to Brazil and back to see their families. I didn't want to mess up morale before our game against Madrid by telling them that it was only a short break, but the team would be off right after the match and I had to let them know when they needed to return so they could make their arrangements. I took my assistant, José Manuel Corral, to one side during our practice on the day before the match and told him the plan.

'Get them in for a quick break now and I'll make the announcement,' I told him. 'I'll say that I want them back here on the twenty-seventh. They'll complain and, when they do, I'll tell them, "OK, OK, make it the twenty-eighth," and everyone will feel like it's a good deal.'

So, we got them in the meeting and I said, 'I know you've got to sort out your travel arrangements for after the game. So, have a good Christmas and I'll have everyone back in for training on the twenty-seventh.'

Bebeto and Mauro looked at each other and then at me with daggers in their eyes. I asked them what the problem was and Mauro, who was the more diplomatic of the two, says: 'Look, mister, when we go to Brazil, we have to fly to Madrid. Then we have to sit in the airport three hours. Then we get on a plane for nine hours until we are home. We lose two days – one day getting there and another day coming back.'

'OK,' I said, with it all going to plan, 'everyone come back in here. I know some of you have a long way to go over Christmas, so, I'll tell you what I'll do. I'll make it the twenty-eighth.' But they were still looking at me like they wanted to kill me.

They went back to their training and the Brazilian pair were barely jogging around the field and so I shouted, 'Hey, come on. You've got to get into this. We're playing Real Madrid tomorrow!'

José gave me an 'I told you so' look, so I got them all back in one more time and said, 'OK, here's what we'll do. For every goal you score tomorrow, I'll give you an extra day off at Christmas.'

I've never seen anyone's eyes light up like Bebeto's did at that moment. Off he went with a spring in his step and the next day it was Deportivo La Coruña 3, Real Madrid 0 – a Bebeto hat-trick. He came straight over to me and said: 'OK, mister, so three goals; twenty-ninth, thirtieth, thirty-first – I see you on the first of January.'

We beat Madrid, they got their holiday and, fortunately, we took care of Real Oviedo on 2 January as well.

I had tried to bring in three or four players of my own over the summer before we'd begun that first season but there were difficulties and they were likely players that hadn't suited the president's ideas. Martin Vázquez and Txiki Begiristain arrived from Real Madrid and Barcelona respectively, but the former had become too injury prone and the latter was not quite the hit he'd been elsewhere. Both were sold the summer after I left, which tells you what you need to know there.

I had difficulty settling in La Coruña despite the fact that I was relatively successful from the off. The team still smarted from losing La Liga on the final day twelve months before my arrival and frustration on the terraces simmered because expectations had increased even with the near miss. My first games in charge were for the Teresa Herrera Trophy, which is hosted by Deportivo every year in August and is one of the most prestigious pre-season tournaments in Spain. We beat Real Madrid in the final and then twice more, home and away, the following week over the two legs of the 1995 Spanish Supercopa. That was Deportivo's second ever major trophy and it made me the only coach to have won the three major titles in Spain with three different clubs. It was a very convincing 5–1 on aggregate. We were totally dominant in the home game and came out 3–0 winners, but we were a little too confident on our return at the Bernabéu and I wanted to get the message to the squad that I didn't want to see them switching off like that when the league began, no matter the occasion.

'My players should feel ashamed of the way we played here,' were my words to the media, but rather than fire anybody up it perhaps began a bit of unease between me, the club and its supporters. Given I'd just beaten Real Madrid three times even before the season had really begun, I might have earned the right to say something along those lines, but apparently not. It didn't help that the man I'd taken over from was a local legend and this was the team that had just won the Copa del Rey. They could walk on water as far as the fans were concerned. So, who was I coming in and telling them that the attitude of their boys was not up to snuff?

The atmosphere in La Coruña can be tricky and Galicia is thought of as a difficult place to win people over. There's a phrase that describes the Gallegos – even if you saw them in a lift, you wouldn't know whether they were going up or down. There's supposedly a secrecy about them. There's only so much attention you should pay to stereotypes but all these parts of Spain are very different and come with their own different identities. The point is that, even though I'd worked in the same country, I was an outsider here. I wasn't yet trusted. If anything, I was a Basque and perhaps it was a mistake to expect that the supporters would think that my way was the correct one when it was the different ideas of their president and former manager that had taken their club to its heights. It all made Iglesias a very difficult act to follow and I remember thinking when he left that this will be a good job not for the next manager but for the one after. On parting, he'd said in the media, '*Le he dejado un equipo bien hecho*,' – I've left him a team well done.

'*Sí, como el pan duro*,' was my reply: Yeah, like stale bread.

The squad had an average age of 29 with none of the regular starters under 25. This was a team that had started very well but I knew that there would have to be big changes pretty soon, which I'd have to try to make in the second year. If I'd been a little more diplomatic in that first year, I might have had more time to get it all to work.

Things weren't as smooth in the league as they had been with those early cup wins and we picked up too many disappointing results to really challenge that year. On our day, we could beat anyone, but I had to conclude at the end of that campaign that that particular group just didn't have enough ambition. I said it in the press partly knowing that it would fire a few of them up, partly because I felt it was true and because we needed some fresh faces with a little more drive, players who were a little more to my taste.

The Cup Winners' Cup had been the one I'd really been aiming for in 1995/96 and we'd had a very good run at it. Of all the medals I've won as a player and a coach, that was the only one missing from my collection and this Super Depor team was just the kind of side to conquer it. We smashed eight past APOEL Nicosia in the first round, beat Trabzonspor 4–0 on aggregate in the second and then, in the quarter-finals, just about managed to overcome the Real Zaragoza side that had won the Cup Winners' Cup the year before against Arsenal, sealed by Nayim's ridiculous last-gasp goal from the halfway line. We never did lift that trophy, though, and I never have had my name on it since.

We drew Paris Saint-Germain, the eventual winners, for the semi-finals and couldn't manage to score against them over the tie. We had two key players missing in Mauro Silva and our left-back Nando in both games, plus our ever-present defender Miroslav Đukić for the away leg along with Fran too. Perhaps we wouldn't have conceded that ninetieth-minute Youri Djorkaeff goal at the Riazor when the visitors won 1–0 in the first leg, and maybe we would have seen enough of the ball at the Stade de France to score one or two of our own in the second, but that's the way it goes and I'm sure I've been as lucky as I've been unlucky over the years on that front. I was screaming for their keeper to get a red card in that second game when he handled the ball outside his area but the referee didn't see it that way.

We finished the 1995/96 season in ninth position without ever really troubling the European places and aimed to regroup in the summer. Bebeto decided to call it a day. At the age of 32 he went back to play in Brazil, leaving the club along with a few of the veterans including defenders Francisco Villarroya and Rekarte, the latter of whom I'd known from Real Sociedad and who had been playing at Depor since leaving Barcelona. We'd scored enough goals to finish in the UEFA Cup spots but the defence needed a lot of restructuring from the goalkeeper forwards. We brought in two new boys between the sticks. The young Czech goalkeeper, Petr Kouba, never really hit it off but that was because Cameroonian Jacques Songo'o came in from Metz and made the position his own for the next five years. He was voted the league's best keeper that first season.

Armando and Jérôme Bonnissel were the replacement full-backs. They were both there for a few years with the former doing better than the latter, but the big signing was Noureddine Naybet for right at the heart of the defence. He was over at my old club Sporting when a Portuguese football agent named Lucidio Ribeiro alerted me to him. Lucidio and I went off to watch Naybet play in a UEFA Cup game in France against Metz, where Songo'o was playing in goal. I wanted them both for Depor but Lucidio said that Jacques was due to sign for another club the next day. I got him to put the brakes on that one and he did so in the nick of time.

Naybet fast became one of my favourite players I've ever coached; a super lad, a great central defender; very intelligent, very able. We picked up a couple of others – Corentin Martins, an attacking midfielder, who managed a decent tally of goals before getting too many injuries, and Mickaël Madar, a big, powerful French centre-forward that we got on a free from Monaco but he didn't hit it off at all. Thankfully, that didn't really matter because the real coup by the president, Lendoiro, was the signing of Rivaldo from Palmeiras. Again, he only stayed at the club for one season but for very different reasons. He finished right up there with the big goalscorers across the league with 21 in 41 games. Barcelona came in with an offer you couldn't refuse of around 4 billion pesetas, which was something like £20 million – a huge sum in those days.

That second year, the 1996/97 season, we went off like a train. We were just two points off top spot in the league in January when Barça came to La Coruña. Bobby Robson was manager and Ronaldo was in his heyday at centre-forward. We went a man down and only lost it to a single goal in the 85th minute. It was the first game we'd lost that season and a few problems started to creep in. I kicked up a fuss because the pitch at the Riazor wasn't prepared as it should have been. The players had been given a few days off and when we got back we all looked at each other agog. It was like they'd lifted it up and plopped it back down again, and it was a bog for our next home game against Athletic Bilbao. It was a shocking wet night with the rain whipping in off the Atlantic. Luis Fernández had just taken over as the coach of Bilbao. It was his PSG that had knocked us out of the Cup Winners' Cup the previous year and he seemed to have the better of me once more when we found ourselves at 1-1 after 26 minutes. Rivaldo was having a very poor time out there and only a few moments later, I told my assistant, José, to get Alfredo warmed up because I was taking Rivaldo off.

'No, no,' he said, 'don't do that,' but I insisted.

So, on went this hard-working midfielder, who was all 100 per cent effort, push, push, push, and off came star striker and darling of the fans Rivaldo. The crowd booed and jeered me and Rivaldo took his shirt off and threw it down at my feet as

Beginnings at Cardiff City, my hometown club. [COLORSPORT]

Rough and tumble against Arsenal at Ninian Park. The way football used to be. [MIRRORPIX]

From Sunday school and into church; signing for Liverpool and the great Bill Shankly. [MIRRORPIX]

Rising highest against Everton, a club I would score against in only my second game. [GETTY]

Kevin Keegan and I: Robin Hood and Friar Tuck or Batman and Robin. [GETTY]

Preparing for the 1974 FA Cup final with Cameron in Formby. [AUTHOR'S PERSONAL COLLECTION]

Liverpool 3, Newcastle United 0; parading the FA Cup with Brian Hall. [GETTY]

Scoring in the Nou Camp – a stadium I would later enjoy more success at as a manager. [GETTY]

A 1-1 draw in the second leg of the UEFA Cup semi-final against Barcelona. Quite a night at Anfield. [GETTY]

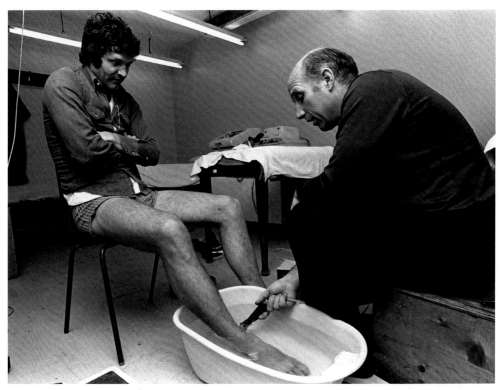

Injuries and trying to stay fit became a theme in my latter years at Anfield. [GETTY]

I used to head out to Southport beach to bathe my ankle in the water when I was injured. Red Rum also trained there. [GETTY]

Winning the European Cup in 1977! [GETTY]

Impersonating Jerzy Gorgoń, the Polish international defender. [GETTY]

With Wales in Malta and the Vetch Field accompanied there by my son, Cameron. [GETTY]

Into management with Swansea City where I would achieve three promotions and celebrate reaching the First Division with the directors. [GETTY AND MIRRORPIX]

Signing the Everton legend Bob Latchford was a coup for Swansea. [MIRRORPIX]

Returning to Anfield in the aftermath of Bill Shankly's death was an emotional experience.

[AUTHOR'S PERSONAL COLLECTION]

After tasting continental football with Sporting Lisbon, my next stop would be Real Sociedad – the first of my three spells in charge there as manager. [AUTHOR'S PERSONAL COLLECTION]

Winning the cup in 1987 and parading the trophy through the streets of San Sebastián.
[AUTHOR'S PERSONAL COLLECTION]

My exit conference at Real Sociedad. To Madrid… [AUTHOR'S PERSONAL COLLECTION]

Familiar faces in Spain… Barcelona's Gary Lineker being one of them. [GETTY]

You might remember this guy beside me, Luis Aragonés: the coach who helped Spain win Euro 2008 – then at Barcelona. [OFFSIDE]

Dinner with lagers in Bilbao with Howard Kendall (Athletic Bilbao) and Terry Venables (Barcelona). We hadn't yet discovered Rioja. [GETTY]

To Madrid and the biggest job in club football. [AUTHOR'S PERSONAL COLLECTION]

A young Fernando Hierro. [OFFSIDE]

Johann Cruyff, one of the greatest players that has ever been became one of the greatest coaches at Barcelona. [OFFSIDE]

Winning La Liga in Madrid still wasn't enough to satisfy some… [AUTHOR'S PERSONAL COLLECTION]

Back to one of the places I call home, San Sebastián. [AUTHOR'S PERSONAL COLLECTION]

Deportivo La Coruña were a difficult club to manage in spite of some fine players including Bebeto. [PA]

Despite some difficulties at Depor, I still had plenty of time to relax and soak up the Spanish culture. [AUTHOR'S PERSONAL COLLECTION]

Only Real Madrid could have taken me away from Beşiktaş and the beauty of Istanbul… [OFFSIDE]

Back with a more experienced player in Fernando Hierro on the training field. [OFFSIDE]

A return to the dugout of the wonderful Santiago Bernabéu. [GETTY]

I enjoyed my short time at Saint-Étienne more than the expression suggests. [GETTY]

Xabi Alonso became a midfield great for Liverpool, Real Madrid and Bayern Munch. I would give him his debut in my third spell at Real Sociedad. [GETTY]

Across three managerial spells I fell in love with San Sebastián and it's people: here I am walking across La Concha beach, and greeting the great Ryder Cup-winning captain José María Olazábal, a big Sociedad fan. [AUTHOR'S PERSONAL COLLECTION]

Another return to Spain, this time with Murcia. [PA]

My second attempt at managing Wales would last a lot longer than my first. [GETTY]

Gareth Bale was just 16 years and 315 days old when I handed him his Wales debut, making him the country's youngest ever player at the time. [GETTY]

Two ex-Real Madrid managers now teammates as TV pundits. [GETTY]

In 2013 I won the Azerbaijan Super Cup with Khazar Lankaran, the fourth country I had won silverware in as a manager. [AUTHOR'S PERSONAL COLLECTION]

One final adventure? Maybe not… I loved living in Casablanca while managing Wydad. [GETTY]

he left the field, but we had the ball in the net before half-time and I turned to the fans and shouted, '*Sí, aplaudid, cabrones!*' – Yeah, you're clapping now, you bastards – and a few other things that were even less appropriate, and they came back even worse. It was like waving a red rag at a bull. It's not the sort of thing I would ever do again but it just came out. Why couldn't I take Rivaldo off? Was there anything in my contract that said I couldn't? But, at the end of the day, it's the supporters who pay your wages, particularly those that go to the games, and they deserve some respect too. To me, though, their jeers had been an indication that they thought I didn't know what I was doing and I was turning round to show them that I did. Sometimes it's very difficult to restrain yourself. I've always felt I've been lucky enough to achieve what I have achieved and that should give me the right to contest people in the way that I've wanted to. I'd won three major trophies in Spain by then. If I was taking Rivaldo off, it was because it needed to happen. It was Alfredo whose chipped ball in caused chaos in the box that led to the goal. If it wasn't for a ridiculous patch of mud in front of the goal line, he'd have recorded the assist; a pity that we went on to let the equaliser in on the 88th minute.

After the game, the president came into the dressing room and gave me a right ticking-off. 'You can't come in here and do this,' and 'What do you think you're doing; ranting and raving?' But I wasn't interested and after that game, my number was up. That was the beginning of the end, even though I was right and the other players, of course, knew it too and stood up for me. Maybe if I hadn't turned round and jeered everything would have been OK, but the president was up for re-election, my relationship with the fans had never been good, and this really rubbed salt into that wound. I announced that I wouldn't be extending my contract beyond the summer a few days later and, shortly after, at the beginning of February, we agreed that I should leave.

There was a lot of unrest after that Rivaldo incident, and there was the state of the pitch and the training facilities – the conditions around us were not up to the standards of the team that we were. But mostly it was because Lendoiro and I had different ideas on how to run a club. There were occasions where he'd sign players without asking me. The classic example was the Brazilian midfielder Flávio Conceição, whom he bought just before the start of the second season. We could only field three non-European players in the team. So, I said to the president, 'Look, I've already got Mauro Silva, Rivaldo and Naybet here. These three, when they're fit, they're always going to play.'

He said, 'No, no, I give you the players, you decide what to do with them.'

'Yeah, but then I've got a problem because this one's not going to be happy. You've caused me a big problem here.'

That was the moment that I knew the two of us were on a collision course. All the good results had held it together for the first half of the season, when we were within one or two points of the top of the league, but the minute we fell away it became too much. They were very difficult circumstances for both me and Lendoiro. We were happy to end it but I think he appreciated the work I'd done there and I appreciated him as well. We had just reached a stage there where it had become impossible. Depor finished the season in third, with the meanest defence in the league.

A few years later, when I was manager of Real Sociedad once more and Rivaldo was playing for Barcelona, I took my team to face the Catalans over at the Camp Nou. Rivaldo was on the field that night as his side took the plaudits but, at the end of the game, he came over to the dugout and he apologised for that moment at the Riazor and gave me his jersey. That's twice Rivaldo's taken his shirt off for me. I liked it better the second time.

10
Turkish delight

TURKEY IS A UNIQUE COUNTRY. IF YOU GO TO TURKEY TO WORK, IN any line of business, then you've got to have your sensors on. You've got to be aware of what's going on around you. This is not like moving from London to Manchester or even Wales to Spain. You're going into a country that is completely and utterly different. You don't have a clue about the language or how things work and there's a lot of trust involved. You've got to realise where you are, and who you're dealing with, what players are like, and what goes on behind your back. You've got to get to know people and get to know who you can trust and who you can't. I went to Turkey open-minded and saw for myself how it works and, for me, it was one of the highlights of my fantastic experience in football management.

For someone from Western Europe to survive two years in a place like Turkey is not easy. Football has been my life, but I like to think I've also learned an awful lot about people's different personalities and mentalities, and not just players – journalists, directors, presidents and supporters too. All of that helped keep me afloat during my time in Istanbul.

I'd been to Turkey with Liverpool once before, to Trabzon, in the east of the country, to play Trabzonspor on the way to winning the European Cup in 1977. It was a horror trip. Take a look at the memoirs of any of the Liverpool players from my era and you'll find an entry on that game. Bob Paisley famously described our team hotel as a 'doss house', the ball as a 'pig's bladder' and he said he 'had better rations in my bivvy in the western desert' during the Second World War. Ray Clemence remembers the pitch that night as having rocks all over it and everyone has a story about how, between the prayer minaret on one side of our lodgings and farm animals on the other, nobody got a wink of sleep. Suffice to say, the place had improved quite considerably by the time I visited Trabzon with Beşiktaş twenty years later, but that first time was terrible. With all due respect, it's one thing to work in Istanbul, another to work in a different part of the country. Generally, the foreign coaches in Turkey only work in the capital or Ankara, where it's a bit more cosmopolitan.

Istanbul is a huge city and I was put up in a terrific place, the Swiss Hotel, right on the banks of the Bosphorus. I used to watch the boats come down to the Mediterranean from Russia every day and wonder what was going up and down inside those shipping containers from one place to another; just exactly what was travelling by right under our noses. It's a very interesting place. I'd do my work there on the waterfront; sit in the cafes planning out my next games, watching how people moved about; watching people in these boat taxis going back and forth between Europe and Asia just fifteen minutes across the water. I'd get on a boat with them sometimes and go across to the other side, have something to eat over there in another continent, and come back again to finish off what I was doing. I enjoyed the bazaars, the old buildings, the temples; top museums they have out there and there was time in my days to go and explore, while still getting all my football matters sorted. Sometimes, I'd head over the old bridge right up to the end of the Straits where the Black Sea starts off and sit among the different types of people over there beyond the city, where I would enjoy all the different kinds of fish restaurants and all sorts. It's a wonderful thing to be able to do, to work in a place like that. It was all part of that same sense of adventure that took me from Swansea to Lisbon in the first place, and it felt exhilarating to be back at it all over again having been settled in Spain for the previous twelve years.

There's a tremendous hustle and bustle in Turkey and Istanbul is a special city for football, with the three biggest clubs in the country all there – Fenerbahçe on the Asian side and Galatasaray and Beşiktaş on the European – and the derbies between them are as fierce as you could wish to get; real football. They were big, big games, ferocious; right up there for intensity compared to everything I'd ever been through. The Beşiktaş/Gala games were the craziest of them all. The only games I've seen close to that are the rivalries in Morocco.

Pelé had played for Santos at the İnönü, Beşiktaş's old ground, and said it was one of the most beautiful stadiums he'd ever played in; very close knit and in a lovely part of town. You could see the Bosphorus right through the stands.

The crowd are right on top of you there; tight, like an old Third Division ground. A game here with a full house was really special.

I had offers from English clubs when I left Deportivo. I'd talked to Rupert Lowe from Southampton, talked to Francis Lee and Mike Summerbee about an opportunity at Manchester City while we played a round of golf in the Algarve, but they couldn't offer me this. Istanbul sounded much more interesting. My brief return to Wales in 1994, which made me realise Britain wasn't home any more, might have been at the back of my mind, but it was much more than that. A few months into the job in Turkey I even turned down the Liverpool job. I met Peter Robinson and Roy Evans in London. Roy, of course, I knew very well and the idea was a kind of a joint role, but things were going very well for me at Beşiktaş. There were no bad feelings. There was no bitterness from when I thought I'd be taking over at Anfield all those years before. That had long gone. I just didn't feel like it was the right opportunity for me. I'd been working abroad since 1984. I'd been relatively successful. I'd become European, I'd earned a reputation as a foreign coach and I wanted to keep that going. With all due respect, I knew that I'd get other offers from Spain when I'd finished in Turkey. My rating was high in Spain and there was the lifestyle that I enjoyed too, and I knew I'd find it difficult going back to the UK. I'd settled. A lot of people go abroad and it doesn't work out for them. They can't settle. It was exactly the opposite for me. I never had difficulty settling in wherever I went. I think that was because I never took anyone with me. I always went and worked with the local coaches and that helped me an awful lot. It was a big plus because it showed them that I had trust in local people, and it made me less insular. I wasn't sitting huddled away with my own people, away from the culture all the time. I was on my own and I had to get up and get on with it. In the end, of course, it was Gérard Houllier that took the Liverpool role, but the partnership between him and Roy didn't last long. Management is not a job that you can share. It just doesn't work that way.

I'd met the Beşiktaş people in Barcelona at the Hotel Princesa Sofia, just up the road from the Camp Nou. We'd agreed terms and I'd signed a two-year contract. I'd had a call from Serdar Bilgili, who was the vice president of the club. He'd spoken to Bobby Robson, who was at Barça, who put him in touch with me. Serdar was the rising star of the club's directors and very much in line to take over from Süleyman Seba, who had himself played for Beşiktaş and was the longest-serving president there. When I arrived in Istanbul, I was very impressed with everything I saw. I saw right from the off what a big club this was.

The first part of my brief was to get to the group stages of the Champions League, which had replaced the old European Cup in 1992. Beşiktaş had qualified for the second round by finishing as runners-up in the Süper Lig the year before to Galatasaray, who were the top side in Turkey at the time. Their manager was Fatih Terim, who was considered as the Godfather of Turkish football. He'd made over 300 appearances for the club as a player, been a key part of the national side for ten years and then returned to manage them both. That Galatasaray team had nine of the Turkish players who went on to become part of the squad that finished a record third in the 2002 World Cup, and any quality they were missing was bolstered by the Romanians in their ranks who included Gheorghe Popescu, Adrian Ilie and Gheorghe Hagi, the last of whom I knew from Real Madrid. They were a very good team who went on to beat the Henry and Bergkamp-era Arsenal in the UEFA Cup final in 2000.

Finishing ahead of this Galatasaray – as was, of course, the other major part of my brief – was not going to be easy. In fact, I had a bit of a disastrous start when we lost 6–0 to them in the pre-season Turkish Sports Writers Cup, which used to be the traditional season-opener. We were well and truly turned over. There were no two ways about it. I was frustrated because I felt at the back of my mind that Fatih had been shown preferential treatment here and there by the referees and officials. He was a big rival of mine but I think he became more sympathetic to my cause after that hammering, which perhaps he shouldn't have, given that we eventually managed to turn the tables on them.

The team I took over at Beşiktaş was not unlike the Deportivo squad I found when I arrived at La Coruña. There was a group of experienced players there whose time was up and it needed some slow rebuilding. A couple of them were good pros who could help me – Ertuğrul Sağlam, the big forward, and the creative midfielder Mehmet Özdilek – but there were others there and they could see the signs early on that maybe it was over for them, and made it a little bit difficult. There was a lot of dead wood.

The right-back captain, Recep Çetin, wasn't my cup of tea. He was a big Beşiktaş club man, though, so I had to be careful. The old president, Seba, liked Recep because he'd come to the club at the age of 22 and become something of a John Terry or Tony Adams-type figure, but by no means as good a player. He wasn't a bad player by any stretch, but I wasn't convinced that his influence was totally positive. He wasn't the brightest and I wasn't as struck on him as everyone thought I should have been, but as coaches, we all have these problems with players. I took a fair bit of stick for either not playing him or playing him out of position. I often did that when I arrived somewhere just to see if I could mix things up a bit and find a few ideas that hadn't been used before to improve the system, the same as I did with Schuster in Madrid.

A bigger problem for me was that the Turkish players, at the time, were not as well schooled in the tactical part of the game. It wasn't like the youth teams in Spain, England, Germany or Italy where they learned these things every day and the upshot was that you might have found an experienced Turkish player who didn't know the difference between ideas like zonal play and man-to-man marking. Mostly, all the defending in Turkey was only man-to-man. Coaches were afraid to play with a back line of four or three because Turkish players would lose concentration too easily and they couldn't understand when it was their zone, when they have to take the man, when they've got to switch players or when they needed to go back to man-to-man style. We were the first to do it. The press were up in arms but I explained it to them and they seemed to accept what I was doing, but not even at Galatasaray with Fatih Terim or with the other successful German coaches in Turkey before – Holger Osieck and Jupp Derwall – did they try this. Now, of course, there's no problem with playing that way in the Süper Lig and with the national team as well.

I didn't have a hand in signing new players. That had all been taken care of before I arrived, so most of them didn't offer much of a boost to the team. Tayfur was a defensive midfielder that made a lot of appearances for Beşiktaş over the following ten years, but the big gamble was on the bald-headed Bulgarian creator Yordan Letchkov. Along with Stoichkov, Emil Kostadinov and Krasimir Balakov, he was part of the golden generation of Bulgarian players who'd dumped Germany out of the World Cup in the USA a few years earlier. Yordan Letchkov made a move to Marseille but had fallen out with the management there and hadn't played for a few months. If the person in charge of recruiting at Beşiktaş had looked, the warning signs were there.

It took Letchkov a while to get back to match fitness when he did arrive and he was influential on occasions, but I didn't have the best relationship with him. He was a very talented, very experienced player, obviously, but with a low work rate. People generally felt that he was a bit lazy in his approach, so fitting him into the side wasn't easy, and that kind of attitude doesn't go down well in a squad either. He was a difficult character too, which didn't help; he was very introverted. His fellow Bulgarian in the squad, Zlatko Yankov, might have kept him company but they were very different players with totally different personalities and, after about six months at Beşiktaş, Letchkov announced that he didn't want to play for the club any more and he went back to Bulgaria. It dragged on in the background. He started training with other teams elsewhere, was banned by FIFA and ordered to pay Beşiktaş for breach of contract. He didn't get on the field again until 2001 when he played for CSKA Sofia and his reasons for it all were that he and his wife couldn't settle in Turkey. But this is football. It's a demanding profession and players fail to settle in all sorts of places. It shouldn't have been difficult for Letchkov. Sofia's only a relatively short hop over the border from Istanbul. I think he just wanted to get back, having realised he'd made a mistake in going to Beşiktaş in the first place. He wanted a way out and he thought that he was big enough to do that, bigger than the club itself.

With the club's high-profile signing out of the picture, then, it was very much a case of looking at the young players that there were and trying to bring them through with the help of some of the seasoned pros. Yusuf Tokaç was a skilful little midfielder and there was Nihat, who was a big success as a forward and whom I later took to Real Sociedad. He made his debut with me at seventeen; an explosive player with a terrific right foot. He scored some spectacular goals and was a super lad who, rightly, did very well. I pushed them through along with two young midfielders named Serdar Topraktepe and Hikmet Çapanoğlu.

Daniel Amokachi was a popular player at Beşiktaş as well. He'd been signed the season before after a short spell at Everton and it was a kind of environment that suited him. He was a big-name player in Turkey. He liked to pick the ball up and run at people. He could whack one in from thirty yards and then miss two or three from five yards, but he was quite a bubbly type of character and good to have around. There were problems with him here and there. He had a back injury that had him in and out of the side that first season, and I had to ban him for a game or two after he came back a few days late without saying anything following Jay-Jay Okocha's wedding in Nigeria over the Christmas break, but we got on OK. You had all sorts of problems like that in those days, particularly as there weren't as many flights as there are now. You've got to stop people taking liberties like that even if you don't want to because, if you don't, you've got fifteen or sixteen other players looking to see what's going to happen, to see what you're going to do. And you can't tell the press when you've got a problem like that with a player. You've got to suffer in silence and they'll often presume it's a great big bust-up when it's not really. You can't tell people why you've dropped your best player because then the problem gets more public and more heated, and you might find that you're finished with that player completely. You might feel let down at times by certain individuals, but you have to manage all that. It can get very complicated in charge of a high-profile football team and having to make these decisions. The public don't always know why you've made them and they think they have the right to know and, in a way, they do. They've paid their money, but if you tell them the truth then you're throwing stones at your own greenhouse. It's often better off for everybody's sake if the fans don't know.

What you have to do at times, though, is make allowances. The Africans going home from Istanbul or the Brazilians from Spain is not the same as going over to Bulgaria or nipping back to Portugal. So, you might not be as heavy-handed in your punishments.

Between the problems with Amokachi and an early injury to Ertuğrul, I was relying on a young Turkish forward named Oktay Derelioğlu to come up with the goals. Oktay had had his break-out season in the previous year but just a few weeks into training in 1997 his young wife committed suicide. I remember Amokachi coming up to me on the bus and telling me that she'd shot herself, like it was something that happened every day over here. It hit Oktay very hard, of course. He was an important player for me over those years I was there but he left Beşiktaş shortly after I did, and he never really settled anywhere after that.

We cruised past Maribor to reach the Champions League group stages. It was a tough tie against what's often been a good footballing side, and we could only manage a 0-0 draw at home, but we then won 3-1 away from home in the second leg which took us into a series of games with Bayern Munich, Paris Saint-Germain and Göteborg. We started with a 0-2 away loss to Giovanni Trapattoni's Bayern team of Oliver Kahn and Lothar Matthäus. We gave a very good account of ourselves despite the result and then won the next game at home to PSG 3-1. That was a good night. It was Ramadan and I remember coming out of the tunnel to the noise. They sacrificed a sheep on the pitch before the start of the game. It was a pretty hostile environment. Oktay scored twice and Ertuğrul once. After a home win against Göteborg we went second in the group. They had a very stubborn, square and solid defence with the great Swedish keeper Thomas Ravelli doing the heroics but Oktay's early goal was enough. If you're in Bayern Munich and PSG's group it's going to be very difficult for a Turkish team to progress, though, and those were the last points we picked up.

We lost 2–1 in Gothenburg in a ridiculous game. The referee blew up against Beşiktaş for a penalty that should never have been and then sent off my goalkeeper, Marjan Mrmić, after 64 minutes before sending off Ravelli as well. We were well beaten in the next game at home to Munich. They were a top, top side. The playing surface at the İnönü wasn't the best and didn't help us, but I certainly wouldn't use that as any kind of excuse. The other teams had to play on it.

With PSG winning that same night, we were out of it before the final group game. We did well and were in with a shout for a while but, as I say, it would have been a major shock in those days for a Turkish team to get through a group like that.

We ploughed away and plodded on in the league. It was a slow kind of progression. The young players were starting to perform and we were still very much in the title race as winter drew near. Fenerbahçe were in the lead but they'd dropped points right before our derby game with them. We were breathing down their necks. Not long before the match, though, it was announced that our form striker, Oktay, had to go off for his national service with the army, which was part of his agreement. The only trouble was, while he was away, he was put on heavy drills and came back with damage to his knee ligaments. I was incensed. He'd obviously been worked really, really hard before this big game and I had my ideas that maybe this was not by accident, but you've got to be careful. You can't criticise the army in Turkey, as I soon found out. It's a criminal offence.

At the press conference before the match I said that it was a strange coincidence that we happened to be missing our top player in a big game like this. How can it possibly be that we're playing a big match on the Tuesday and Oktay has to go away on Sunday and Monday to do military service? Someone in the club or somewhere should be saying no, that we need him for that game and he should go another time. So, I said that someone somewhere had made it happen.

There were a few differences in the press as to exactly what I said after that but, what with those inconsistencies, the fact it was all through translation from English and back, and that it was twenty years ago, I don't remember for sure, but it's very possible that I made comparisons to the old communist regime from the

Soviet Union, which didn't help matters. By the time I was in charge of Beşiktaş, you could do anything in Turkey but the army was sacrosanct and, to be honest, it was ignorance on my part, but in front of journalists in a press conference when you're frustrated that your top player can't play in a big game, then strange things can and do happen. I just felt that Oktay was representing his country as much by playing with Beşiktaş in Europe as he was doing his duty with the army. He was out there in Paris, scoring goals, and in the international team and everyone around Europe was talking about him. I wasn't necessarily against him doing his service, but I felt he ought to have been protected while he did. The room went so quiet. They all knew it was such a big story and they wanted to get every word but I was very, very angry and wanted to make this point because Oktay was my player. I'd developed him. I turned him into a player that would fight and play for the shirt. Oktay had become really motivated. So, for him to come back injured like that made me very angry and I did not want this to happen again.

Of course, the papers were up in arms. The military high command got involved and sent a memorandum to the president asking for an investigation. I wasn't the most popular person in Turkey that week. The Beşiktaş president Süleyman Seba was a decent fellow but he was upset about this. He's the most Turkish Turk I've ever known, so it was something that was difficult to deal with. Over the years, I have had the tendency to put my foot in it like that on more than one occasion and in more than one country, so it wasn't altogether a new experience for me. In the end, I apologised in a statement read to the press that said: 'I have no business with the military. I showed no disrespect to anybody. I merely felt sorry for the injury to Oktay, who is a member of the national team, and I expressed that. I am a person who loves Atatürk. I apologise.'

It sounds like something a PR department would come up with but I really am a big fan of Kemal Atatürk, Turkey's founding father. I've read with great interest his history over the years and that was a useful thing to be able to say. If you're in a country like Turkey and you've got a lot of time on your hands, you should pick up a few things about the place. Thankfully, it all blew over fairly quickly in the end. There were a lot of people who wanted to make more of it than they really needed to have done.

The president of Fenerbahçe, Ali Şen, got himself involved in the run-up to the game and for a while afterwards too. He came out and said that he'd have sent me packing were I manager of his club. So, I called him a clown to the media, said that we all laugh at him and he'd won nothing in football compared to me. I never shied away from any kind of thing like that. It was all part of the game out there. They could be like children sometimes in Turkey with the way they argued and, when in Rome, sometimes you need to do as the Romans do. It's not always objectively the right thing to do, but you've got to understand where you are and that you can't let people walk all over you. I was black and white all the way. You've got to support your own team over there and it can be pretty ferocious. 'Galatasaray özel, choc uzel Fenerbahçe çok güzel, ama en büyük Beşiktaş,' – Special Gala, very special Fenerbahçe, but the best Beşiktaş. That was the line I used out there. I didn't speak much Turkish but I could manage that and they called me *Gally Hoger* – Welsh coach.

I didn't always know what the press was writing anyway because I didn't speak the language and I wasn't there long enough to learn it. I couldn't read an article and tell you what they were saying, which was a disadvantage, so I had to have Tayfun Ozusakiz, my translator, with me all the time to fill me in. That's why I say that you've got to have your confidence in these people. You don't want people leading you the wrong way to get you to say something because they're trying to move you out.

Ultimately, the derby against Fenerbahçe finished as a 2–2 draw, but we had the ball in the net on three other occasions, only for all of them to be adjudged offside. That speaks for itself. I don't think I've ever participated in a game where there's been three goals disallowed for offside. I had to be restrained by security guards at half-time when I went to have a go at the ref, and I was subsequently sent to the stands. It was a natural spontaneous reaction. Sometimes you can't always get the best view from where you are, but if someone disallows three goals for offside in a big Istanbul derby, when one of your players has already been taken out before the action, then it does raise your suspicions. I don't know any coach worth his salt that wouldn't complain about that.

We faded away in the league that year and finished sixth, but we had to change a lot of things and it wasn't really until the second season that we had any kind of consistency about us. Where we did succeed in 1997/98, though, was in the cups. We beat Galatasaray in the Turkish Cup final on penalty kicks. Hagi missed the first for Fatih Terim's side after both legs of the tie had ended 1–1, and they never recovered from there. We had a young goalkeeper that day, Fevzi Tuncay, who'd kept us in the game with a string of saves in that second half before shutting out

Hagi at that vital moment, and then we played Galatasaray again in the Super Cup – called the President's Cup – a few months later in the capital Ankara.

Fatih Terim was probably the most successful coach in Turkish history and he was a cute customer. He was a trickster and he'd get away with little psychological plans of his. I never really trusted him. Any goodwill that he might have shown us after that opening friendly defeat of the season had long since dried up after our tussle in the league and after we'd taken the Turkish Cup off him too. What I remember most about that Super Cup game was when we went out into the tunnel before kick-off. The Galatasaray team should have been waiting there with us but they weren't out yet. I was looking at my watch. We'd been told to be in the tunnel ten minutes before the start of the game. We were there twelve minutes before and when there was seven minutes to go – and Fatih's boys still hadn't lined up – I turned my players round and told them to go back into the dressing room. Just as we were going back in, Galatasaray began coming out and both Fatih and the match delegates told us to stay there or we'd get a fine, but I told them, 'No, no, I don't mind about any fine. Carry on back to the dressing room, lads. They can stand out here and wait four minutes for us and then we'll come out when we're ready.'

It was just to let them know, we're here and don't mess about with us. Fatih, I think, was used to getting his own way. It was important that my players knew they were just as big as their opposite numbers. I think it gave them the feeling that we weren't going to let them trample over us, and we went out and we beat Galatasaray 2–1.

We didn't play well in that first half of the Super Cup. Alpay Özalan was one of the best centre-backs in the country; a young guy. I liked him very much. I supported him, I encouraged him and I told him what a good player he could be if he concentrated. He could play in England, or anywhere in Europe if he worked hard, and he deserved it, but Alpay was terrible in that first half. No focus, no concentration and, because I'd heard a rumour that Fatih Terim wanted to sign him and because of the way he was playing, I was getting angrier and angrier while I was watching from the bench. So, I went into the dressing room just before the half-time whistle to wait for the players. Alpay came in laughing. I closed the door behind him, went right up to him, grabbed him by his shirt and really gave it right to him. Alpay's a big guy but the more I laid into him, the smaller he got. Normally, I'm very calm. That's not something I've done very often. It must have been quite a funny scene with me shouting in English and my translator, Tayfun, in between us speaking the Turkish equivalent to Alpay. I get the feeling Alpay would have understood anyway. He always made sure he tried hard after that. Everybody did.

Two trophies was a pretty decent haul, and I was rewarded with a contract extension and the chance to make changes for that second year. Beşiktaş needed to go places. I moved out some of the older players, including the captain, Recep, and brought in a few foreigners of my own who'd impressed me from what I'd seen of them in the Spanish league.

I loaned a Nigerian centre-forward called Christopher Ohen, who'd been on the books at Real Madrid as a youngster and had been playing with Compostela. I signed José 'Chemo' del Solar, a Peruvian midfielder whom I'd known from his time playing in Tenerife, and Jamal Sellami, the Moroccan captain whom Noureddine Naybet had recommended to me. He was just the type of holding player I needed to tie the team together. Last of all, there was a local lad, Ayhan Akman, who was a promising Turkish international; a No. 10-type with a lot of quality. I liked him. I'd seen him the season before playing for Gaziantepspor – a side from a city in the south of the country.

We started well that second season, the 1998/99 campaign. We were a better side in the league and very quickly found ourselves at the top of the table fighting it out for the championship with the usual suspects. We'd have got there sooner had it not been for a two-game stadium ban after some crowd trouble in our draw against Gaziantepspor. The referee made a series of poor decisions and this can be incendiary in Turkey, where the emotions run high as it is. Fans ran onto the pitch and there was some general confusion between them, the referee, the linesmen, the opposition players and some of our own as well; pushing and shoving and all sorts. Our defender, Alpay, who later played for Aston Villa, got himself a five-game ban for his own assaults on the match officials, but these were normal things in Turkey. If they didn't happen to you, they happened to the opposition.

We didn't get so far in Europe. It was the Cup Winners' Cup once again and while we did a comfortable job on Spartak Trnava from Slovakia in the first round, we went out at the next stage to a John Carew-inspired Vålerenga. We'd lost by a single goal in Norway as they pumped the ball long to the six-foot-five giant every chance they could, but then it all seemed to be going OK when we were three goals up at half-time in the home leg, thanks to two from Oktay and one from Tayfur, with Ohen doing a lot of good work. We then conceded three to the Norwegians in the space of eleven minutes, which was just crazy given that we had the best defence in the league.

Domestically we started the season with a fifteen-game unbeaten run, and it was only a loss to our old enemy Galatasaray in December that cut our lead at the top down to two points. We were going really well. We were going to win the league. And then Real Madrid came in for me.

I was happy at Beşiktaş and the club were happy with me. I'd survived there nearly two years, which isn't easy, and I'd become part of the footballing scenery in Turkey, but I got a call from Lorenzo Sanz, the Madrid president, whom I'd known from when he was there working under Ramon Mendoza as a director. He was a different character from Mendoza; shrewd and experienced at the club. Guus Hiddink had been in charge for a short spell but Lorenzo could see that Guus had not managed to get control of a dressing room of superstars drunk on their successes after achieving the club's long-awaited Champions League win the season before. Madrid were sixth in La Liga and struggling, really struggling, and Sanz wanted someone who knew the place to come and sort things out.

Now, Real Madrid is not just any kind of job. When they come for you, you've got to go. Things had been going very well for me but while there's uncertainty everywhere in football, there was a particular uncertainty managing in Turkey. I always had the feeling that if we lost two or three games on the bounce, I'd be on my way. So, it made a lot of sense to go.

I was coming up to two years in Turkey and that's normally enough for those of a Western European temperament. It's a volatile atmosphere over there. The people in high positions in football clubs there often act spontaneously, coming to regret their decision the morning after. They'll realise a few days later they've made a mistake, but they should know better. You've got to be there and live it 24 hours a day and you'll get the idea. Arguments blazing up out of nothing outside your hotel or wherever; you'll sit there and watch it happen around you, things that you wouldn't see in other parts of Europe. Wherever you go, you've got to realise that the rules are different and be prepared for what happens. The ideal thing to do is not react too strongly. The lack of patience and the difficulty of trying to explain to people can be wearing, even though you might know you're right. Even if your words get blown up into a big reaction, that's not necessarily a bad thing. You have to hope that in the time after, the player or person in question will come to see your side of things, or hopefully the events of the future will prove your point. You put your point over and hope it has the required effect.

I would have to say that the Turkish fans, and the Moroccans, are the craziest. They are the most fanatical supporters I've ever worked for. I enjoyed that because I was reasonably successful in those places and won trophies, but I had seen the other side of it after difficult performances. Things could get really heated out in the stadiums. Fire bombs, missiles flying onto the pitch left, right and centre; really desperate stuff. You have to find your own way of coping with that. During one derby game away at Galatasaray I remember a drinking bottle whizzing past my head and landing on the turf. I picked it up, pretended to drink from it and waved my thanks to the opposition fans who'd thrown it. I stopped myself from actually taking a sip from it because I wasn't sure what the liquid inside was.

Things get particularly nasty when the fans aren't happy with what they see. Then the players know they need to keep a low profile – maybe more so than the managers. There are places you might have to steer clear of; they had to be very careful where they went and what they did. Fortunately, I was successful, but I wouldn't like to have been unsuccessful.

There is an inferiority complex in Turkey with football and you see it especially in the press. It increases that sense of pressure. More than in other places in Europe, they expect results too quickly. Board members and supporters are manipulated by this, so there is never enough patience for foreign managers and foreign players. If they do not succeed immediately, it is a disaster and this is why many do not succeed in Turkey. The big clubs want success in six months. Sometimes managers get sick of it and they leave, and sometimes they are pushed. If you look at Vicente del Bosque, he came to Besiktas in 2004 and after seven or eight months he was gone because they said he doesn't know anything about football! Then he left, and a couple of years later took over the Spanish football team and won the World Cup and the European Championship. It's ridiculous. So, that is the main problem with football in Turkey, but it is getting better.

The fans on the streets were always friendly to me and have been since I've left, and I've come across Turkish fans everywhere I've been. I had no idea at the time of how many Turkish people live in Germany, not until we played a pre-season tournament in Cologne that first year. We were sold out for every game with the stands packed full of Beşiktaş ultras in their black and white strips. Again, ignorance on my part, but that's what managing in these places is about – learning things, and I learned an awful lot during my time in Istanbul. It was very much a successful spell in every sense of the word; winning two major trophies and travelling into Europe with a Turkish side is a good experience – to go at the head of a Turkish expedition like that and to travel to Germany, France; there's a responsibility there and massive support wherever you go.

It's not for everyone. Not everybody can cope with that kind of crazy atmosphere, the unpredictability and often fiery tempers, but if you can't take the heat in Turkey, well, then you don't stand a chance in Madrid.

11
Madrid and the media

YOU CAN CRITICISE A PLAYER IN THE DRESSING ROOM, BUT IT HURTS them a lot more if you do it in the press and in my second spell at Real Madrid, I wanted to hurt them. Managers are a little bit frightened to do that these days because the people in the press will eventually turn on them when results go badly, even though you've given them good copy in the past. The fact is, though, that the press will probably turn on you regardless, so you may as well say your piece.

I remember criticising Real Madrid players in the media the first time around after a defeat and Ramón Mendoza said to me, 'Here we dry our dirty linen on the inside of the house,' to which I replied, 'Yeah, well I tried that for three weeks but it's not dried so I had to open up the windows and hang it outside.'

You have to decide for yourself which approach is going to work for you. You can't always sit there and take the flak and protect players. It depends when, who, how and if there are players there taking advantage of you. Then you have to let them know, otherwise you will die a slow death.

It works with some players – it fires them up and they want to prove you wrong – and it doesn't work with others, those who become detached and mentally stick two fingers up at you. You've got to know which ones are which and when it's best to do what. You've got to know when it's beneficial and when it's not. Everything you do as a manager has got to be what you think is in the best interests of the football club and if that means ruffling the feathers of your players in public, then so be it.

Going into Madrid that second time, in February 1999, it was like going into Baghdad. This was not the most disciplined group I'd ever worked with, not like my first time there. There were more foreign players for a start. The three-man ruling had changed just a few years before and Real Madrid had gone to town, signing the best that the world had to offer. The homegrown ethos of the days of *La Quinta del Buitre* had been lost, never since to return, and the era of the Galacticos had begun.

There was still a Spanish core to the side and even one member of the Quinta still on the field. Unfortunately for me, it happened to be Manolo Sanchís. Hierro was still part of the team too, but this was a completely different Fernando Hierro to the nineteen-year-old whom I'd brought in ten years earlier. It wasn't the same young lad I'd take off when I needed to make an attacking change, not someone who was as happy to listen and learn as the one I'd worked with before; but he'd played for the Spanish team since then, he'd captained his country, captained Madrid, been named in FIFA's World XI three years on the bounce, so that's understandable even if it made things more difficult for me. He always had a lack of pace but was very skilful and intelligent, and read the game well, all of which easily overcame his issue with speed. It surprises me to see that he's gone into management; I didn't think he would. He was always more involved in the Spanish FA and directorial kinds of matters. I'd never seen him make a move as a coach but good luck to him and, interestingly enough, he's done it at a lower level with Real Oviedo and later with the Spanish national team at the 2018 World Cup, so credit to him.

My strike pairing was very much a Spanish affair too – Fernando Morientes and Raúl. They worked well together. We played 4–2–3–1 with Morientes the main centre-forward and Raúl just behind. They were both good professionals. Raúl walked with the air of someone special, which is how he was regarded by everyone at the club. I say he was a good professional, but he wasn't always professionally correct. He was only in his very early twenties but already becoming a legend at Real Madrid, having made his debut for them at seventeen. He was fantastic for sniffing out the opportunities at goal. He had a big voice in the dressing room, a big voice in the club – maybe too big – but you can't take away his record. We're all different though, coaches as well. My opinion will be different to others and a lot of coaches sit on the fence and don't want to say anything too controversial. I would never criticise Raúl, but I don't think we were 100 per cent fans of one another.

Raúl was a big friend and a fan of the Argentine international midfielder Fernando Redondo, which helped me a great deal in terms of getting on with the players, because Redondo was a top professional. I was only with him for a short spell but he made a profound impact on me with his attitude, ability, work ethic and respect. He was an important figure both where he played in the middle of the pitch and in the dressing room as well. He had the respect of most of the players and he took Raúl under his wing.

Being foreign in itself was not a problem, to which Redondo, an Argentinian, was testament. The real issue was that this group of players had finally done what the club and the fans had asked of them, they'd won the Champions League in 1998. But it had completely gone to their heads; some more than others. In the previous season, under Jupp Heynckes – whom, of course, I played against plenty myself in European competition – this group, which included the so-called Ferrari Brigade of Clarence Seedorf, Davor Šuker, Predrag Mijatović, Roberto Carlos and Christian Panucci, had beaten Juventus 1–0 in the final in Amsterdam. Then almost the next day it was Ferrari, Ferrari, Ferrari; each of them turning up at training with the cars they'd bought on their win bonuses and attitudes to match.

Heynckes was sacked just eight days after the final. Apparently winning Madrid's first European Cup in 32 years was not enough to make up for the poor form in La Liga, which had seen the club finish fourth. The next coach, the former Madrid player José Antonio Camacho, lasted just 22 days before differences between him and Lorenzo Sanz saw him lose his job without even taking charge of a game, and so in his place came Guus Hiddink. He began the 1998/99 season in earnest, but got sacked himself not much beyond the halfway mark of the season after a 1–0 home loss against Athletic Bilbao had seen Madrid drop to sixth place and with Champions League qualification looking a lot less than certain.

Hiddink was no spring chicken. He'd been around the block enough times to manage anywhere and Heynckes was the same. They're two coaches I've always had a hell of a lot of time for. I knew them both very well personally, so I knew what I was walking into. I knew it was going to be difficult. If there were problems of the nature that they couldn't handle, then they were going to be big ones.

When I arrived at the end of February, it was a very difficult time. There was no drive among the players. There was a general malaise caused by a few bad apples in the group, which was enough to drag the team down and keep them there. Most of them weren't training hard enough and they were not as fit as they should have been. They looked jaded, they looked tired and it's very difficult to change fitness when you go in late in the season like that. That's the point when players are going to feel it most and if you've not properly prepared for it, then it's too late by the time you've got there. The only way I was going to get this lot to perform was by a different means of motivation, and for many of these puffed-up players it was telling them that they weren't as good as they thought they were in public that proved most effective.

Some of them took it with good humour. I remember after one game in Tenerife, which we eventually won 3–2 but had really struggled in, I said to the media that I'd sweated more on the bench than some of my players had on the pitch. Morientes joked in reply that I'd put on a bit of weight recently, so maybe that wouldn't do me any harm. I got my point across, we laughed about it and let it go by.

Over the years, I'm sure that my way of doing things was good for the media. I gave them good copy, but it was more than that. I knew how to work my way around them to make sure I'd said the things that I wanted and got the messages out to the people who needed to hear them. A bad manager will just consider press conferences a bind, but a good one will use them for their own interest. Players know what's been said, so it's like speaking straight to them but with a very big audience. When I go into a press conference, I know full well what I'm going to say and what I need to get over. If I don't get those questions asked to me, I have to steer my answers over until I get to those points. Very often, there'll be three or four things I want to get across. With the passing of the years, you become an artist at it. I never went into a press conference blind, not knowing what was going to happen. Besides, what you've got to remember, when you go into a press conference, is that you're going to be stuck in there, so you might as well enjoy it. That was my attitude. I wasn't going to go in there with my head down, particularly after a bad result. I knew where the bullets would come from, so I'd sit down for five or ten minutes before I went in there, work out what I was going to say, open the door and go out guns blazing. More or less, I knew the questions they were going to ask and who was going to ask them.

I see managers now, though, and they go into a press conference and I don't know what they've gone in for, because they've said nothing. They go in with a glum face if they lose. They go in if they've won and praise the opposition just to make their win look better. And that's it. When I went into a press conference, I went in to say something. Not everyone's going to like it but if the media go along to a press conference, they want to leave thinking it was worthwhile. Why are we all doing it otherwise? Nowadays, if you've seen one press conference, you've seen them all. It's as if the managers are told, 'Be careful what you say!' right before they go in. You know what all the top players are going to say as well: 'It's a very difficult match, we take one game at a time, they're a very strong side, they beat Chelsea 3–2 last week.' Well, we know that. That doesn't tell us anything that's worth hearing.

I didn't behave like other managers. The media always enjoyed my press conferences because I'd always give them something good. They used to use a lot of my phrases. They asked me once if the criticism I was getting at Madrid was affecting me at all and I replied, '*No, para mí es como agua en la espalda de un pato,*' – it's like water off a duck's back – which I knew full well was not a phrase common to the Spanish language. They all looked at each other blank for a minute until I told them to think about it. 'You don't think a duck is concerned about having water on its back, is it? So, like we say in England, it's like water off a duck's back,' and they enjoyed that so much that they still use the expression in Spanish. It was a bit of fun but I knew that at the same time it would take the focus of the room away from the original issue of whether I was in a tricky situation at the club or not. I've answered the question, and they've got something they can print.

Another time, I was asked if I'd thought about using a psychologist to get the players' attitudes straight but I replied that, '*Psicológicamente, no creo que sea una buena idea*' – psychologically, I didn't think it would be a good idea. It was the answer I'd heard Shanks use once when he was asked the same thing. The fellow in the room didn't quite know what to make of it when I used it on him, but the rest of his peers thought it was hysterical.

There was another line from Bill Shankly that I used in a Madrid press conference and became famous for it. It was something he said to me on the phone while I was at Swansea. He said, 'After a game, don't think about your team for the next match. After a game on Saturday, don't even think about it until Monday. On that Saturday night, you're going to want to leave them all out. Then on the Sunday night, you'll think about it and say to yourself, "He didn't do too badly, alright, I'll make nine changes." After training on the Monday, you'll think, "Those two wide players, they look OK, and anyone can have a bad game, I'll make seven changes." And you go through the week like that until, by Thursday, you want to make just two changes but, if you do that, they'll think they're the ones that were responsible for last week's mess. Finally, you arrive on Friday and think, "Oh, forget it, I'll keep the same eleven bastards who played last week."'

That went down very well in Spain. They could see the funny side of it and they could see the reasoning behind it too, and a lot of coaches and managers who listened to me and learned from me said that I was right and that it was a great way of putting it. Even supporters from teams go home from the match and think along the same lines. You know you do. Then the week goes by and you're talking at work with your mates about who you'd pick and then by the weekend you're ready to give them all another chance again. Never make decisions straight after a game.

Any manager who's not happy to sit in a press conference is in big trouble when they get to a club like Madrid, where your every movement is under the microscope. With Tuesday or Wednesday games to contend with for most of the season, it got to a situation where I'd end up with press conferences on a Friday before the game, on the Saturday after the game, on the Monday or Tuesday before the European fixture, then after that fixture too – Friday, Saturday, Monday, Tuesday and all round again. It was ridiculous, so I changed it while I was there to one single general press conference on a Wednesday where the media could ask my opinion on Arsenal or about putting someone on the moon or whatever they wanted, and I gave them as much time as they wanted. Soon after, a lot of other managers decided to do the same.

My brief from Lorenzo Sanz was to get this team into the Champions League positions by the end of the La Liga season. So, I can't say that the first leg of the quarter-final tie against Dynamo Kyiv in that current year's competition, just a few days after I got the job, was particularly high on my list. Of course, I wanted to win, but this did not look like a Madrid that was capable of pulling off the same heroics as the previous year, even if we did have enough to get by the Ukrainians. As it happened, it was also a particularly good Dynamo of Andriy Shevchenko and Serhiy Rebrov that we had to contend with, under the great Soviet coach Valeriy Lobanovsky. They were a top side, and we weren't. When we could only manage a draw in the first leg at the Bernabéu, I knew we'd stand little chance of making it through, particularly with Dynamo fresh from their winter break and Madrid virtually unable to make it round a pitch for ninety minutes. We went out 3–1 on aggregate and Kyiv only narrowly missed out to Bayern Munich in the semis, who then famously lost at the last gasp to Manchester United in the final.

Back in La Liga, Barcelona were way out in front. No one was going to catch them. Then there was Mallorca, Celta Vigo, Deportivo La Coruña and Valencia between us and the second place that meant automatic qualification for the

Champions League, and slowly but surely we began to reel them in. We lost to Celta and Atlético Madrid but it was a tight season with lots of the top sides taking points off one another and we fared better than most. With the last three games to play, we clawed our way up to second, but still had two tricky fixtures against Deportivo and Mallorca – both of whom could have caught us if we didn't take the points – either side of a trip across the city to face Atlético. At the same time, we drew Valencia in the semi-finals of the Copa del Rey and had midweek ties to play either side of the two left in La Liga. The league was obviously more important with regard to what I'd come here to do. So, when we went to the Mestalla for the away leg of the cup, I didn't play a lot of the first-teamers – no Raúl, no Roberto Carlos, no Hierro, no Mijatović, no Panucci – and, after we went down to ten men when Fernando Redondo got sent off in the 26th minute, the floodgates opened and Claudio Ranieri's team recorded one of Real Madrid's most humiliating defeats – 6–0. Needless to say, the home leg was something of a dead rubber.

I took a lot of stick for that result in Valencia but we beat Mallorca and then Depor in the final game, which we had to win to finish runners-up to Barça. Raúl got two and we won 3–1. *Misión cumplida*, as they say, and I felt very justified by my choices.

Now that the season was over, I was finally able to do something about the Ferrari Brigade and bring in players that would be more useful and more disciplined instead. Relations between Real Madrid and Šuker had broken down after some pretty strange comments in the papers about transfer dealings at the club, which he later claimed were made up by the Spanish press. Either way, everyone involved was angling to get Šuker a move away from Madrid, which was fine by me.

Panucci had already made his plans too. He was a good player; a classy player. He'd won the Champions League with Milan and Madrid, which speaks for itself. With him and Roberto Carlos in the squad, we were very strong in the full-back positions. Any defensive problems he might have had were overcome by the terrific attacking possibilities that he gave the team. It's very similar to Marcelo's position in the modern Madrid. Whenever I managed a team that played against Roberto Carlos – as I did on a few occasions – I would try to get the front players in behind him all the time, drag central defenders across and then look to get into the space created as much as possible but, at the same time, you've got to be aware of the attacking options that they had with him, and, of course, his free-kicks as well.

When he was part of my team, I had to make allowances for Roberto really – particularly away from home or in big games. Against the lesser opposition, you didn't have to worry about it. Madrid only had to play a team at the same level as them once every six or seven games – Champions League or one of the top three or four in La Liga. In those bigger games, you'd have to tell the centre-halves and midfielders to be aware of the danger. If you were a left-sided centre-back and you had Roberto Carlos as your left-back, you had to be well aware of what was likely to happen.

In the dressing room, Roberto went with the hares and the hounds, as they say in Wales – he tended to say what it took to stay onside with all the different factions. I'd been speaking with Lorenzo Sanz as the summer was approaching about the players we needed next season and both Roberto and Panucci were still very much going to be part of the set-up.

I headed off to Mallorca for a couple of days and my friend, Mauri, who runs a restaurant out there, came up to me saying that Panucci had signed for Inter for the next season. I couldn't believe it. Panucci had been saying to me, 'It's fine, mister, I'll be here, no problems,' but Mauri was good friends with Franco Baresi's brother, Giuseppe (who had a very good, if not quite as stellar, and almost as long career with Inter at the same time as Franco was with Milan), and had got word.

So, we went away to play in Santander in the league and the whole team was sat down in the team hotel. I said, 'It's strange. My friend in Mallorca tells me that Panucci has signed for Inter. It's amazing some of the nonsense that goes flying about.' Panucci sat there in silence until I turned to him and pointedly asked, 'Isn't it?' And then, after a moment, he sprang to life and with all the romance he could muster said: 'Oh, mister, when I drive the car out through Barcelona, I go up over the Alps, I see Milan below the beautiful mountains and my heart is with my family . . .'

'Oh, shut up,' I said, stopping this embarrassment. He had already signed the agreement. It was that kind of nonsense with those Madrid players all the time.

The one member of the Ferrari Brigade that I really did want rid of was one who stayed – at least for a few months longer than I did. In a dressing room of petty jealousies and pointless spats, you'd very often find Clarence Seedorf was involved somewhere. He spoke his mind, which is no bad thing. The trouble was that what was on his mind was not worth hearing. He was caught on camera having a punch-up with Ivan Campo at the Intercontinental Cup in Tokyo while

Hiddink was still in charge. There was another incident on the pitch where Seedorf and Hierro argued over who would take a free-kick. I never saw what happened but the reports were that it continued into the dressing room with the two having to be pulled apart by the other players. Seedorf obviously had ability – you don't get four Champions League winners' medals with three different clubs without ability – but with all the rest he brought at the time, he wasn't worth it. This was a very different Seedorf to the considered man you see on your TVs as a pundit nowadays. He was only young, in his early twenties, with plenty of titles and accolades with Ajax and Madrid already, and it had all gone to his head completely. It seems he matured during his long spell in Italy.

Over the summer, I signed Geremi from Gençlerbirliği in Turkey to replace him. Geremi was a Cameroon international and I'd seen just how good he was up close when I'd been working at Beşiktaş. I took some criticism at Real Madrid for signing him but they made a huge profit on him when they sold him on to Chelsea four years later, two European Cups and one Ballon d'Or nomination down the line. I'd seen him playing and thought, 'You can give me him before Šuker and Seedorf any day.' When the press got wind of it, they were firing questions at me all over the place. 'Who's this Cameroonian that Real Madrid have signed from the first division of Turkish football?' So, I replied, in Spanish: 'You people here, you never speak to me in any language other than your own. Geremi speaks four different languages.'

Geremi would also go on to win a gold medal at the Olympics and two African Cup of Nations titles with Cameroon. At Madrid they were all 'Seedorf, Seedorf, Seedorf,' but, in my opinion, Seedorf didn't like training. Seedorf didn't push himself.

I went over to my house in Zarautz, just along from the coast from San Sebastián, for a few days' break a couple of weeks into the 1999/2000 season, but I got called back to Madrid by the president to confront Seedorf and his agent about why I wasn't playing him. I wasn't interested in arguing. I had my reasons for not playing Seedorf and I doubted I'd be able to persuade him and his entourage that I was right. Instead, I just laid down the facts of the matter, which were that Seedorf had three years left on his contract and I had six months. 'The normal thing is that if I don't play him, I'm going to go before he's going to go. He's a squad player here but, if I've got everybody fit, Seedorf is not going to be in my starting line-up. I can't say it any clearer than that.'

But they kept asking why I didn't like Seedorf. In the end, of course, I did go before Seedorf, but he followed just a couple of months later. Apparently, del Bosque didn't miss him either, and maybe what happened to him at Madrid was a harsh lesson. He was young, but he picked himself up in Italy and went on and achieved some important things in football – but not before he came out with some comments in his book a year or two after leaving Spain. He said that I'd taken money for signing Geremi and Elvir Baljić, another player I'd picked up from Turkey, which was, of course, nonsense. So, I took him to court. When the case finally got in front of a judge, Seedorf didn't even bother turning up. It was just his lawyer. I felt sorry for her. She was on her own and I had the president of Real Sociedad with me as a character witness, I had the ex-secretary general of Real Madrid backing me up, I had two agents who'd had dealings with those clubs in the past – they all spoke in my favour. Nobody came forward to support Seedorf's claim and this was an ideal opportunity for anyone in football who might have ever seen me do anything untoward whatsoever to come forward. Seedorf's team had obviously tried to find them but nobody did. Seedorf was obliged to pay the necessary compensation and his book was taken out of print.

Predrag Mijatović had the good grace to leave for Fiorentina over the summer. He'd scored the goal that had won the Champions League in 1998 but he'd turned thirty and had been *viviendo de las rentas*, as they say, living off the rent since; living off his past glories like Šuker and rest of them. Raúl and Morientes were doing more damage up front and, what's more, everybody knew that a twenty-year-old Nicolas Anelka was on his way from Arsenal. There had been a lot of noise surrounding his signing and he'd spent virtually all summer training on his own in London because Wenger wasn't at all happy at the way Madrid had gone about doing the deal. So, when he came, he wasn't really as fit as he should have been and that caused a bit of a selection problem. I liked Anelka. I wanted to use him but I couldn't straight away. He fitted in nicely with Geremi and Samuel Eto'o, who'd been coming through the ranks. They were a good threesome and were together most of the time. Eto'o made his debut with me in a Champions League group-stage game against the Norwegians of Molde as the season began. He played on the right side in those days; a pity for the club that they let him go to Mallorca as they did in the summer of 2000 following a successful loan to the Palma club.

The 1999/2000 season got off to a decent enough start but with two games and two victories under my belt, I lost my first-choice goalkeeper. Bodo Illgner was a very solid player for Madrid. He'd taken over a few years earlier from the ever-present Paco Buyo, who'd been at the club when I won the league with *La Quinta del Buitre*, a decade before. The big German, Illgner, though, spent more time in the swimming pool than the training ground. He always seemed to have some kind of niggle or problem. Albano Bizzarri was the second choice and this was a goalkeeper that was not to my liking. He was not up to it but he had been signed by the vice president, Juan Onieva, which made things a little bit more difficult. I was never forced to play him. I was never forced to play anybody; people tried to force me but I never bent to any of them. Instead of Bizzarri, I wanted to try out an eighteen-year-old Iker Casillas who we'd promoted to the first team that year.

I remember seeing Iker for the first time a few months before. There was a week of selection issues and I'd organised a game with the youth players so that four or five first-teamers didn't lose momentum. There was Iker, then just seventeen years old, making a terrific save after one particular move by a sweeper. There was a clearance and then another superb save by Casillas. I was almost asleep until then and I got up to applaud.

He got his debut in the Basque Country. We were playing Bilbao in the old San Mamés – La Catedral, as they used to call it – which was traditionally a tough game. If you took the fixture list and looked at where Madrid were likely to drop points, Bilbao and the San Mamés was one of those places. On the morning of the game, we trained in Bilbao and I asked Iker if he fancied playing that night. So, in he went and we drew 2–2. He threw one in but he was OK. He looked so small in between the sticks, I remember that. Then, on the Wednesday, we had a game in Athens with Olympiacos, which could be a tricky fixture with the crowd and the travel, and we drew 3–3. So, we let three in that day and then the following weekend we played at home against Deportivo in a match we drew 1–1. A Brazilian, called Djalminha, who was extremely left-footed, shot with his right and it went in. It must have been the only goal he ever scored with his right. I gave Casillas one more start at home against Molde, which we won comfortably 4–1. So, that was four games in two weeks for Iker in Europe, in La Liga, in Athens and in Spain, and after that he'd started to wobble slightly. His head was spinning a bit and I noticed, so I told him that he'd dipped his feet in and now it was time to come out again and have a bit of a breather. It's often like that when you're blooding very young lads. For the first few games they play without a care but you've got to keep an eye on them for any knocks to their confidence – particularly goalkeepers – but Casillas had broken the ice and he was a good competitor with unbelievable reflexes. It was clear he was the future, although it was the last game he ever played for me. Illgner was fit for a spell and Bizzarri filled in the odd game while Casillas was taking stock.

With our sights trained more on Europe, things took a bit of a dip in the league. Our decent start was marred by a few too many draws as well as a home loss to Valencia. Next up was a trip to the Camp Nou to take on Louis van Gaal's Barcelona, who were six points ahead at the top of the table; we couldn't let that gap get any wider. I'd come up against Van Gaal once before, when he was coach of Ajax and I was at Deportivo, during the Teresa Herrera pre-season tournament in 1996. After the game, I went to the Ajax dressing room with a Deportivo shirt and asked if I could exchange one for an Ajax Amsterdam shirt and Van Gaal stood there with his stiff voice and said: 'First, you have to write a letter to Ajax football club in Amsterdam with the shirt and the details . . .'

And I thought, 'Who is this man?'

I just turned around and walked away. I had no idea what else to do. It's one of the few times in my life I've been dumbstruck. You have to rate him as a manager. You have to recognise what he's done, but we never exactly hit it off.

The night before the game, the radio stations had wanted to speak to both managers at midnight because, of course, people go to bed in Spain much later than they do in Britain, and there are two big radio stations over there – the Cadena COPE and the Cadena SER. I was always pretty much more with the COPE. José Maria Garcia was there. He was one of the most famous sports journalists at the time and I did stuff for them when Spain played, but the two were big rivals. The Madrid public relations officer came over to me at dinner and said that Garcia wanted me live at midnight and then came back a few moments later saying that the SER wanted me at the same time. Both refused to record the interview and both refused to budge. Now, if I went on with SER, COPE would hammer me, and if I went on with COPE, SER would hammer me. So, I told them both to stuff themselves and I went to bed at 10.30 p.m., and they both hammered me. That was one of the main reasons I said I'd only do one press conference a week after that.

The game itself was a cracker. It's remembered as one of the most entertaining Clásicos, at least for the neutrals. Raúl scored early with a lovely near-post header from a short cross from the byline after some great work from the Brazilian Sávio.

Then Barça got two back with Rivaldo and then one from range from Luís Figo in the second half. Shortly after, though, Patrick Kluivert got himself sent off for having a go at the referee after a strong challenge from Iván Campo. He totally lost his cool and I have no idea what he said to him, but it was a straight red with no violent conduct whatsoever. His teammates could barely get him off the pitch and the rest of the match went on at that tempo, with challenges flying in all over the place and Barcelona still keeping Madrid out. Finally, with 89 minutes on the clock, Raúl broke through for his second, which he lifted over the Dutch keeper, Ruud Hesp. It was such a composed finish for such a young lad and at as high-pressure a moment as you'll ever see. The crowd were always whistling when we played there and Raúl put his finger to his lips to hush them as he ran along the hoardings. It's a famous Madrid photo.

It was a big result, but we still stuttered in the league following two more draws and a loss at home to our city rivals, Atléti. At the same time, though, the most important thing, as far as I was concerned, was finishing top of our Champions League group in our final three games, which we were playing midweek in between. We lost the first 2–1 away in Porto with Mario Jardel, in his pomp at the time, scoring both. We won at home to Olympiacos and that meant that we went to Norway needing to win against Molde to finish top of the group, but at the same time, we had a tricky game on Saturday against Rayo Vallecano in Vallecas in Madrid, which is a difficult little ground. Now, it's a game that Madrid should normally win but, on this day, Rayo were top of the league with Juande Ramos as the coach.

We went to Molde, and I knew we were going to qualify, but also that we needed to top the group. I gave a few of the lads a rest – Raúl, Morientes, Hierro – and we won 1–0. We came back to Madrid and I had to play Albano Bizzarri in goal. Bodo Illgner was out and Casillas was still regrouping. By half-time at Rayo, we were two goals down. Bizzarri had been at fault for both – terrible decision-making for one and fumbling the ball for the other. By this point, the president, Lorenzo Sanz, called all the directors to go to the Rayo stadium because they were going to get rid of me at the end of the game. They'd decided this at half-time. So, we went out in the second half. Morientes was sent off for complaining to the ref about a clear penalty that wasn't given after the Rayo keeper, Kasey Keller, took him out, but we still managed to score three goals and win the game 3–2 with ten men.

At the end of the game, we walked towards the dressing room with the elation of having turned this game around and there were ten men, the ten directors, standing there waiting for me like ten undertakers with long black coats on. Rayo's such a tight little ground that the dressing rooms are behind the goal, so there they all were lined up in front of it unable to do the thing that they'd gone there to do. I didn't know whether to laugh or cry. When I went out for my post-match comments to the press, I laid the blame at Bizzarri's feet. I told them that he'd had a poor evening, that some of his goalkeeping made me weep. He'd cost us our previous home game against Atlético Madrid a few weeks earlier by getting himself sent off early in the second half. This was not a one-off issue. He needed to pull his socks up. Right after, the directors told me that I couldn't say that and that I'd have to rectify my comments the following day at the training ground, but straight away I said, 'No. Whenever I say anything to the press, I think about it very carefully; about what I'm going to say, and, if I say something, it's because it's in the interest of the club and everybody here for me to do so. So, as we say in English, you'll see pigs flying before you'll see me change my statement.'

Bang. The next thing I see it's the headline in the *Marca* newspaper of me saying that there are pigs flying over the Bernabéu. That was it. I was dismissed. They claimed that they thought I was talking about the club president and calling him a pig, but it was utter rubbish; just an excuse. I was sacked at Real Madrid after winning two games away from home. That has to be some kind of record. I had to leave the job because I refused to say sorry. They wanted me out; maybe they felt they couldn't manipulate me as they wanted, maybe it was the Šuker/ Seedorf thing. I don't know, but they used that as an excuse to get rid of me because they couldn't get rid of a coach who'd finished top of his Champions League group and beaten the team at the top of the league with just ten men. If I'd come out and said, 'Sorry, I shouldn't have said that,' I'd have been the walking dead; just waiting for something else to happen until they got rid of me. But I won't work like that. You can't work with a gun at your head.

I left and Vincente del Bosque took over. Within a couple of weeks, Seedorf had been sold to Italy. Del Bosque had gone to Sanz and told him that Seedorf had to go. Madrid ended up winning the Champions League in Paris that year. I'd managed a lot of that campaign and I'd got the team into a qualifying position in the league the season before, for which I don't feel I've ever had quite enough recognition given the mess that the side had been in. When you analyse it, my second spell at Madrid was not the flop that some people thought it was. I did exactly what Lorenzo Sanz had hired me to do but, not long after I'd done it, his support for me had dried up.

That group of players – the Ferrari Brigade – they loved themselves and I was brought in there by Sanz to bring them down a peg or two and that, by definition, is a problematic job. The long-term result is that you get rid of the nasty players but it's a result that you never get to enjoy because, by definition, you're confronted by such a battle in the short term that there's bound to be a lot of casualties later on and one of them will probably be you.

It's an unspoken rule that you don't talk about players in the press the way I did that year. It applies to footballers everywhere but in particular at Real Madrid. There is a sense that you don't do this, even if you think this is right. You can tell the players and you can deal with it directly with them but you don't use the press as the messengers. Times may have changed, but there's a certain parallel to Mourinho's time at Madrid. The players accepted some of the criticism but what they didn't accept was Mourinho using the media to do it. What a lot of the players felt was that you don't play it that way because, if you do, you'll lose, because we are stronger than you. I think I was brought in, in 1999, in part because of the hope that I could be as strong as the players at a club where that's very rarely the case.

For that reason, I feel like del Bosque's first Champions League partly belongs to me. Maybe Madrid wouldn't have won it if I had stayed, because the relationship had become difficult, but I think they might never have won it if I hadn't been there either. I'm still waiting for my win bonus.

I went to watch the final that year in Paris and the only thing I did feel truly resentful about is that I had a contract with Real Madrid but they said that, to receive my owed wages, I had to sign a confidentiality clause that didn't allow me to speak about anything that had happened thereafter. I know that Rafael Benítez signed one after he left the club in 2016. He came out when he was sacked talking about what a grand club it is and how it's been a big honour, but I told them I couldn't sign that because I knew that, if I did, and then one day I happened to say something in an interview, that there'd be trouble.

They say you've got to bite your tongue; *pasar por el tubo*, they say in Spain – they make you go through the tube – but, when I die, I'm going out with a bang, not on my knees. This was not fair and not right. I'd left Beşiktaş, where I was very happy, and, with eight months to go, they got rid of me. The least they could do was pay up the rest of my contract.

I ended up having to take Madrid to court and I had to wait ten months after that to receive the money I was owed, plus interest and the freedom to say what I wanted. It was very uncomfortable during that time and I didn't particularly feel like taking on another job. I wouldn't have been able to concentrate on it.

Ultimately, they're Real Madrid and they can bypass everything and do what they want. At least they did pay up eventually. It disappointed me that they acted in such a way. Sanz had been a friend of mine when he brought me in. Florentino Pérez took over as Madrid president during proceedings and he could have quite easily sorted it out and not let it go all the way to court, but he didn't. They're the only two occasions in my life where I've had to go to court – with Madrid and with Seedorf, and both from this short spell. I'm grateful for to my lawyer, Javier Urdangarin, for helping me put the record straight. It doesn't make me proud to have done so but it gives me satisfaction, at least. To go to a court in Madrid with Real Madrid in the other corner is not easy for a Welshman, but you've got to fight your corner. I've seen lots of Argentines and Brazilians and Spaniards and Italians at Real Madrid, but I've not seen many Welshmen. It makes me feel proud and I'm proud to be Welsh.

Over time at Real Madrid, I think the politics has got worse and it's played out in public more. Now, they have a president in Florentino Pérez who has a public persona of never interfering, but privately is the worst nightmare of a manager because he's imposing on him, telling which team to pick, he's bad-mouthing him and he's filtering things through to the press. At least I had the advantage of having a president like Lorenzo Sanz who, while he might be saying things in the press, at least he was doing it openly. I was aware of what was going on even though I could see the alliances around the club shifting all the time. Wherever you are, once the players turn against you, and they go to the president, you need the president to stand firm or else your authority disappears. The flying pigs moment was when Sanz decided he wasn't going to do that any more.

Sanz was no shrinking violet himself. He knew I'd take the players on and he knew that, even if he didn't get the results on the pitch that he wanted, that I'd do the dirty work so that the next guy could. Madrid is a very political club. If the players aren't to be trusted, then the president isn't to be either.

*

12

Sociedad, three times for a Welshman!

BY THE AUTUMN OF 2000, NEARLY ONE YEAR ON, I WAS SATISFIED that the problems with Real Madrid had been solved. I felt a lot freer to take up coaching opportunities once that court case over the remainder of my contract had been concluded. In October, I received an offer to work in France, for the first time in my career, as manager of none other than Saint-Étienne. It was Lucidio Ribeiro who'd set it up once again and it was a very attractive proposition. For me, Saint-Étienne was one of the biggest, if not the biggest, and best-known clubs in France with a great history that, of course, I remembered first-hand from that famous European Cup quarter-final of 1977. I'd played there with Liverpool and I knew what Saint-Étienne meant to football supporters in France. I remembered the stadium. It had been remodelled one or two times since my last visit but it had that same closeness and feel about it. It was the place where David Beckham had got himself sent off against Argentina in the World Cup just two years earlier. Super ground, big support, terrific training facilities; I could see that the people there were quite excited to be getting a manager who had just worked at Real Madrid, but I hadn't been their first choice. Funnily enough, the chairman, Alain Bompard, had initially called on my opposite number from that 1977 fixture, the big Argentine Osvaldo Piazza, but Piazza had just signed up to take over at Independiente in his home country and the club refused to let him go. So, there I was, available again and ready for another challenge.

I didn't know much about Ligue 1, but I've never known a great deal about the football they're currently playing wherever I've gone. I go in and get on with the job as I see it and the job this time was certainly a complex one. With ten games already gone Saint-Étienne were at the foot of the table with just seven points, having conceded twenty goals, an average of two per game. That stat told me everything I needed to know. That would mean that we'd need to score three per game to get enough points to survive, so it was pretty clear to me that the solution was to tighten up at the back and, going forward, to do whatever was necessary to get this not-long-since-promoted team back to resembling the side I played against when I was with Liverpool.

Robert Nouzaret was the manager who had brought the team up in 1999 after a three-year absence from the French top flight, but a bad string of results in the early autumn had got him the sack. Worse still, the club had become embroiled in a scandal over fake passports. The transfers of Brazilian striker Alex Dias and Ukrainian goalkeeper Maksym Levytskyi were put in the spotlight after a game against local rivals Lyon. The former had slipped in using a Portuguese passport and the latter with one supposedly from Greece, but as it turned out during the course of the following months, the documents had been falsified, so that wasn't the best business to have rumbling along in the background when you're trying to save the club from relegation.

I didn't know a lot about the team, but I had a good idea of the style of play I wanted to put in place to stop them conceding so many and the kind of structure I wanted at the club to give any young talent the chance to shine. I was put up in a super place, La Poularde, a hotel with one of the best-known restaurants in France in a quiet little town called Montrond-les-Bains, which is about thirty minutes outside the city of Saint-Étienne. It's a small town, very quiet. Not a big city like it's neighbour, Lyon, by any means. I settled in there, got used to the drive in and out of training and I thoroughly enjoyed it. It was different, working with different people, in a different league. It was a real football club and I got on very well with the president, the players, the assistants, the other coaches, goalkeeping coaches, everybody there. It was a good set-up. Very quickly, I caught on that the coach of the second team could be very useful to me. He knew all about the younger footballers at the club, he knew the league better than I did and, because his parents were from Tarifa, near Cádiz, he spoke perfect Spanish. So, Rudi García became my first-team assistant, and what a good little stepping stone that's turned out to be for him.

Off we went, travelling through France, playing these games and often against a familiar face or two. We took on the previous manager, Robert Nouzaret, with his new club Toulouse, and beat them 1–0 at home with five minutes to go. I got my taste of yet another local derby when we visited Lyon and lost to a goal in the ninetieth minute to our rivals as managed by Saint-Étienne club legend Jacques Santini, whom I had also lined up against in that fateful tie of 1977. Perhaps the biggest run-in of all for me, though, was when I came face to face once more with an old enemy of mine from Spain, Javier Clemente, who was now in charge of Marseille. Javier was manager at Athletic Bilbao and there for my very first derby when I arrived at Real Sociedad in 1985. I was a foreigner and he was very much Basque and against foreign signings. He said a few unpleasant things about my appointment but, later on, I must admit, I got on quite well with him and he did, on more than one occasion, acknowledge the work that I had done. Javier always liked a bit of a fight in the press and I've certainly never been one to back down from one, so I was always happy to have battles with him. I enjoyed having that back-and-forth kind of relationship and I expect he did as well. In that sense, we weren't that different and, over the years, of course, our paths have crossed many times and I think there's mutual respect. We've both won trophies in Spain and that's not something that happens by accident. When I was at Real Madrid that first time, Javier was in charge of Atlético Madrid. So, we had a Madrid derby, a Basque derby and this rivalry in France too.

Javier seemed to follow me around quite a lot in those times. Later, when I went to Real Murcia, he was at Tenerife. I bought a house in Zarautz in the Basque Country and so did he. I couldn't get shot of him. We'd bump into each other out for a walk every now and then. We sat down for a coffee once or twice, but we generally kept to the part of town nearest our respective clubs – Javier in the west towards Bilbao and me closer to San Sebastián.

On this occasion in France, it was Javier who walked away with the bragging rights. At Marseille, he had a young William Gallas in his side, Bruno N'Gotty and former World Footballer of the Year, George Weah, at centre-forward. Weah opened the scoring with just ten minutes to go, but despite Saint-Étienne equalising, Javier's team stole it at the end. We'd deserved to get something but that was the way it went. We won a game and lost a game, won a game and lost a game; kept our heads above water. In twelve games, I picked up five of Saint-Étienne's nine wins that season and nearly half of their total points but after our match away at Lyon in December, the phone rang and everything changed. It was

Luis Uranga, the president of Real Sociedad. The Basques were fighting for their lives at the bottom of La Liga and he wanted me to take charge immediately.

Maybe I was a little bit out of order with Saint-Étienne but, as difficult a thing as it was to do, I felt that if Real Sociedad had come back for me, I had to go back there and try to dig them out of the mire. I'm not afraid of those difficult choices because, as I've said many times, you've got to make decisions. No matter how difficult they might seem, you have to make the one that's right for you. I had a home in San Sebastián. The most important club for me was Real Sociedad and the call of help from them was a big one. Luis Uranga was a close friend of mine. He was a director when I first went there and he spoke perfect English, which was a big help to me at the time. Luis had since moved up to become the president of a club that was now in deep trouble. They'd appointed Javier Clemente as manager for the 1999/00 season, which in itself caused a fair bit of division, and I was very surprised because I'd certainly never see myself managing at Athletic Bilbao. Javier had not done a particularly good job and left after just one win from the first six in the following campaign. So, the club put Xabi Alonso's father, Miguel Ángel 'Periko' Alonso, in charge. Periko had been a key part of Real Sociedad's golden generation of the early 1980s and later signed for Barcelona. He'd done a few lower-division coaching jobs, generally around clubs in the Basque Country, but he'd done nothing at this level and it hadn't gone well for him with just seven points from ten games. He wasn't cut out for it, really. Periko Alonso was born in San Sebastián. Everybody knew him and it was a very big responsibility for him, but the pressure of the matches and the results every week was too much for him and he explained to me that he had to stop. After he stepped down from the job he said he'd never manage again – a very strong statement to make – and he didn't. There must have been something about the work that he recognised didn't suit him at all. Luis Uranga always had a lot of confidence in me and he'd reached straight for the phone.

Within a matter of hours, I was on a jet from Lyon to Biarritz, which the club had sent to get me, and then I drove from there to sign for Real Sociedad in San Sebastián. They weren't happy at all in Saint-Étienne and I could understand that, but I said I was sorry and explained that, for me, Real Sociedad is my club. They're like family. Players change clubs and managers change clubs; a lot of times they do it for money, a lot of times they do it for ambition, but there are certain places that you never really leave, or at least they never leave you, and Real Sociedad was that for me.

Saint-Étienne were paid compensation but they went down that season. Their results took a nosedive after I left. They were found guilty of the false passports debacle, the two first-teamers in question were banned for the rest of the season and the club was docked six points. With that stacked against them, maybe they would have got relegated all the same, but if I'd stayed I'd have fancied our chances. So, part of me was sorry to have left. It was a very interesting, if short, period for me. I had no complaints at all about the way that I'd been treated at the club. It was just unfortunate. I remember Rudi wanting to come with me but I had to tell him that it was difficult there with staff at Real Sociedad and that I always went to these places on my own. So, Rudi stayed and did what he could there before eventually winning the league and cup double with Lille many years later and having a good go at Serie A with Roma after that, all of which he thoroughly deserved.

Upon returning to San Sebastián, there was a big job on. With almost half the season gone, Real Sociedad were at the bottom of the league with just thirteen points to their name. The only positive, as far as the table went, was that it was shaping up to be a very tight season. Javier Clemente had put two players out on loan to Eibar in the second division, which I didn't agree with – a young centre-forward, Joseba Llorente, and a nineteen-year-old Xabi Alonso. The first thing I did was to get them back. I knew of them and I wanted them with me because at times like that you need all your players around you so that you can work with everything you've got and decide what's best based on that. Besides, one man's meat is another man's poison, so I wanted a closer look at these players for myself. I started gingerly with Xabi, playing him for an hour or thirty minutes at a time because, fitness-wise, he was a bit short. Xabi was a bit one-paced – he always was, actually – but he had terrific vision and it was just a case of easing him in slowly but surely. I noticed he was a bit slow off the mark but he was great in control of the ball, so I put small poles down for him to tiptoe through quickly in training just to get him faster off his feet. I did the same thing for myself at Liverpool to get a bit of sharpness. Very quickly, he ended up that season as a regular starter in the side and he never looked back. I think his father had been a little bit reluctant to put Xabi and his brother, Mikel, into the team because of what people might have thought, but it was the right time for Xabi to make the step up. We played a 4–2–3–1 with Xabi alongside Iñigo Idiakez and there was good protection for Xabi because he was well surrounded by our experienced regulars, so it afforded him that little bit more freedom to do what he does best, an ability that took him to Liverpool, Real Madrid and Bayern Munich – a career path not too dissimilar to my own. Xabi knew those players around him well. He knew their game from watching them for years from the stands and, because they were local players and he was a local lad, they were very welcoming to Xabi and he felt comfortable enough to play. That's the way it is for young footballers in the Basque Country.

Apart from Xabi and Llorente, the only other changes I made were to bring in two defenders – Luiz Alberto, whom I'd just worked with at Saint-Étienne, and Júlio César, whom I'd known from my second time at Real Madrid – both Brazilians, good pros and successful at the club. Luiz I liked a lot. His transfer to Real Sociedad was part of my compensation agreement. We offered more money than he was worth, really, but he justified his value in the end. He could play centre-back or a midfield holding position. Typical Brazilian footballer, he liked the ball at his feet. Good build, good stature; maybe he wasn't the type of centre-back that the Basque people were accustomed to – more of a ball player, less of a big and solid and hit-them-hard marker, but he could look after himself. César was another good player but never got enough game time stuck behind Hierro, Campo, Iván Helguera and Aitor Karanka in the pecking order at Madrid. His was only a loan, so he didn't stay at Sociedad as long as Luiz, but both were good signings.

It was a difficult time to go, get to know players and get results, so the more I had that I already knew, the easier and quicker it made that transition, and time was something we didn't have an awful lot of. It was a big job on to keep the club up. They'd signed too many foreign players after the ruling had been relaxed. They'd gone a bit crazy and hadn't signed the right ones. There was no plan. We were beaten by the big clubs in the league but got wins against most of the rest and, with a good late run, dragged ourselves up the table. We won away at Villarreal, which is never an easy place to get a result, beat Málaga and got a draw at Zaragoza which virtually guaranteed our survival with two games to play, but what I saw in that final couple of matches did not sit comfortably with me.

Real Sociedad faced Athletic Bilbao at the San Mamés in the penultimate game of the season. A win for us would guarantee La Liga survival, something which Athletic had accomplished the game before. There was an incident in that derby game, which we won 3–1 – and we were very good that night, we were good value for our win – but there was a case where Urzáiz, the Bilbao centre-forward, who was terrific in the air, missed an unbelievable chance from five yards out. It was harder to miss than it was to score and that raised a few eyebrows. There were people who thought that maybe Bilbao had let it happen so that we stayed up – a Basque thing, you understand – and then Real Sociedad obliged by gifting Osasuna three points in the Pamplona side's final game at the Anoeta to ensure that the three Basque teams stayed up in the top division at the expense of Real Oviedo.

I wouldn't put that out of the question. I saw things on that final day that I didn't particularly like. We hardly went into the last third of the field. It was a little bit after the Lord Mayor's show. We'd been under pressure for five weeks and, the week before, we were finally safe. Maybe there was a little bit of a lull. Osasuna had to get something from the game to stay up, so they were at the races that much more than we were. So, whichever way you looked at it, you could say that it was obvious that relaxation crept in but, at the same time, it really wasn't a pretty sight – especially from the Basque players in my side. To give an assured opinion on it, to say it was a fix, you'd have to be 100 per cent certain of it, and I was only 99 per cent sure, so that's the way I left it, but, as a professional, I didn't like what I'd seen at all. But, of course, when it's working in your favour, you think a little bit differently than you do about it when it goes the other way. In normal circumstances Urzáiz would have scored, and in normal circumstances, we would have beaten Osasuna in that last game because we would have had to and, in normal circumstances, Osasuna would have gone down, but things were hush-hush in the Basque Country. Oviedo went down instead and I don't think they've recovered since.

That summer should have been a chance to put the squad right but there had been elections at Real Sociedad just a few weeks before the season ended. Luis Uranga stepped down after nine years in charge of the club and José Luis Astiazarán took over. Astiazarán was a former youth player at Real Sociedad who'd become a successful lawyer and eventually a director after he hadn't quite made the grade as a footballer. I knew him and got on well with him from my years in San Sebastián but he had his own plans when it came to who should be coaching the team. As new president, he wanted me to move up to become a kind of technical director or general manager with a responsibility for signing the foreign players that would work best at Sociedad. My record at signing foreigners for the club was very good – Kodro, Xavier, Oceano. Valeri Karpin was another; I'd bought him during my second time at the club and he came back again in 2002. In 1994, I'd sent my assistant to watch him playing for Spartak Moscow because they were in a position where they had to let four or five of their players go. He was a terrific pro. Very competitive. He started as a wide player, but came in as more of a right-sided midfielder. I remember when we went on a pre-season tour to Portugal, Karpin had got an ankle injury the day before we were meant to travel. He had it all strapped up. On the flight over, he spent his time hopping up and down the aisle. He was already starting his recovery. It's a small detail but it tells you everything about him.

Darko Kovačević was another I signed. He'd already spent three years at the club from 1996–99 before heading off to Juventus but he wasn't such a big hit in Italy and it was an easy choice to bring him back in 2001. When he returned, he formed one of the deadliest strike duos in the club's history with Nihat. He was in the line of the old Yugoslav-type No. 9s, a big player for Real Sociedad. The two were a classic big man/little man pair. None of these players I signed disappointed. None of them. Now, possibly it was because I knew the environment there in San Sebastián, because I knew the people and I knew the players, but if you did a poll of the best ten foreign players at Real Sociedad, you'd probably find that at least seven of them were signed by me – and that's after nearly thirty years of foreign players being allowed to sign for the club. I was only there for about four or five of those years.

Many of my signings made money for the club as well, so everyone knew I could do the role of sporting director or something similar, but I wasn't sure I was quite ready for it. I was confused, to be honest with you, which is not a position I've often found myself in. There was a part of me that thought it would be great; comfortable, living in San Sebastián, travelling about, but I still had that desire to be the coach and felt I was getting pushed into a corner.

There was a lad called Juan Manuel Lillo, who was a Basque from a village just outside San Sebastián. He'd done very well at Salamanca, taking them up from the second division to the first. He was doing quite well with spells at Oviedo, Tenerife and Zaragoza and they thought it would be good if Lillo was the coach and I was making the signings, but I felt I was getting pushed out and I was very uncertain. It was a difficult time for me. The comfortable thing would have been for me to agree. I was well respected. I'd managed there on three occasions and this could have been an easy way out into a kind of early retirement, if you like, but it wasn't something that convinced me. I knew I could still be successful as a coach. It was in my blood.

Astiazarán had virtually agreed that Lillo would take over. He was on his way and I had to intercept the idea. It didn't go down well and, six months later, in March 2002, I was dismissed. Astiazarán wasn't too happy to do that. Maybe I'd forced him into a little bit of a corner. I always had a good relationship with him. He was a young chairman. I'd seen him come onto the board and he became successful later on as the president of the Spanish Football League Association. Real Sociedad was my club, San Sebastián was my city and the last thing I wanted was animosity.

I didn't get a chance to sign the players we needed until the winter when we were already, unsurprisingly, towards the bottom end of the table, so it made it easier in some way for Astiazarán to make the decision. Lillo went elsewhere. He eventually took charge of the club in 2007/08, following relegation. A Frenchman by the name of Raynald Denoueix took over my work in earnest for the 2002/03 season and got Real Sociedad to finish runners-up in the league that year with the players and the team that I'd built. It was something of a last hurrah for Real Sociedad before they went down in 2007. I'd signed Dutch goalkeeper Sander Westerveld from Liverpool, Kovačević and Nihat from Lazio and Beşiktaş, and a very serious, very concentrated lad called Bjørn Tore Kvarme whom I'd worked with at Saint-Étienne and was probably too nice and laid-back to be a defender, but you get all sorts in a football team and it's good to have a mix of personalities.

We also had Basque players like Xabi coming through. Javier de Pedro was another who made his debut with me. He wasn't a great trainer but had lots of quality, a terrific left foot and an excellent understanding with another one I developed called Agustín Aranzábal, who played at left-back. They were good mates on and off the field, both left-footed, both ended up playing for Spain, like Xabi; brilliant for the overlaps and communication.

You don't just put a team together like that and it clicks, you need a bit of time for them to gel. That team was a team of international players that I'd made. Raynald Denoueix came in, but he'd never achieved anything before and never has since, and that speaks volumes.

I've never regretted turning down the chance to move upstairs at Real Sociedad. It had seemed right for a moment, but when it came to the crunch I decided against it. I think maybe that upset their plans a bit and it turned a little sour. I was

53 years of age and that's young for management these days. I didn't think I was ready to leave that life. I'd not long since been at Real Madrid and I ended up still coaching fifteen years later in Africa, still winning trophies. Once a coach, always a coach, for me. I couldn't sit still and do a job like that. I'm not interested in politics. I could never be a director. I'm a football man. I'd get frustrated that I wasn't on the sidelines doing it myself. I've always been the coach and I've seen others doing these jobs and they're not for me. When I've finished coaching, I'm done. I'm finished in football.

13

Sicily and the Mafia

PEOPLE MIGHT THINK OF XABI ALONSO, IKER CASILLAS, GARETH Bale or Aaron Ramsey as the most significant players I've helped to develop, but the success story that means most to me is that of Guly do Prado. I met Guly at the training ground in Catania, one week before my second game in charge of the club, the biggest game of the season, the Sicilian derby at home to Palermo. It was a fixture that Catania had not won for twelve years. All around the town the talk of the game was in the air. There was no point trying to go for a stroll to clear my mind of it.

'Ah, Mr Toshack,' someone would say, 'Catania–Palermo; you know this is a very important game for us?'

Even if I'd had no idea of local rivalries, it wouldn't have taken me more than a few yards in the streets to understand all about it.

Coming to work at Calcio Catania in November 2002 had been something of a risk. It was the first time I'd managed a team outside of the top flight for twenty years since I'd left Swansea. I'd achieved a lot of things in Spain and been at the top of the game there, but I was running out of clubs with the right kind of challenge where I hadn't already been and I'd always liked the idea of trying Italy out for size. The languages are very similar, so I knew that wouldn't present too much of a problem, but the style of play out there is very different to what I was used to, as are the people – the players and directors – and the way these clubs are run.

With reference to the last of these, Catania was a particular risk. It was owned, along with Perugia in Serie A, by the infamous Italian businessman Luciano Gaucci. In a country with something of a history of eccentric presidents, Gaucci was even more eccentric still. Very outspoken, he'd often fill a few column inches with his criticisms of one referee or another if he felt Perugia had been hard done by and he sought out publicity by any means possible. The more controversial the better as far as he was concerned. Italian football was never as good as the Premier League or La Liga at global marketing, and this was Gaucci's way of bringing more attention and more money to his club. He signed the Japanese player Hidetoshi Nakata and the first Chinese and first Korean footballers, Ma Mingyu and Ahn Jung-hwan, to play in Italy to increase Perugia's appeal in Asia, the latter of whom he sacked in 2002 after Ahn scored the winning goal for his country which knocked Italy out of the World Cup that year.

Luciano also tried, unsuccessfully, to sign two top female football stars to play as part of the men's team in Serie A. The first, Germany's Birgit Prinz, turned the opportunity down in December 2003 and then the Italian Football Federation closed the loophole in its rules that had made it a possibility before the second candidate, Hanna Ljungberg, could agree. Instead, Gaucci had to be content with shocking the world by getting Colonel Gaddafi's son, Al-Saadi Gaddafi, on the books at Perugia, which gives you an idea of the kind of circles that Gaucci moved in. Gaddafi, of course, was an embarrassment on the field and off it. He made one appearance for the team before he was banned for testing positive for anabolic steroids.

Maybe the story that should have been the worry for me was when Luciano installed the first ever female coach of the men's football team Viterbese Calcio, which he owned in the lower leagues of Italian football. Carolina Morace was a very famous player for the Italian national women's team but she soon handed in her notice to Gaucci after the president tried to have too much say in her coaching and playing staff, not least of which was a male assistant.

Luciano had put his 23-year-old son Riccardo in charge of Catania, though, and when I met the pair at the Gaucci family home, they made assurances that Riccardo wouldn't interfere with footballing matters. He had done well since taking over the team two years previously in 2000. He'd brought Catania up from the third tier of Italian football to the second for the 2002/03 season, but the team were already flirting with relegation and I was brought in, the fifth coach of that calendar year, to make sure that it didn't happen. There's no doubt that there were alarm bells from the off but, as I say, I'd always wanted to work in Italy and it was a short assignment so I knew that I wouldn't have to put up with the Gauccis for too long if things weren't to my liking.

The first game, we lost in Siena 4–3. What a beautiful little city and a lovely ground, but it was quite easy to see why Calcio Catania was in the position that it was. It was the first chance I'd had to look at them and the team were shipping goals all over the place. We worked in our first week on the defensive side of things but all the talk with all the players and the staff and everyone else was the big match the next weekend. It was everywhere you went. There were ghosts coming out of the closet all over the place. People were talking of the Sicilian mafia bribing players, fixing the game and all kinds of things. If we'd turned up at the ground and Marlon Brando's Godfather had been the referee, it wouldn't have surprised me. It was very tense everywhere you went.

My assistant coach was a famous Italian international, a centre-forward called Francesco Graziani who had played in top Italian sides like Torino, Fiorentina and Roma in the 1970s and 80s, and had also coached Catania the previous year. What I remember most about him was his mobile with that horrible Nokia ringtone that went off every second of the day. Diddle-er-der, diddle-er-der, diddle-er-der-der; followed by his loud salutation every time he answered it, 'Amigo mio!' – my friend! I didn't have a mobile phone at the time. I think that put me off for a fair few years after.

Part of Graziani's job was to fill me in on the players in the squad and that was no mean feat under the Gauccis. All of a sudden four players might arrive on loan from Perugia because they weren't getting a game in Serie A. One or two might disappear off in the other direction. You never knew who was coming and who was going but, despite all this movement, it was another young lad hanging around at the training ground that caught my attention. Guly do Prado was a twenty-year-old from Brazil who didn't speak any Italian. He didn't train with the squad because the last coach hadn't fancied him. Instead, he'd fallen back into the role of a general dogsbody. He fetched the water and the sponges for the players. He'd bring them their boots and maybe go off for a run on his own to keep himself fit. He seemed more like a junior or assistant to another Brazilian-born boy at the club, the team's top striker Luís Oliveira, who had himself been around Serie A for the previous fifteen years or so. All the same, Guly had bags of enthusiasm and I could see in the way he ran that he was a good athlete so, with a few days to go before the derby,

I called him over and said: 'You. Train with us.'

'No, no,' he replied, 'I can't try because I only bring my shoes. No football boots.'

'Try,' I said.

We had a little practice game and I thought, hang on a minute. He had something about him. You could tell straight away that he had intelligence and a good sense of positioning. When his side attacked, he arrived from deep positions, which is not something you can always teach somebody. Guly had been touring Italy with his team from Brazil, Portuguesa Santista, when the Gauccis had seen him play. They brought him over to Catania but then nothing. He was stuck there, not training, because they thought he was too young. Often in Italy, if you're not a big name, then they don't give you an opportunity. So, to begin with, he was training on his own and then going home, and then training some more and nothing. Nobody cared what he was doing, so it was something of surprise to him and everybody else around the club when, based on what I'd seen in that practice, I picked him to start in the Sicilian derby of 2002, a game where Catania had not enjoyed victory over island rivals Palermo for twelve years.

It was a night game at Catania's Stadio Angelo Massimino, right in the heart of the city. The stands were packed with supporters, flags waving, fireworks going off in the sky and flares in the crowd Catania red, the noise of the singing bouncing off the tribunes and bangs of the pyrotechnics. Smoke from the flares billowed off the stands and I remember, as it cleared, a banner in blue and white across one end that read 'Welcome Mr Toshack, you won't miss the Bernabéu'. I'd experienced all kinds of derbies wherever I've been but this was something special. My friend Mauri, the restaurant owner from Mallorca, was in the stands that day. It was him who had set me up with the job at Catania via an intermediary. He's an Inter fan but he wanted to see how I was getting on and he knew the Sicilian derby would be too big to miss.

'Mafia versus mafia,' he described it, 'the best game in Italy!'

The supporters of these two clubs are real fanatics. They knew all the players inside out but in the stands that day, when they saw the name do Prado on the teamsheet, Mauri said that nobody had a clue. Guly had not played one match; not a first-team game, not reserves, nothing, and they were not happy about this. Word got around that Mauri was a friend of mine and it got very awkward for him. Mauri believed in what I was doing but everyone started telling him that I was crazy, asking him who this do Prado was and virtually pinning everything on poor Mauri.

After ten minutes, though, it was clear that Guly was the best player on the pitch. He ran the game from midfield. He was first to every ball, cut passes out, dispossessed the Palermo players easily and then burst forward into attack. After thirty minutes, Catania scored. Guly had made the pass. Nobody was questioning Mauri or Guly or me any more. Oliveira made it 2–0 in the second half and Catania won the day.

It had been a very tight, very tense game; difficult for the referee. It was a relief to see a friendly face when Mauri walked across the field towards the dugout to congratulate me while the players were on the pitch saluting the crowd. On his way back to Mallorca the next day, Mauri stopped to get petrol not far out of the city. Mount Etna was rumbling. It's a very important thing over there. Everybody lives in the shadow of the mountain. It's a big, big personality. Everybody looks at it all the time. He asked an old man what was going on, if there was going to be a problem and the old man said, 'No, no problem. The volcano is very happy because Toshack is here.'

The day after the win, I went with Graziani to the town centre. We walked past a clothes shop and the fellow who owned it came out and put his arms around me. '*Eh, grazie, signore, grazie,*' and he gave me a black leather coat. A few more steps later and another shopkeeper ran out and gave me a pair of sunglasses. Then a shoe shop and it's, '*Que numero, mister, que numero?*' By the time I got back to the car I had a completely new wardrobe. I don't like to think what would have happened if I'd lost the game.

With Guly in the side, after a few games, there was an order in the team that wasn't there before and the beginnings of a belief that we could win, but I wasn't really there long enough to change things properly. We lost so many games by the odd goal in the last five minutes. When you perform major surgery on a team – new personnel, a new way of playing – it takes a period of time for those cuts to heal and the side to fully rehabilitate, but that kept getting set back by the ridiculous president we had to deal with. Riccardo Gaucci, the son of Luciano, had played some football in the past and he thought he knew more about it than the managers and other staff at the club. It became virtually impossible to work with. Generally, I've respected all the presidents I've had, whether I've agreed with them or not, but this one was something else. It was different to any boardroom conditions I've ever had to work under. He went through a hundred players in his four years running Catania, many of them sent from Perugia to supposedly help us out.

But these were players who were not match-fit, whom I'd not seen play, and the expectation from Gaucci was that I'd just drop them into the first team. He didn't appreciate that they wouldn't be ready or that it would upset the group. He called his own team out in the press for having a Serie C defence when he'd provided Serie A-type players and by that point I'd had enough. I couldn't tolerate his lack of respect to my players and my work any longer and, after three months at the club, I handed in my notice. Napoli away was my last game. We lost 1–0 and I got sent off for complaining to the ref. I remember the goal. The lad was about ten yards offside. It was ridiculous. I finished it three days later. There were so many difficulties, of all sorts, particularly with the president. It was a nightmare.

At lunchtime on the same day, some of the players called me into the referee's room where they had Riccardo Gaucci and were forcing him to make concessions and take me back. I think some of them could see we'd been moving in the right direction. It had been going OK. We'd pulled away a bit from the relegation situation but we were still involved and were by no means picking up points every week. It certainly wasn't enough to make me change my mind. Then, later that night, at about midnight or one in the morning, they came to my hotel to persuade me. A big group of supporters were there with them. I was sleeping, ready to go the following day, and I got this call from reception telling me that there were twenty fans making a row and waiting for me downstairs. 'Mr Toshack, you have to come down.' I had to get up and go down and they were saying, 'No, no, you don't go, mister, you stay here,' and I said, 'No, I've signed the papers now, they're with the federation, it's too late.'

'No, no,' they replied, 'we've got the papers,' and they had too. They were waving the contract termination in front of me. They had a new contract and they were holding the president in the dressing room at the training ground ready to sign it. I had a terrible feeling that there was going to be no way out of this, like they were making me an offer I couldn't refuse! It was a bit of a frightening experience. Eventually I convinced them that I couldn't carry on and that it was in the best interests of everybody that I left. I checked out of my hotel very early the next day; very early indeed.

As for Guly, he was spotted that day at the derby by Riccardo Gaucci's father, Luciano, the president of Perugia, who couldn't believe what this talented kid was doing down in Serie B. Guly spent the best part of a decade in Italy playing in and around some decent sides – Perugia, Fiorentina, Cesena when they were in the top flight – and, eventually, he got his move to England with Southampton where he put in over a hundred appearances and became something of a favourite. I bumped into him at Swansea in 2014 when the two clubs met in the Premier League. He was still a good lad and it was very pleasing to have played a small part in his success.

So, there are jobs that outsiders might look at and think of as mistakes but, for me, Catania was not one of them. It was never going to work but I enjoyed my time in Sicily. It was impossible not to. It was such a beautiful place. Throughout my four months, Etna was erupting. It was one of the most explosive periods for the volcano for the last 150 years and I had a ringside seat as the mountain opened up fissures of magma across its flanks and burst spumes of ash so high into the atmosphere that it came down as far away as the Greek island of Cephalonia. It was incredible to watch how people's lives were interwoven with Etna; how it had been for centuries in Catania and the little towns and villages even closer to the foot of the mountain and as far up its slopes as they'd dared to build.

I remember waking up in my hotel the morning after the seismic activity had started. It was a bright sunny day but the streets were covered in this thick layer of soot; the cars, the roofs, the pavements, everything. It was like it had snowed the wrong colour; black instead of white. I had to watch the second team play with an umbrella because the cenere, as they called it, the ash was falling from the sky. The players trained with masks on and everyone on the sidelines – the coaches, the supporters, the families – were all with umbrellas up on this beautiful, blue-skied day. I'd seen a lot in football but this was unique.

The police were kind enough to take me up the mountainside as far as they would go to see the lava. It was fascinating to speak to the people in the villages there and listen to how they respect the volcano and how they've learned to live with it. They talk about it like it was a person: 'Oh, he's angry today,' and things like that. It was in sight wherever you were. On my days off, I'd often go to Taormina. Richard Burton wasn't the only Welshman to have fallen in love with the place. I'd sit there and soak up the life, read the Italian newspapers and watch the volcano; the puffs from its cinder cone, the red-orange lines of molten rock zigzagging across its face. Further down the coast you could see the Cyclopean Islands where Odysseus had supposedly tricked Polyphemus and then been cursed to spend years lost at sea. It all added to the magic of the place. It must be the most picturesque place I've ever worked. It might have only been four months but the beauty and the culture of Catania has always stuck with me. We played one game up in Venice, where you're taken to the stadium by boat and then straight from the dock into the dressing room. We played in Napoli where Maradona had become a legend. If I hadn't been in football, I wouldn't have seen these things.

Played ten, won four, lost six, doesn't look like much on paper but it was an unforgettable few months. The travel, the culture, the language, working with young players in a country I'd not been to, imposing a different style of play, trying to right the way a club goes about its business and the risk taken in doing so: of all that gets talked about with Real Madrid, Liverpool and Swansea, in many ways, what happened on and off the field during my time at Catania tells you more about me than anything else.

14
International management

WITH INTERNATIONAL MANAGEMENT, YOU'VE GOT TO JUDGE THE job by what the fellow had when he went in and what it looked like when he went out. What happens in terms of results is mostly down to timing. It's a lottery and it really depends on the situation of the side when you arrive, because it's not possible to turn things around quickly – not even two years could be long enough with only about seven matches in the calendar and so much time in between them. You can't buy. You can't sell, and I'd have sold a few if I could. You're stuck with what you've got and your only decision is whether to work with what's in front of you or to move them out and push a new lot through. That was my situation when I took over the Welsh national football team in November 2004.

At the time, what was considered Wales's golden generation of players had failed, yet again, to qualify for a major international tournament under Mark Hughes. They'd come close to Euro 2004 but lost out to Russia after a two-legged play-off that produced just a single goal. It was heartbreaking stuff for Wales but a lot of what I'd seen through the recent campaigns hadn't looked too clever to me and I'd said as much as a pundit on TV. So, when the Welsh FA announced that they were looking for a successor, the time finally felt right for me to answer the call. It wasn't without some sense of trepidation that I threw in my hat.

As much as I'd always referred to Wales as home, it hadn't felt that way when I took charge of the nation's team for a one-game spell ten years earlier. I knew it would be different this time. I had the space to take it on, which I hadn't back in 1994, when I was the manager of Real Sociedad for the second time, and I had tried to do both jobs at once. It's easy to see now that it could never have worked, but I was 45 years old back then. I'd not long since won the championship with Real Madrid. I thought I could have managed eight or nine teams at the same time in those days, I was experienced and the possibility of taking over Wales at international level excited me. Leading out your own country is a dream job for any manager. At the same time, my allegiance to Real Sociedad was very important to me. The club was very close to my heart and San Sebastián had been my home for a decade. The people in charge there understood the importance of the opportunity. They trusted me if I said I could juggle the responsibilities and gave me permission to do the two jobs. I'd played for Wales as an Under-18, an Under-21 and as a full international on forty proud occasions, but when I returned to Wales for training and for our match against Norway at Ninian Park, it was definitely a shock; not what I had expected at all.

We lost the match 3–1 and what I'd seen then I was not particularly enthusiastic about. With the squad, there were a lot of things discipline-wise that I thought, 'Hang on a minute, this is completely new to me in the way of organisation, timing, punctuality, all sorts of things.' It was a group of players that should have done a lot better than they were doing. The likes of Neville Southall, Andy Melville, Chris Coleman, Dean Saunders, Ian Rush, Gary Speed and Mark Hughes certainly shouldn't have been losing on their own ground to Norway. It was a decent Norway side but their FIFA ranking of second in October 1993 was very inaccurate. When we played them, they only had a smattering of top-level players. It was an experienced Wales side, but in the three or four days I'd been with them I saw a lot of things that I didn't like. I got the impression that some of these players were coming down for a break, not to win a football match.

From what I'd seen in that short period, I knew that I wouldn't be able to put things right in Wales from where I was over in San Sebastián. I could see it needed someone on the spot all the time to make the changes. Mike Smith, who had been manager when I played, was my assistant and I remember him saying to me, 'You're doing too much. Let them get on with it.' But that's not my way. I have to be very hands-on.

The reaction of the crowd at Ninian Park was also a bit negative too and that didn't help. Granted, I'd been important for their rivals at Swansea but I was a Cardiff lad. I expected more. During that trip it became quite clear to me that people at home were not fully behind my appointment. In all the time I'd been away I'd not forgotten Wales, but Wales had forgotten me. They liked Terry Yorath

– both the fans and the players – but the FAW had decided not to renew his contract after his near miss with World Cup qualification, which had only been one penalty kick away from success. I played in the same schoolboy side as Terry. We were in the national team together; he captained the team that I played in and I was always very good friends with him, and I remember, when I got the job, going up to Leeds to speak to him. There was no animosity. He had finished and that was it. It could have been anyone going in. It didn't matter but I still had to bear the resentment for the country and it probably didn't help that, to some eyes, I was a foreigner. Terry was very popular with the media, the players and the fans. After that final game against Romania in 1993 in the qualifiers for USA 94, there was a dinner for him at the Angel Hotel in Cardiff. He got a standing ovation from the press. A lot of people felt like it had been a glorious failure, so when he didn't have his contract renewed, it was a big shock. The expectation from everywhere was that Terry would stay on as manager because we'd only just failed, plus he had recently lost his son, Daniel, who was only fifteen, so a lot of people felt that to carry on under those circumstances, and with the work that he'd done, it would have been the right thing. For whatever reason, though, the FAW decided that they wanted a change and I wasn't made fully aware of everything that was going on when I walked into the role.

I remember the press conference in Cardiff when my appointment was announced. There were only about twenty chairs set up because attendances at Welsh press conferences, at the time, were sparse, but 150 journalists turned up. It was packed and I got quite a grilling in that room, which, if I'm honest, took me by surprise. That's when I first realised that it wasn't going to be as simple as I thought. There were questions about how I was going to manage both jobs and there was anger about what had happened with Terry.

The match itself was not a nice thing to witness either. Wales had been playing all these big games at the National Stadium with fantastic support in front of 40,000 fans and then, suddenly, with the game just a friendly, we were back at Cardiff City with only a 10,000 attendance, the first fixture since the disappointment, and it was a pretty negative atmosphere. The players and fans were still very supportive of Terry. They were still chanting his name and, when we were three down, a few started chanting, 'Toshack out'. It was a mood that you just wouldn't expect.

I realised that I wasn't tapped into everything that was happening from over in San Sebastián and that I wasn't as popular as I thought. I felt Wales should have been a lot happier about my appointment. I'd managed Real Madrid. I'd won La Liga. As Welsh managers go, none had achieved what I had, and I was quite happy to get back to Spain after I'd dipped my toe in the water. When I did arrive back in San Sebastián, though, there was some criticism about what I was doing and I saw that this wasn't going to be the bed of roses that I thought it might. If I'd stuck with it, I knew that neither side would be happy with the situation and I don't think I'd have made a success of either of them. Wales would be a full-time job. I'd need to be in the UK all the time and I had to admit that I'd taken on too much. In the end, my allegiance had to be with Real Sociedad. The people there had been good enough to let me try it out. I was two years into a project with them and, what with the culture shock of the set-up back in Wales, it was an easy, if embarrassing, decision to have to make. I'd seen the house from the inside, and I hadn't liked what I'd seen, but when the chance came again in 2004, the situation was different. I was ready for the job, and, to some extent, I think Wales were too.

I'd had a short spell at Real Murcia at the beginning of the year at a time when I hadn't quite wanted to return to management, what with all the legal business going on after Seedorf published his book in May 2003. I had only taken the position at Murcia in January 2004 as a favour to the president whose family I'd known when I was in Madrid. It was the club's first season in La Liga in 15 years and they didn't really have the quality to compete. The previous managed, Joaquín Peiró, had organised them well enough to defend but, by the turn of the year, Murcia only had one win with the rest of their points coming from 10 draws. Under me they won another four, which included a victory over a Real Madrid side with David Beckham in it, but we had many more losses and the overall effect wasn't very different. Murcia finished bottom of the table and I experienced relegation for the first time since my Swansea days.

Like Terry Yorath, Mark Hughes had been a popular Wales manager, particularly with the players. He was the same kind of age as them and he'd played with them. I'd voiced my opinions as a pundit that might have upset a few of them too, but if you're on television then it's your job to say what you think and how you see it. Unlike ten years earlier, though, I came back home with my eyes open and a plan already in mind.

These players had just failed and they were not as good as they thought they were. They thought they were part of this golden generation of Welsh talent who were playing for big Premier League clubs, but, with the exception of Ryan Giggs and Gary Speed, none of them had won anything significant. In the end we had to get boys to replace them. The team who made the semi-finals at Euro 2016 had eleven years together before they took the stage in France – five under me, one under Gary Speed and five under Chris Coleman – and just look at the way they work for each other. There are players there playing at bigger clubs and with bigger careers than any of Mark Hughes's lot ever dreamed of, but it still never gets in the way of their attitude.

With an average age of over 28 and rising, it was also the right time to make a change. The squad I inherited had had their turn at trying to qualify for major tournaments and shown they couldn't do it, even in their prime. If they were not good enough, I knew I had to move them out and push a new lot through. This team with the older players might have got more points in the first two years, but they were never going to get us where we wanted to go. If I didn't go in and rip it up now, I'd only have to do it further down the line. I knew that if I did it on day one then there was a good chance that in four years' time we might have a side that could get to a major finals.

Obviously, it had to be done slowly. You've only got six or seven games each year to effect your changes in international management, so bedding in players is a longer process and I'd need a few of the old guard to take us through the transition. You can't throw a team of eighteen-year-olds into top-level football and expect them to pick up good habits. I had the support of the FAW. In fact, I think they were quite happy for me to do it because I think they knew it needed to be done. But these experienced players, they all had their friends in the press. I'd been working abroad for a long time and because I'd gone abroad to get my success I think there was a lot of jealousy involved. I knew I was putting my head on the block with the way I was about to do this and there were some clever people around who would have been quite happy to see me fail. I've no doubts about that.

We had the usual talk and most of the players could see what was coming for them and many of them were very good about it. Robbie Savage complained about the eating habits we laid down and just about anything else he could think of. It was probably his way of venting frustration about what he knew would be the end of his Wales career. He thought he was a lot better than he was, and that happens particularly when players get older and more desperate to play. I gave everyone a chance to prove me wrong but I had a pretty good idea that I didn't want Robbie Savage around. I just didn't like him as a player. He didn't score goals from midfield, he generally wasn't disciplined on the pitch and you got the idea that he felt it was all about him out there. I called him up for my first squad in February 2005 even though he was struggling with an injury. In the end, he wasn't fit in time to face our opponents, Hungary, so it gave me the opportunity to try something else and, with Carl Fletcher and Carl Robinson in midfield instead, I liked what I saw. They did what I asked of them, and I never looked back. There was still a lot of talent around from that older group elsewhere, though: Giggs, John Hartson, Mark Delaney, Speed, Craig Bellamy. Wales always had half a team. Jason Koumas was a fantastic player but you just couldn't rely on him.

A handful of them, including Gary Speed, retired straight away – most of them were ready to finish anyway. They'd just brought in the ten-day international break schedule, which meant players taking time away to be with Wales that they might otherwise use to go on holiday with their families. So, for some of them there was pressure from home, knowing that I might take them away to be part of the group and not even play them, particularly when their footballing friends and neighbours were off to Dubai or wherever, and knowing that, sooner or later, they'd be replaced by younger lads.

It was a long, long transitional period. It had to be. Firstly, I needed to find these younger players, and I had an idea of just the man who could help out with that. Brian Flynn had been interviewed for the Wales job at the same time as I had, along with Gérard Houllier, Ian Rush and the French manager Philippe Troussier, who'd had success with international teams in Africa and parts of Asia. I knew Flynny from my playing days in the Welsh national team in the 1970s and 80s. With over a hundred caps between us, we'd got to know each other very well. What's more, he had been working down the road as manager of a fourth-tier Swansea City and he'd saved my old club from relegation from the Football League by bringing through 21 young players to the first team there in just one season, all culminating in that famous 4–2 victory against Hull at the Vetch on the final day of the 2002/03 campaign. Flynny was just what I needed. I had a connection with him. It was just a one-to-one arrangement and we trusted each other.

Flynny was brought up on recruitment being the key to success. He went to Burnley from Port Talbot in 1972, moving 250 miles away when he was fifteen because he knew he had a chance of playing in their first team before he was twenty. When he got there, there were boys from the North-East, there were boys from Scotland, there were boys from Wales, there were boys from all over the country, from everywhere. Their recruitment was fantastic, and it had to be. They sold to survive and they'd reinvest back into their youth policy. So, Burnley's coaching and recruitment in the 1970s and part of the 60s was the best in the country, and Flynny took those ideas to Wrexham for his first managerial appointment in 1989.

He never had a chief scout. It was just him, his assistant and his coach and they did all the recruitment. You gain a real player knowledge like that when you're watching games every night of the week, and he turned it on again when he took over that bad situation at Swansea all those years later. Swansea needed ten players in eight weeks, otherwise they really would have been relegated. Flynny was able to identity and bring in those players in a short period of time because he'd had all that practice. So, then there he was with me at Verdi's cafe in the Mumbles talking about doing it again, but this time for his country.

The main problem with the Wales youth system was that the team structure wasn't doing the senior squad any favours. There was an Under-17 manager, an Under-19 manager and an Under-21 manager – Ian Rush, Neville Southall and Glyn Hodges, respectively at the time – and I thought, 'I don't like this.' The Under-21 manager obviously wanted his team to win for the sake of his own reputation, but if I had a player at twenty years of age who was good enough for the seniors, then I wanted him in my team. I just felt there was a bit of a selfish attitude and not enough thought for the collective. I put Flynny in charge of the lot. They all played at different times, so it was easy enough to do, and it turned out just as we wanted. As soon as he thought he had one that was ready, all he had to do was tell me and I'd pick them for the first team. I trusted him completely and he never let me down. Of course, it just so happens that the first player we tested out this fast-tracking system on was Gareth Bale. The senior team were going off on a mini-tour, staying in Bilbao and Austria, and Gareth had been with Flynny in the Under-17s. He'd been to two tournaments and he was just breaking into the Southampton first-team squad and I remember Flynny telling him that there was no way he would have a career at left-back. He'd have to be a forward with the talent he had or he'd be wasting it.

'Sixteen?' I asked Flynny. 'Bit young, isn't he?' But Flynny reminded me that it had never bothered me in the past, so I was good to my word. Gareth made his debut against Trinidad and Tobago, breaking the record for the youngest Welsh cap; from that point in, he only played one Under-21 game. It was working.

We fast-tracked the players because we needed the numbers and because we knew it would develop them more quickly.

You've got to be brave when you're making decisions on young players. They see you being brave and it'll give them that much more belief in themselves. They have no fear, and when you go onto a pitch and you're not afraid to make a mistake, your confidence rockets sky-high and that's what we tried to give to the younger groups.

I was twenty when I made my debut for Wales against that incredible West Germany team. I played my first game at Wembley Stadium against England at the same age. For any young lad, that's a huge, huge thing and, of course, as a Welsh lad there was a lot of pride because it was always a big battle between Wales and England. That gave me an enormous boost and the desire to do the same for younger players. There have been a lot of players that made their debut under me – Gareth Bale at sixteen, Aaron Ramsey seventeen years of age, both with Wales; a lot of players at Swansea, Xabi Alonso at nineteen years of age for Real Sociedad, Casillas at the same age for Madrid. Some managers aren't so keen to offer those chances but it's helped me through wherever I've been.

The real genius of Flynny's recruitment, though, was digging up those players who were nothing to do with the Welsh set-up when we got there. Either they'd slipped the net somehow or they didn't know they were Welsh in the first place. He'll tell you that it was just a case of being in the right place at the right time but Flynny was everywhere, so the chances of him missing anyone were virtually nil. If your dog was Welsh, he would have known about it. He built a database of every single player in the UK with a Welsh surname and then went on to first names. He'd also look out for Welsh spellings like Rhys instead of Reece and such. There was always a chance with any Davis, Evans, Jenkins, Williams and the rest. Flynny scouted everyone like that. He found Ashley Williams that way. Ashley was an easy one in terms of mileage because he was only at Stockport. Flynny knew Jim Gannon, the manager there, well. He phoned him up and checked on Ashley and found out he was from the heart of the Black Country and then got Jim Gannon to look and see if he had any Welsh blood in his family. On all contracts, they have the birth place of your parents and that's a good clue to your grandparents too. Jim phoned Flynny back an hour later and said he thought his grandmother was born in Bangor. Flynny hadn't seen him play at that stage but he'd heard he was good. Now, he went to watch him and straight away Flynny said he passed the football test. He phoned me up and told me to ignore the fact he was playing for a fourth-tier side. So I did. He was 21, he was raw, his background was non-league, but long shots come off sometimes. I sent Roy Evans, who was my number two, over with Flynny to watch him again and by half-time Roy said he'd seen enough. He'd do us proud.

Flynny's favourite story, though, is the way he found Hal Robson-Kanu. Brian Flynn was made welcome at every training ground in the country because he wasn't a threat to the coaches and managers. He wasn't there to pinch their players. He was there to promote them, and it was a huge feather in their caps – particularly the youth-team coaches – if one of theirs got to international level. So, through a lot of research, he'd found out that Reading had a couple of possible Welsh players in Simon Church and Jake Taylor, the latter of whom has not done so well, sadly. If Flynny was in London, he'd head over to the Reading training ground to watch a game or just to watch them train. He'd talk to the coaches and find out how they were doing and they were honest with him.

One afternoon, Flynny was sitting in the Reading canteen and Glen Little went over to him. Flynny knew Glen from Burnley. By all accounts he was a good character on and off the pitch and a bit of a card, which was something that Flynny liked about him. Glen knew the reason Flynny was there and he pointed over to this young lad in the corner and gave him that old joke, 'Hey, he can play for Wales, Bri, 'cause he goes on holiday to Wales.'

Flynny felt bad for this lad, so he went over to introduce himself. He explained to him that Glen Little was taking the mickey out of him (Flynny) and not this lad, but the lad tells Flynny that he does go on holiday to Wales every year. Flynny asked him why he goes and the lad said they've got a caravan that his family takes down to Tenby. 'It's brilliant down there in the summer,' he said, 'we go down the M4, we pick my grandmother up in Caerphilly . . .'

At this point Flynny said, 'Hold on, what's that?'

'Yeah, she was born there.'

Flynny hadn't seen him play but he went over to Brian McDermott, who was the Reading manager, and Brian told him that he'd got real hopes for Hal; that he was only nineteen but close to the first team – he'd already played for England at Under-19 level but that was no barrier to him choosing another country for senior level. So, Flynny stuck around to watch him train and he liked he what he saw.

Flynny left Hal for a couple of weeks to cool off. He'd passed the first test, the football test, that's the acid test, but the next one is, do they want to play for Wales, and the only way you can find that out for certain is to ask them face to face. Do you feel Welsh? You get a reaction off a player like that. That's the real question. It sounds funny but when you look into someone's eyes and they answer, you know if it's the truth or not. You know how they feel about it.

So, Flynny went back down to see Hal. He told him he'd seen him play and that he'd left him a couple of weeks to cool down, and then he asked him if he wanted to play for Wales. And straight away Hal said, 'No.'

'That's fine,' Flynny said, 'I like people who are positive, but remember one thing, Hal. My nickname is the Rash. You never know when I'll turn up and you'll never really get rid of me.'

So, each time Brian Flynn was there to see the others, he'd pop in and see Hal and ask him if he'd changed his mind and he kept saying no. In the meantime, Flynn was in touch with Hal's dad, who was working feverishly in the background to persude him. Flynny and Hal's dad would talk quite a bit on the phone and Flynny would tell him to be patient, that Hal was only nineteen and that there was no deadline.

Maybe a year later, Flynny gets a call and it's Hal's dad asking him to come and see his son. He went straight down the following morning, having a pretty good guess at what would come next. He asked Hal the question again – did he feel Welsh – and this time his answer was, 'Yes, I'd like to be considered.'

So, Hal came to try us out away with the Under-21 squad off to Austria in May 2010. He played, came and linked up with the first team on the Sunday in Cardiff and less than two weeks later he was off with us in the seniors playing in Croatia; when he got back he said he'd loved every minute of it.

Williams and Robson-Kanu would start at Euro 2016. The players Flynny found didn't always work out, though. The fallout rate was high, as you might expect. We were casting the net as wide as possible. For every five we dug up, there'd probably be one or two who'd make it to the seniors. That's normal, and even when we had assembled what we felt was the core of the country's next generation, we knew there'd have to be a lot of settling in, but there was a good feeling in the camp and I hoped it would see us through. My squad was young and I knew there'd be some very tough times for them ahead. For the first time ever, I'd gone into a situation where a lot of what I had to do was damage limitation.

They were seventeen, eighteen and nineteen years of age, these players, when they first came into the squad. It was difficult for them at this top level and the Germans, Russians, whoever the top seeds in our group were, they didn't care whether we were rebuilding or not and we still had to play them. That's the trouble when you're a low-ranked team in these qualifying groups. It's even harder to get through because you're having to play better teams than the more established sides. Wales have always had at least two big guns to contend with every time and we were in some tough groups. For Euro 2008 we had Germany and the Czech Republic, who were ranked first and second in Europe. The qualifiers after, we had Germany and Russia, who were one and three. You can't tell your half-ready players that you're not going to qualify. You find a way of playing those teams that still allows you to get what you want out of the game, and playing three central defenders meant that I could protect the team from being on the end of too many car crashes, as I'd call them – shocking results. We had a fair few but we'd have had a lot more if I'd have set us up differently. We got some decent results. We drew 0–0 with Germany away from home in Euro 2008 qualifying.

I took a lot of stick playing three at the back, but you look at the Wales team under Chris Coleman at France 2016 and it was the same system. It's in vogue again. Juventus play it, Chelsea and Tottenham have been playing it; all in different ways but it's the same system. The players that you choose in the positions are what make it attacking, defensive or more focused in certain areas of the field. Now, the players we had weren't as familiar with these kind of tactics as the ones I was used to coaching in Spain, but they got it.

We went to Austria in 2005 and played this system with a sweeper, two centre-halves, two full-backs, and three midfielders, with Giggs and Bellamy up front counter-attacking. We lost 1–0 but Bellamy was one-on-one with the keeper on three occasions and Giggs once or twice. At the end of the game, the Austrian coach, Hans Krankl, who'd played for Barcelona in his day, was embarrassed. I can remember him turning his head down in shame as he shook my hand. He knew he'd been beaten tactically but luck had seen him through.

The exact way we set up wasn't always out of choice, though. If you're a big club, you can pick your own group of players. You can have what you want for each position in your system. I couldn't do that with Wales. I was limited to what I had. I'd have an idea of the system I wanted to play against a given opposition but, at that time, early in my tenure there, it was really a case of waiting to see who turned up with Wales. And, at that particular time, we went through a couple of years where people pulled out of squads all over the place. It was well known with Alex Ferguson and Giggsy that you could forget about friendly games, and with some of the older players getting the hump you never quite knew who might call time and when.

We went to play in Azerbaijan for a qualifier in 2009. We met up in Reading beforehand to discover that we only had ten realistic starters and three subs, and those ten who turned up were the ten that played. Fortunately, I could put a system out with them all involved: Wayne Hennessey in goal, Ashley Williams, Craig Morgan, Lewin Nyatanga, Chris Gunter, Neil Eardley, Aaron Ramsey, Joe Ledley, Dave Edwards, Robert Earnshaw and Simon Church. Most of these players were in the second tier, the Championship. There were no Premier League players in the side. We had to call up a couple of others that were non-league to make up the numbers. Ramsey was a teenager at Cardiff City at the time but he was outstanding that day. He had a temperature and probably shouldn't have played. After the game, he sat down and he was coughing and he was spitting everywhere. We won 1-0 and I can honestly say that it was one of the most satisfying results I've ever had. I know people might think that a win in Azerbaijan was nothing but, I tell you what, to go to Baku with that group of players and to win that game in those circumstances, I was absolutely delighted.

All the players now, they break their necks to get to Wales no matter the game because, a decade later, they're like a family. When they first came in, though, they were young lads in awe of the one or two more experienced players who were still around, and who were possibly not the right type of experienced players to help these young ones along. Maybe that's why it took a little bit longer than it might have. We were missing an experienced goalscorer on a number of occasions. We had a small core of them coming through but rarely were there two of them available at any one time. Earny was there for us and came back when he could but the one we had to rely on most was, in some ways, the one we actually wanted around least.

Craig Bellamy was a talented footballer but sometimes what he brought you on the pitch could be complicated by his attitude off it. Occasionally, he could cause problems where they weren't necessary and you always felt there was a possibility that he could upset the applecart. On his day, though, Craig Bellamy could be a threat to any defence, and we needed to have him in the team. We had a lot of young players and although, in my opinion, he wasn't the ideal person to have around, the positives just about outweighed the negatives. By about 51 per cent to 49. Maybe it's no coincidence that the moment he left, Wales qualified for a major tournament.

He had nine different clubs over an eighteen-year career. So, a lot of managers signed him but a lot of managers got rid of him as well, and, if you look at the managers that Bellamy has played under – Benítez at Liverpool, Bobby Robson and Graeme Souness at Newcastle, Roberto Mancini at Manchester City – all were trophy winners, but none of them ever won anything with Bellamy in the team. Apart from a substitute appearance in a League Cup win under Kenny Dalglish, the only major honours he's picked up are a shared Community Shield and a Scottish Cup with Celtic; mind you, I don't know anyone who's played for Celtic and not won anything. Considering his ability, that says it all for me.

That lack of experience that our young group had could be very frustrating, very difficult in certain moments. With all due respect to Chris Coleman, whom I've known a long time, since he was ten or eleven years old when he used to play for Swansea's youth side along with my boy, Cameron – he didn't have that problem. It's the same system but I didn't have the Gareth Bale that played for Real Madrid, I had the Gareth Bale of Southampton. I had the Ramsey who was still at Cardiff, the Joe Ledley who was still at Cardiff; the Ashley Williams and Joe Allen of a Championship Swansea. It's totally different. We might have closed out a few more games like our fixture in Moscow, in September 2008, for the World Cup 2010 qualifiers. The Russians went ahead with a penalty from Roman Pavlyuchenko right after Gareth Bale had missed one for us, but he made up for it. I pushed him up into the attack for the second half and he burst through in the inside-right position. He crossed the ball and Joe Ledley stuck it into the net to make it 1–1. It was the first time Gareth had been played there. It was before Harry Redknapp had him doing it with Spurs. It was just a shame we lost the game to a late goal from Pavel Pogrebnyak. Heartbreaking. With that bit of belief you get when you gather caps, we'd have picked up the points and maybe even got close to a major tournament ourselves.

Ryan Giggs played for me for a few years, certainly in all the competitive games that he could. He retired when we played the Czech Republic at Cardiff in June 2007 when we drew 0–0 as part of the Euro 2008 qualifiers. I brought him off in the ninetieth minute so he could get the applause of everyone there in the

Millennium Stadium. There's a famous photo of him coming off and I'm shaking his hand in the dugout. I think Fergie had said to him that if he wanted to carry on playing at United, he'd have to give up international football, because he didn't fancy the idea of him trying to do both. Fergie wasn't very happy with players going off on international duty at the best of times but Giggsy, at 34 and slowing up, was a prime candidate to get that kind of 'advice', for want of a better word, from Sir Alex.

I think probably, more with Wales than with England, managers tended to give us grief over the players coming away, particularly for friendly games, and they were just as important while we were trying to build. As the years have gone by – and I've been a club manager myself – I think they're increasingly reluctant.

The more I look back at it now, everything was against us, but I always believed in myself. I'd done things that hadn't been done before in the game and this was a big challenge, but I could push through that terrible draining feeling of a bad run because I knew I was on the right lines from the off – all these players had tried before and they weren't good enough. We had the pressure from the press saying we had to play the biggest Wales stars, but we knew that it hadn't worked. I couldn't say I enjoyed it. I enjoyed getting positive results against the big teams; the 0–0 draw in Germany in November 2007 in the last game of the Euro 2008 qualifiers. Then we'd mess up as we had done in Cardiff against Slovakia in October 2006, when we lost 5–1 in our second game of the same campaign and recorded the heaviest defeat for Wales on home soil in 98 years. Paul Jones won his fiftieth cap that day and shaved a five and a zero into his crew cut. I told him after the game he should take the zero off there to commemorate how many he'd conceded. To go back over to Slovakia one year later in September and put it right with a 5–2 victory, though; that was terrific. I could take all that, the highs and the lows. What I did find very difficult to take in my time with Wales was injuries.

By 2009, four years into the job, I felt we had the right group and it was starting to come together. They knew the systems, they knew each other and they had enough caps under their belts to know what international football was all about. We put all that faith in young players and by those latter years, 2009 and 2010, it was paying off. We played Scotland in November 2009 in Cardiff and we were brilliant. We beat them 3–0 in George Burley's last game in charge and I remember saying to Flynny that we'd cracked it. We'd just have to be patient now and we'd have that team qualifying. Within four months, five of those players had to have major operations; Rob Edwards suffered ankle ligament damage, Bale had knee surgery, Ramsey broke his leg at Stoke, Joe Ledley had two hip operations and Jack Collison would later have to pack the game in completely after a number of serious problems. These were big players. We're talking about having the heart of the team ripped out. It was just so disappointing, just when we had moved the older players out too. We were stuck in no-man's land for personnel and it was typical of what we'd had to contend with all the way along.

In August 2010, before our game against Luxembourg in Llanelli, I'd watched all our plans falling apart yet again. I'd been doing the rounds, looking at some of the squad playing their club games in the days leading up to the match. I went to Ashton Gate to watch Bristol City play Millwall on Saturday, 7 August. Sam Vokes came off injured with a torn hamstring. Then the next day Cardiff played Sheffield United and I saw Ched Evans leave the field as well. Finally, in our first training session on the Monday, before the international game on Wednesday, Simon Church walked off and that was our three young strikers all out. That was a classic example of what happened to us. It was six years of watching that unfold; six years of the most frustrating management. I've never talked about luck outside of this period. I've won major trophies in five different countries and I've never blamed luck wherever I've been, but this spell with Wales was just unbelievable.

Really, the final straw had been a friendly in Croatia, our penultimate game before the first qualifiers where I thought we'd really be ready. I'd gone out of my way to get that game arranged because Montenegro were to be a rival of ours in our Euro 2012 qualification group. They played a similar type of football across the old Yugoslavia, so I thought it would be good but, by the time we got out there, we had fifteen players unavailable. In the end, we could only scrape together a squad of seventeen. It was soul-destroying. We'd managed to get a top side away from home as preparation but we got there knowing that only three of our starters would be performing and seven or eight of them wouldn't even be in the eventual squad.

We had five Welsh debutants that day, frankly, because we had to. Hal Robson-Kanu made his first appearance when he came on for Earny, and Neil Taylor, who played for non-league Wrexham, came on at left-back for the second half, and what a plucky little performance that was. He took a hell of a whack, which turned out to be a genuine injury, but he said nothing and stayed on, the bugger. He was up and down the line to the finish. Andy Dorman got his first cap that night starting in midfield, and Christian Ribeiro got his as a sub nearer the whistle. The last new lad, Mark Bradley, he didn't even have a club and he was on the pitch for his country. He'd just been handed his cards by Walsall a few days previous. We played well, as it went, but lost the game 2–0 to a Croatia packed with the likes of Luka Modrić, Darijo Srna and Ivan Rakitić.

We had no Ramsey, no Bale; both out due to operations they needed to have. There were five or more out through injury and another five who'd retired. It was impossible. We had been so unlucky over those years. We were threadbare like that for far too many encounters. We'd regularly find ourselves selecting players from the third tier of English football. Not even England or Italy sides could have contended with luck like that.

We started that Euro 2012 qualifying group with a bad loss in Montenegro – a team we really needed to beat if we were going to get anywhere. It was my last game in charge. On the plane on the way home, I went and had a chat to the president of the Welsh FA, Phil Pritchard, and told him, what with all my frustrations with injuries and the like, that it was wearing me down. I'd do the next two games against Bulgaria and Switzerland and then review my position. I did not even last that long. The newly appointed chief executive, Jonathan Ford, recommended an immediate change. We sat down and worked out a solution and off I went. Ford was not my kind of operator but I must say that I had the utmost respect for his predecessor, David Collins.

It was hard leaving all of our well-laid plans after such a long time getting everything ready. We knew we were building something that would last. A lot of managers are cynical with the way they consider their tenure and mine and Flynny's eyes were wide open. We knew that the team wasn't ready at the time. We knew we'd be doing all this work for someone else. We knew that, when they got to fifty caps, they'd be flying. Look at them now and that's what they've got. There'll be a record number of them hitting the century mark in a few years' time. The FAW told us it wasn't working: our strategy, our youth team set-up consolidated all under the one coach. They've kept it though, and I've no doubt that, if they'd have given us longer, we'd have qualified. We might even have done it earlier. Chris Coleman made it happen but the work Flynny and I did was the catalyst, and if you look at the fourteen players that were fielded in that semi-final against Portugal in 2016, eleven of them made their debuts under us and we had left six years earlier. I'd told Flynny that I wanted the average age of the team under 25 within three years of us starting. We did it in two.

It'll be interesting to see what happens to this Wales side. After the success at France 2016, we were all expecting more from them in the 2018 World Cup qualifiers, particularly in view of the fact that there were no outstanding teams in the group. There was a great deal of parity between Serbia, Austria, the Republic of Ireland; and Wales were the highest-ranked side of the lot. So, to finish third, having only won four games out of ten, it was an obvious let-down, but it's not the punches on the jaw that soften up the champ, it's the pats on his back, and maybe some of these players received a few more plaudits than they should have done.

It's quite clear that after the Euros other teams studied Wales a little bit more. The players' profiles increased so people knew a lot more about them, but it's still disappointing to see them go out to an untested Republic of Ireland team. I know these players really well. I remember them coming in when they were teenagers and I still think that they've got one, or probably two, more tournaments in them before it has to be rebuilt again.

The current people in charge are fortunate enough to have benefitted from the work of their predecessors on and off the field. The Welsh FA and football public should never underestimate the groundwork put in by Brian Flynn during his time in charge of the intermediate sides. Well done, Flynny.

You can never say never in this business. Anything is possible, and there have certainly been some enquiries over the years, but I can't say that a return to international management would be my first choice. I gave it another crack straight away with Macedonia and I couldn't say it went a whole lot better.

15
Father and son, Macedonia

THERE'S NOT MUCH TO LIKE ABOUT TRAVEL, BUT YOU'D BETTER GET used to it if you're going to be in football management. Everyone in the game has got to do it to some degree, even if it's just the length and breadth of your own country as you work your way through a calendar of away games. The luckier ones among us get to compete in European competition, which adds even more time in takeoffs and landings, waiting around in transit lounges and hotel rooms. A lot of top managers and players don't embrace it, but I've always been interested in different cultures and languages wherever I've found them; coffee bars on the Bosphorus, villages in the shadow of Mount Etna. No job has tested my love of travel more, though, than when I was head coach of Macedonia.

I had moved back to Spain, where I'd been living for a year since finishing the job for Wales, when I was lucky enough to get the call. It was Borko Krunic once again, who put me in touch with the people at Macedonia. I'd always had a soft spot for the football played by the old Yugoslav countries. Borko had helped me bring both 'Jimmy' Hadžiabdić and Ante Rajković to Swansea so successfully all those years ago, and it was an opportunity to work with a whole squad of internationals, even if the country was a fairly lowly ninetieth in the FIFA world rankings at the time. I was in my sixties by now and ready to try new things and new experiences.

I used to have to travel the best part of a day just to get to Skopje. The first leg was a journey across the north of Spain to Barcelona, then I'd catch a 6.30am flight to Vienna where I'd wait for a few hours before I got the seventy-minute connection to the Macedonian capital. On the way back, the layover in Vienna was so long that it made more sense to leave the airport and head into town to enjoy the city before catching the evening return. You have to make the most of these things and the streetside cafes of Vienna were certainly a lot more interesting than its airport.

I've never been one to take people with me to the places where I've worked, as you probably know by now. I've always gone in there and put myself alongside the coaches and staff who've known the idiosyncrasies of the club and the culture of the city, but this time it was different. There isn't that same sense of longevity and tradition in international management and, besides, I wasn't going to live in Macedonia, so I chose an assistant with whom I was already familiar instead. My eldest lad, Cameron, had not long started in coaching and I could see that him coming with me would be a good experience for the both of us. Cameron's playing career had been cut short when he was just 23 with a diagnosis of diabetes that meant his fitness levels were never going to sustain what he wanted to achieve on the pitch. In the fifteen or so years since, he'd been working as an executive at the Pfizer pharmaceuticals company in London and living with his family in Cobham. At the same time, he'd been working on his UEFA A Licence through the Welsh FA, to whom he'd been reporting as a performance analyst. He'd watch Wales's opposition and compile dossiers on what he'd seen for the managers in charge. On top of that, he'd managed the Kingstonian youth team and later been on the staff at Neath in the Welsh Premier League. He'd been paying his dues and it was a good opportunity but not without its hurdles. It meant him taking five weeks off in annual leave, but it was super to have him working with me and a fantastic opportunity for a young manager to work at international level, so knowing Cam, it wasn't something I thought he'd pass up. His first challenge was running it by his wife and two young children, and maybe there was a sense of history repeating itself there, if in a smaller way. Just like when I chose to manage abroad, Cameron knew he'd have to spend some time apart from his family in order to invest in their future. They had spoken about it before and knew that, objectively, it would be the right move, just as Sue and I realised when I had my chance to go to Lisbon all those years ago.

Having lived it as a boy, perhaps it was harder for Cameron because he was fully aware of the difficulties, but it's a lot easier now with the Skype and with modern travel options. I know he missed out on a lot by his father not being around so much after he was thirteen, as can happen with any football family. Perhaps these days it's different but, back then, the pay wasn't anything like what it is now, which made relocating your whole family a lot more precarious and not really viable. Back then, when a decision was made to live apart from your family and you have thirteen-, eleven- and nine-year-olds, as I did, it's a big call. They just assumed I'd always be at Swansea, the local team, and doing that job, and then I go to Portugal and they think, 'Oh, he'll be back.' We couldn't have predicted what the outcome would be and they certainly couldn't really process it all that at that age.

My younger children, Sally and Craig, were schooled in South Wales, where they were born, and the family always came out to visit me wherever I was, but it still put a big strain on family life. From the other side, though, managing those clubs that I did, that was a dream and I know that they didn't want to keep me from that either.

Cam and I didn't have long to settle into the job. We took over the team on 7 August 2011, midway through Macedonia's Euro 2012 qualifying campaign. With six games already played, the previous coach, Mirsad Jonuz, had been dismissed after picking up only four points with a win away at Andorra and a 2–2 draw at home to Armenia. We had three sessions to prepare the team for a game that if not won would mathematically end Macedonia's chances, and it was the toughest game of the group – away to the favourites, Russia.

One of the big challenges of working with this squad of players was that virtually none of them played in the local Macedonian football league, which was a poor standard anyway. One or two of them plied their trade in the bigger European leagues but, generally, they were a disparate bunch, which meant that we didn't know much about them and they didn't know much about each other. They were based all over the place – Ukraine, Croatia, Sweden, Slovenia, Serbia, Italy, Cyprus, Germany, Russia, Switzerland, Turkey, Poland, Belgium, Azerbaijan and, of course, Macedonia, but never more than two in the same division, let alone club. At one point, we named 24 players from 16 different countries. When you're manager of Wales, you're looking at two – Wales and England. The players were fantastic, though. They never missed a friendly or any kind of squad session at all, no matter how hard it was to get back to Skopje. In fact, it was the exact opposite of the Wales squad I'd taken over back in 2004 where there'd be eight or ten players dropping out of the less competitive fixtures for not very acceptable reasons.

Even so, organising a squad that far-flung had its challenges. The Macedonia communications officer, a man called Mario, had his work cut out. He'd tell them, 'OK, we'll meet at the team hotel at six p.m.,' but they'd arrive at all sorts of times. They did their best to get there but a lot of these players had to take three flights to make it. All it would take would be a small delay on one of the legs of the route and everything would spiral out of control. There was really was nothing anyone could do. To a man, though, they were all committed to playing for their country. Goran Pandev was the one superstar of the side and his life was a little easier thanks to his private jet, but he was as dedicated as the rest of them, despite his commitments to Inter, and he was always very good with the others in the squad. You never got a feeling of resentment from them and he'd give a few of them a lift back to Italy if it helped make their connections.

Aside from Pandev, I had some decent pros. There was Nikolče Noveski, the captain, who played centre-half for Mainz in the Bundesliga, and Goran Popov at left-back, who later played at West Brom. The other young full-backs had good legs too. They could move and could get into a number of positions and do what we set for them and, between them and the more experienced players on the list, we were able to set up a system to thwart and make things difficult for anybody, but we had a big lack of ability necessary at international level in the last third of the field to conjure things up. Pandev was superb but he played a little bit deeper off the centre-forward and we lacked punch. Without a quality No. 9, we just never had enough to threaten the opposition as much as I would have liked. So, we tried to be solid, organised and counter-attacked which, if you've managed Real Madrid and played at Liverpool, that's a different mentality to have, but I'd had to have it with Wales too.

Ilčo Naumoski was an option in the striker position. He had a good career at Mattersburg in Austria, he'd played in Europe a bit and he was a real livewire, but him and Pandev didn't get on. We did include him in the squad for a friendly against Luxembourg but the camp was not right with him there, and what he added as a centre-forward didn't justify his effect on the rest of the players. He wasn't interested in defending on the transition and that didn't suit what we were trying to do as a team. So, between him and Pandev, it was no contest.

There were one or two other players that came out in the media saying that they'd been frozen out under me and Cameron. They had links with a journalist at Macedoniafootball.com and were able to make themselves heard, but there was nothing personal going on there no matter what was said. The truth is that you get given a list of players worth considering by the Federation in a situation like this and, for whatever reasons, some players weren't on it. The one interesting exception was Yani Urdinov. He was a Belgian-born Macedonian pro and his past was a bit chequered. He'd had a disagreement with the previous coach who'd told him he'd never play again – at least until one of my assistants, Boban Babunski, pointed him out to me. Babunski had played in Spain in his time, so his Spanish was very good, and I had a decent relationship with him. Urdinov had played for PSV at youth level and Babunski knew that he was capable. We watched him and gave him the opportunity to play for the national side again. Certain elements of his game were basic but he responded when we told him what to do and not every player can do that; that's your first pass, that's your second pass, that's your default; you don't try and do that last thing you tried to do, etc.

We worked hard on defensive shape and the organisation of the team without the ball. We played four at the back with two sitting midfielders and had expectations of the wide players to work hard too, and it was all governed very well on the field by Noveski and all of his Bundesliga experience. There was little that was spectacular but there were good pros in there, including a very decent journeyman centre-midfielder by the name of Nikola Gligorov, whom I later took to Khazar Lankaran in Azerbaijan.

As I mentioned, Russia away was the first game. The Luzhniki Stadium is a massive venue and we got there that September with the Russian team a little down on their luck – only four wins out of six, so far – in a group that included Armenia, Andorra, Slovakia and the Republic of Ireland. The Macedonia team had listened well and the game was going to plan. We kept the home side largely quiet and then, with five minutes to go until half-time, Pandev broke away and got brought down by the keeper for what should have been a penalty. It wasn't given and then, as can often happen when the game is feeling cruel, the opposition went straight down the other end and scored. Russia had more about them in the second half and dominated the play better but, despite a chance Popov had to level at the death, that was the way it finished. We ended up losing 1–0 but everyone seemed to know afterwards that we'd done a better job than the other side. With what they had, they were up against it and they hadn't been expecting that. When we got back to the airport to fly out of Moscow, the Macedonian Federation were there and said they'd never seen a Macedonia side so disciplined, organised and hitting on the counter at the right times. It was just a shame we never got the result that the performance deserved and, just one game in, we were already having to look to the next qualifying campaign.

We played Andorra a few days later back in Skopje, but there was a little less intensity knowing we were effectively playing a friendly. We missed a lot of chances again and won just 1-0. The score should have been higher and I could see why this team had big difficulties. Without any out-and-out goalscorers, we knew that we were never going to beat anyone 3-0. It was always going to be 1-0, 2-1 or 0-0 results at best and that's a hard way to play. It takes a lot of focus and ninety minutes is a long time to do it for without any slip-ups. The only bad result was a 4-1 loss away to Armenia, who still had an unlikely qualification in their sights. We were without Pandev, who was serving a ban, and our central midfielder, Veliče Šumulikoski, who got himself sent off halfway through the game when we were already 2-0 down. Henrikh Mkhitaryan and his countryman, Yura Movsisyan from Krasnodar, were too much for us.

We had a go playing three at the back for the final game against Slovakia at home, but it didn't go particularly well and it finished 1-1, which was about par for the course anyway. We had a break until February the following year and I'd lined us up a series of friendly games before the 2014 World Cup qualifiers began later in the year. The first of those friendlies was the only other result that I felt was unacceptable. We lost 2-1 in what was supposed to be something of a confidence-builder away to Luxembourg. We'd taken the lead early but Luxembourg equalised in the second half and then the same striker, Maurice Deville, grabbed another in injury time. He had only scored three goals in his 34 international games when the final whistle went that day, and two of them were against Macedonia.

They used to call the old Yugoslavia the Brazil of Europe because it produced so many technically good players, but a lot of those national teams that have come out of it also have the same problem with their mindsets. They start well but, if they have a setback, they find it difficult to deal with because they're often missing that edge of belief. We did a lot of work on it but it's very difficult to iron out a mentality like that. I saw Macedonia recently, since leaving the job, playing against Italy and they were leading 2-1 with fifteen minutes to go. Then, all of a sudden, their legs turned to jelly. They lost 3-2. Macedonia don't believe they can win, whereas the mentality of Italy is that they cannot lose. Macedonia lose playing well, Italy win playing badly. It's amazing that you can get such different mental strengths on the same field. So, when we held Portugal away 0–0 in a friendly, it was very, very satisfying.

We knew there would be games that, on paper, there'd be no point going into, but that's not the way football always works out. I told the players when to press, when to go in, and we managed to frustrate Portugal. They didn't have an answer to the puzzle that we set them. When you have players like Cristiano Ronaldo, Nani and Ricardo Quaresma all looking to burst through and you manage to close the space where it's important, it's a great feeling for the people in the dugout.

I do remember one moment, though, when there was a free-kick about 35 yards out, just before Ronaldo got subbed. He put the ball down, stood there astride as he does and, as the wall backed off, just as he was about to take it, we were looking on from the technical area and, maybe because it was a friendly and I felt I could, I hear myself shout out, 'You'll never score from there!' Cristiano turned round and gave us a big smile, a bit like a shark might before it eats its dinner, and I thought, 'Oh, no. Here we go.' He didn't score though and, as he jogged back, I shouted after him, 'I told you.'

Ronaldo took it in good spirit. He came off after 65 minutes or so, and he made a point of coming over and shaking my hand. He was brought up at Sporting where I had managed and he was a Madrid player too, where I had been successful. We spoke to each other in Portuguese and, after the game, he came into the dressing room and gave me his shirt. It was a quality gesture, and a very good day for us. Everything was coming together and you could see that the Macedonia players believed that we could organise them and that we could make them competitive. It was a massive result, which made it an even bigger pity that just three days later was our last game in charge.

The Macedonia Federation wanted to make changes. The president that had brought me in, Hari Hadži-Risteski, had become very ill and was moved out. He'd been in charge for a decade. After the Federation elections in July 2012, Ilčo Gjorgioski took over the role. He was a much younger man, who had played in the Macedonia leagues virtually all his career and had just resigned as coach of one of the division's top clubs. He wanted to bring in his own people, and changes at the top like that are always telltale signs that you might be losing your job. A new regime needs new ideas, so it makes no sense to keep the old manager running the show. The official line was that they wanted us to move to Skopje, which was a bit of a joke given that 95 per cent of the squad was based outside of Macedonia. We'd have been better off living in the Ukraine if a more consistent contact with Macedonian footballers was what was required.

It's a shame because we felt like we were doing a good job. Over the eight games in charge, we'd realised what we had and how to get the best out of it, and we knew that there were two or three players coming up from the Under-21s, possibly in time for the next qualifying campaign, that might well have made a difference. Two of them were Babunski's sons, one of whom was with the Barcelona youth set-up while the other one was with Real Madrid's. We'd laid down a structure or a way of playing so that, when they played for two or three games and came back, they'd know what we were about and the principles of what we were trying to achieve. It could have been the beginning of a better spell for Macedonia but I'm sorry to say that, after I left, they went backwards, which disappoints me. When I took over in 2011, the side was 103 in the FIFA rankings. When I left they were at 81 but then it all went crashing down until they bottomed out at 162 in 2016. Fortunately, they recovered and are back up at 77 for 2018. I put young players in and blooded them but the new people that came in left them out and brought back the older ones. Maybe a few of the players had been frustrated by certain aspects of what I'd been doing but, generally, there was a feeling among the squad that it had been going well.

I wasn't sure how well Cameron and I would work together and I'm sure he had the same doubts, what with all the shiny new toys of modern coaching, training and business-management skills that he'd learned trying to get along with my hands-on experience, but in the end it was very good. We had different methods but our ideas on the game were the same and we both had the same expectations of the players and of each other. A lot of what Liverpool was doing during the 70s and what I've taken on is part of what's been formalised by coaching courses anyway – don't train hard right before a game, work in small areas in the early part of the week, then move it out for fitness towards the middle of the week and then bring it back in again with the intensity down to work on more tactical elements just before the weekend; not rocket science.

I'm not one for having huge numbers of assistants with specialised jobs all sitting on the bench with their tracksuits and I'm not one for all the data that's involved now either. If my midfielder hasn't done the job I've asked him to, I'll know about it. Now, you can go to the machines and screens and get all his clips and have a look and see his high-speed running stats and accelerations but I already know, and you only get that by being an experienced manager. The more games you've watched, the better you become at it. If you have an understanding of software, then that can help to bring you to that level a lot quicker, but you have to be very careful how you utilise that information. It can come back to bite you. You can get lost in that data or a player can use it to state his case for how he's got everything right when maybe it wasn't quite the job you wanted him to do. In one situation you might want an all-action midfielder of yours to sit deep, screen the centre-back pairing and occasionally go into the wide areas to provide defensive cover. That might not look that impressive on ProZone, but that's his role. So, you have to understand the context of the numbers and strike a balance before giving a player too much information. I'm not sure how useful it is for the players to hear all of this either. For most of them, you just want to give them one or two points to work on each game and that might be it. If you put too much in a player's mind, then they'll forget to play the football that they already do well.

Maybe people think it's an easy ride for Cameron to be in football and to have John Toshack as his dad but it works the other way. As a footballer, he was a mark. The other team knew the name of the No. 10 and tried to make sure he didn't get a sniff and, as my assistant at Macedonia, I had to show he was there because he deserved to be, so I had to make sure the work he did was top quality. That's the way it has to be.

Whatever disappointments there might have been at the time our work together ended, it's been fantastic to watch Cam's coaching career go from strength to strength. He started coaching the Under-19s at Swansea at the start of the 2013/14 season, a year after we finished at Macedonia. He won two consecutive FAW Youth Cup titles with his team until the 2015/16 season when he was bumped up to the development squad to compete in the Professional Development League. They made the play-offs of the second division, which Swansea were in, in Cameron's first year and then he got them promoted by finishing eleven points clear of their nearest rivals. Then in their first season in the Premier League 2 top flight, he's taken them up to fourth place, finishing just behind Liverpool. On top of that he got his lads to the final of the Premier League Cup in 2017/18 – the cup competition for the same age group – and only missed out on penalties to Aston Villa.

I'd say he's a chip off the old block but Cam's very much his own man. I'd like to see him in charge of a first team soon. I'm sure he'll get there. I know there was talk of the job at Barnsley at the beginning of 2018 but I wonder if, like me, it will be Swansea that will give him his first chance?

16

Champions of Morocco

IF YOU THINK IT'S EASY TO GO TO MOROCCO AND WIN A championship or to take a job in Azerbaijan and lift the Super Cup, then I suggest you go and try it. I've seen plenty of European managers take over teams in other parts of the world and struggle for any success.

There were aspects of my job in Morocco that were a lot more difficult than those of Madrid. The language barrier is one obvious example. It's very difficult to have a long conversation of any kind of football depth with a player when you have a language problem, so that conditions the way you work. There's no point in trying to establish a more nuanced style of play if no one can understand it. It's good to be able to work at that kind of level as a manager but, if that's the only way you can do things, then you're going to come unstuck, and there are plenty of other non-footballing problems that are going to get in your way too. It's not as simple as you think.

In March 2013, seven months or so after my tenure at Macedonia had ended, I received a call from Serdar Bilgili, by this time president of Beşiktaş after Süleyman Seba had stepped down. He wanted to know if I would be interested in coaching a team in Azerbaijan. Khazar Lankaran were a relatively new club owned by Turkish business partners of Serdar based in Istanbul and I decided to meet them, thinking it could, at least, be an interesting idea. I'd been to Azerbaijan with the Welsh national team and was very impressed with the capital city Baku – great restaurants and shiny shopping malls – but I couldn't say I'd heard much about the Azerbaijani Premier League which, as it turns out, is not very surprising since it had only existed since 1992. There are about ten teams contesting it each season, but that's fluctuated over the years depending on the number of businessmen with deep pockets over there whose dream it still is to entertain Barcelona and Real Madrid in their very own stadia. With four qualification-round places to be won in both the Champions and Europa Leagues, from the outside, the odds look good. So far, though, only one team from Azerbaijan has made it to the group stages of the bigger competition and that was only just recently in the 2017/18 season, when FC Qarabag found themselves alongside Chelsea, Roma and Atlético Madrid.

For the president of Khazar Lankaran, Mübariz Mansimov, a boyhood Beşiktaş fan, it was about getting the chance to play the Istanbul club but, despite picking up one league title and three domestic cups in its very short existence, since formation in 2004, they'd only mustered a single win in Europe across twelve attempts. I travelled to Istanbul to meet him thinking, 'Nothing ventured, nothing gained.'

You do have to visit these places. It really is an eye-opener. These people live a fantastic lifestyle and sometimes I found it embarrassing to be sat at the table in luxurious places watching them click their fingers and be attended to immediately. Even though they were the owners of all these five-star hotels and restaurants, my upbringing in Northumberland Street, Canton, Cardiff, with Mum and Dad, meant that I could never act in a similar way. It was quite awkward.

Regardless of these supposed perks, the offer on the table was an interesting one and I accepted. The favour that was asked of me for this one was to rescue the club from relegation – something I was getting used to. A Romanian named Mircea Rednic had been the last serious manager in charge before a string of short-lived appointments had sent the club into a nosedive. He'd filled the playing roster with some very skilful first-division compatriots of his at the expense of much in the way of local talent. There'd only been three or four Azerbaijani starters per game maximum and, while that hadn't made him entirely popular with the supporters, winning the Azerbaijan Cup had – at least until Mansimov lost patience after a second successive failure to make it through the early qualifying rounds in the Europa League. Europe was a long way from his mind when my services were called upon, though. Like a few others across the continent, the Azerbaijan Premier League splits into two in the final stages of the season. Khazar were very much in the bottom group.

When I arrived in Lankaran, I understood why they had wanted me to agree the terms of the contract in Baku. It's one of the smaller major cities of Azerbaijan, with a population of just 51,000 compared to the 2.4 million people in the country's capital. There's a lot of very nice national parks not too far away from Lankaran; lots of trees, lots of birds, lots of fish, but not that many people. Sitting right at the southern end of the country on the coast of the Caspian Sea, a three-hour drive from Baku and just north of the border with Iran, it's home to Azerbaijan's largest population of Talysh people, who were originally Iranian. They have their own dialect too, which was going to make learning the local language even trickier that it might have been already.

I realised straight away that this was no ordinary club; no ordinary situation. To start with, all the players lived, slept and ate in the one compound where the stadium and training facilities were – all within 100 yards walking distance of the accommodation. Talk about living in each other's pockets; everyone would have breakfast together, then walk across the road to the training ground and, when the session finished, would head back to their rooms for a rest and then dinner at 7 p.m. – together again. We did not live under a military regime, it's just that there's not a huge amount to do in Lankaran apart from a couple of coffee bars, a restaurant or two and half a dozen shops. In fact, the best part of Lankaran was the training ground, without a shadow of a doubt. There were good facilities for watching videos with the players, a tidy little gym there. The stadium pitch was available as well so we could train on it whenever we wanted. It was a good surface and good space for 15,000 people or so. Everything else outside was very basic. I went out for a walk a few times but apart from the city centre, there's just miles and miles of sand. You've really got to love your football if you go to work in a place like Lankaran.

There were five teams based in Baku and we had to play each team three or four times, so we made sure we travelled at least two days before those games and returned two days later or so, so at least the players had some kind of release and respite from the monotony of Lankaran. We were all very happy when we went to Baku, which seemed to work out as every ten days or so. When the players' families came they stayed in Baku too, which gave another reason for everyone to enjoy our visits to the capital. Living in each other's pockets like that is a situation I'd never been in before. It's unique in football as far as I know. It had its advantages – everybody was there, so you could call a training session whenever you wanted – but the fact that it was so rare tells you that it wasn't the ideal situation. Great facilities, but it could drive some of the players stir-crazy.

I was completely engulfed in my work there. There was really nothing else to focus on. Fortunately, I wasn't required to spend quite so much time at the compound as the players. I stayed in a hotel in town – the only one acceptable. It had a super apartment attached to it which was very comfortable. It was like a holiday home with three bedrooms, a big lounge with my TV, a kitchen, a terrace to sit on out front and access to the hotel swimming pool just 100 yards away. I'd have a bit of breakfast then jump on my bicycle and pedal a few miles down the road to the club which, at the age of 64, wasn't a bad thing. At least it kept me moving.

We did enough in the remaining fixtures of the 2012/13 season to stay in the league and reach the cup final. There were terrific scenes at the airport in Lankaran when we returned from our semi-final first-leg victory against FC Baku, who are one of the big sides. I wouldn't have minded but we were only 1–0 up. Fortunately, we finished the tie off at home 2–0 because there was a lot of interest before the final itself in the national stadium against another top side from the capital, Neftçi. They had already won the league title and were without doubt the best side in the country. My starting line-up included a Spanish goalkeeper, a Romanian centre-back, a Brazilian left-back, a midfielder from Macedonia and another Brazilian at centre-forward. There was a bit of a split between them and the local lads when I arrived, but the players had done their best to make up their differences. It wasn't easy for the foreign lads, particularly the Brazilians. A lot of the people in these places speak English but you still need to make an effort if you want to settle. We all had to try and learn a little Azerbaijani – another thing that makes working in these places a lot harder than you think. Fortunately, there's a similarity between the Turks and the Azerbaijanis, which put me in good stead.

The cup final itself was a good, hard battle. We played well, even though Neftçi were clear favourites. We took it all the way to penalties after a goalless draw but, for the first time in my life, we lost a cup that way. Perhaps I'd been lucky with my goalkeepers before. This one was no Arconada. He never got to any of them.

We had the opportunity of putting that defeat behind us when the federation decided that the Super Cup would be played for between the league winners and ourselves as the Azerbaijan Cup runners-up and, with our second bite at the cherry, we did beat Neftçi 2–1, despite having a player sent off, and thereby entered the Europa League in July. However, it all finished a bit sour there for me a few months later.

Our first opponents were Sliema Wanderers from Malta and we won that confrontation after a 1-1 draw in on the island was followed by a 1-0 win on home soil in Lankaran. The next trip was to Israel, where we faced Maccabi Haifa. We were beaten by a couple of goals but I thought if we could get off to a good start in the home tie, we would have a chance. How wrong can you be? We missed a couple of great opportunities in the first five or six minutes and then, suddenly, we were three down after fifteen. We just totally capitulated. It ended up 8-0.

I was looking around and just thinking, something's not right here. My team looked like they threw it completely. I got the idea that I'd been cheated by certain players. How often has a team lost 8-0 at home – especially after a good fight in the away leg? You've only got to look at that. As a coach, you don't have many other alternatives in that situation but to hold your hand up and say that your pride has been dented and that this is something that's never ever happened to you before. The feeling came over me that I was a long way from home. This was part of the old Soviet regime, Iran's just over the border, and I realised I had to get out of there. This was not healthy. I'd always been one for a bit of adventure, but maybe this was an adventure too far.

I resigned straight after the final whistle, but the owners wouldn't accept it and I was persuaded to stay on. However, the next couple of months were very uncomfortable. They started to bring in other assistants and other staff as if they were just preparing the ground for the next manager who'd already been agreed, and I could see that it was going to finish to their schedule rather than mine. I'd been round the block a few times. You can tell these things. The owners had a certain respect for me because of my CV and because they were Beşiktaş supporters and they knew I'd done well there. So, they knew that there were aspects of this job that weren't totally down to me. Successful businessmen like these people, their football knowledge might not have been as extensive as other owners, but they were no mugs and they knew that they'd made some signings that were maybe not the best and that it was a difficult job. Whatever you say, though, it's not easy to lose 8-0. You can be pretty bad and not lose 8-0. Eventually, we agreed to end it after a poor performance in a game in November, and I made the long journey to San Sebastián via Baku, Istanbul and Barcelona.

Everything had been made all the harder by the death of my mother, who had been in a care home for the elderly in Cardiff. The home was about 200 yards from where my daughter, Sally, was living with her husband Huw and their three girls

– Megan, Lili and Holly – and while I was working so far away from home, it was, at least, comforting to know that Sally and her kids were daily visitors. I'd made the long journey from Baku to London and on to Cardiff while I was still working in Lankaran and arrived in time to see my mum at 9 p.m. on a Monday evening. She was clearly in some discomfort and I was warned that she could go at any time. I stayed with her for an hour or more and then left, only to be called two hours later and told that she had passed away. I'm sure she had hung on until I'd got home. She was stubborn like that.

I had some time to reflect now and watched a lot of football in Spain and in Wales before getting another call about a job in Casablanca. I've never had an agent pushing my name here, there and everywhere. I've very often stumbled across jobs through friends that I've had or people I've worked with before. In early June 2014, seven months after finishing in Azerbaijan, it was an old acquaintance, the Portuguese football agent Lucidio Ribeiro, who brought my next job opportunity when he called me out of the blue at my house in Mallorca. I'd known Lucidio for some time. He'd been instrumental in the signing of the Moroccan defender Noureddine Naybet during my time at Deportivo La Coruña in 1996. I'd watched Naybet play for Sporting Lisbon in Paris and was very impressed by his leadership qualities to such an extent that I persuaded the Deportivo president to sign him. Lucidio spoke to me about the possibility of a coaching job in Casablanca with Wydad Athletic Club, who I'd watched some twenty years earlier in the city during their derby game with local rivals Raja Casablanca. I remember at the time being blown away with the 60,000-strong support in the ground and the extraordinary atmosphere, and I'd ended up taking a Raja player named Jamal Sellami to Beşiktaş in Turkey. It was an eye-opener for me to see how feverishly local games were followed in other parts of the world. I'm not sure what I'd expected, but these aren't matches that are well documented in the newspapers of the places where I've lived. You might have an idea that a passionate Moroccan league exists, but to sit there among the noise and the banners and feel the heat of the spectacle makes you take notice of what's going on in the game in places like North Africa.

Part of me was wary after my experiences at Khazar Lankaran, but I travelled to Morocco with an open mind and, after meeting the club officials, I felt confident enough in who they were and what they were trying to build to sign on the dotted line for this big club that was in decline and had suffered from years of problems.

It was rundown, the facilities were not the best and the supporters had become impatient, but the new president in charge had grand ideas to spruce the place up, and they started by getting an ex-Real Madrid coach at the helm.

I began working in the middle of June and straight away accompanied the team to Lisbon where Lucidio had organised three pre-season friendlies against Portuguese first division opposition, all of which we won. Very quickly, the fog of disappointment of the previous years had lifted and expectation was in the air.

The friendlies had given me a decent look at the players in my squad and the time to use a couple of different systems of play to see how I could get everyone to fit. I had an ex-Wydad player named Hassan Nader alongside me translating. He spoke perfect Spanish after a career that had taken him to Mallorca, as well as a few clubs in Portugal. What's more, while most of the players spoke Arabic, French is a second language for most, which isn't a long hop from what I could understand myself. So, this was not the same situation as in Lankaran where Azerbaijani was a total mystery to me. Working in Morocco was also an opportunity for me to call on Roberto Ufarte from the Basque Country once again. He had played for me, and later had been my assistant, at Real Sociedad, but it also happened that he spent the first eight years of his life growing up in the Moroccan city of Fez, which made him doubly useful in this role when it came to getting my message across to the players. Plus, of course, Roberto knew all my training methods so everything seemed nicely in place when we started the season at the end of August.

We got off to a solid enough start, winning a couple of home games and drawing a couple away. Those eight points put us in the top three, and from there we never came out of the leading positions. By the middle of October, we were at the head of the league and, apart from a slight slump in January, when I lost both goalkeepers for three weeks, we were always in command.

It was a fascinating first twelve months and very rewarding too; travelling the length and breadth of the country, meeting the different people here, seeing how they live their lives up in the Atlas Mountains and on the fringes of the Sahara; the nomads of the desert, the market traders in the souks of the cities. There was a lot that was new for me outside of football and those kind of experiences go a long way in terms of blowing out any of those cobwebs you might have been carrying around inside you.

Trying to manage a team during the month of Ramadan was another challenge I'd not really come across elsewhere. I'd dealt with the odd player who couldn't eat and drink during the daylight hours before, but never the entire squad. Training had to be arranged carefully with plenty of rest breaks. We needed special houses for rest nearby and the travel arrangements had to be made so that the players could break their daily fasts in the evenings in the right ways and at the right time. It was something the club and the players did every year, of course, but I certainly had to rethink a few of my methods and ideas to fit around everything else that needed to happen. Apparently, you can teach an old dog a few new tricks.

My team was pretty well settled when we came to the final challenging months, which are often the trickiest of any title push, and I was fortunate that we were able to steer clear of injuries. I had a keeper who was capable of making outstanding saves but who was also likely to lose concentration and offer a present to the opposition. The two full-backs were steady, good professionals but it was incredible the number of times I had to repeat things to them. I remember the great Bill Shankly telling me that, very often, you have to tell some players the same things two or three times before they make it stick, but if you have to tell them four times, then you'll need to get rid of them. Shanks would certainly not have had the patience with these two, but then you can afford to set the bar a little higher when you're working at Liverpool.

My centre-backs were a pair of thirty-year-olds; very experienced and vital to our success, and in front of them I also had a couple of journeymen midfielders who were not the greatest in possession but certainly made life difficult for their opposition. They firmly shut down the centre of the field and it was very tough for any opponents to make any way through the middle of the park. That meant that, at times, when we had to take the initiative, we were found wanting, but the good points outweighed the bad. It also meant that we could play to our strengths, which were in the forward positions.

I had a twenty-year-old who was already an Under-23 Moroccan international called Walid El Karti, who played behind a front man. He had bags of energy and was as honest as the day is long; a good team player. If you asked all the other players who was the most popular in the side, it would be Karti, hands down. If he scored more goals, he'd have been in a top side in Europe. If you're playing in that position, as a sort of second striker, you need to chip in with at least eight or nine a season, but he never got onto the scoresheet as much as he should have. I can imagine other coaches not picking him for a bit until they knew him a bit better. If you've seen him play for a couple of matches, then it's quite easy not to understand his value to the team, but if you see him over a period of time in training and see him in more games, you'll understand. He had the tendency to run down a few blind alleys and sometimes there was too much traffic high up the pitch for him but, if that was the case, he could still do his business if I brought him back into a deeper position. A couple of times, I thought I'd have to leave him out but, come Saturday or Sunday, I'd always play him.

The goalscoring was mostly left to the three players who played in attack beyond El Karti. Two of them were foreigners – Malick Evouna from Gabon, who finished leading scorer in the championship with sixteen goals that season, and Bakare Kone from the Ivory Coast, who fell just short of double figures. The other was another young Moroccan lad called Reda Hajhouj, who chipped in with eight. It was his breakthrough season for the team. He's a wide player with good pace and movement, able to come in from wide positions where it wouldn't be so crowded – given the way I had the team set up – and score goals.

We won a comfortable 3–0 away in Agadir in the penultimate game of the season to clinch the title. I was obviously thrilled to have won this championship, but I have to admit that I did so with little or no knowledge of the other teams, the players or their coaches. I know it seems an incredible admission and an indictment of the level of professionalism, but I knew everything I needed to know about my own players and my own team. I knew my own players inside out. I knew what they could do and what they couldn't do from working with them every day. And I never bothered about the opposition at all in the two years that I was there. Maybe for certain away games where I knew it was a difficult place, I might make a tactical change, but otherwise, no. I concentrated 100 per cent on my own problems and never set up in reaction to what I thought my opponents would bring. We never went into the games totally blind. We sat down and watched a thirty-minute video of the opposition's previous match and the players worked things out for themselves. It's one of the advantages of being one of the biggest clubs in the division. Of course, you're going to get surprises, but generally speaking, it's the other teams that have to adjust their game to you and, when they did present us with interesting problems on match day, we had the resources and I had the experience to tweak things as needed.

A successful first year, then, where we were only beaten on three occasions, where I'd picked up the manager of the year award, as voted for by the league's players and coaches, and where we finished as champions to represent Morocco in the African Champions League. It was like an Indian summer for my career; to win a championship in front of 70,000 people, it gave an awful lot of satisfaction to me and to a lot of other people who'd stuck by me.

I was well aware that the second season would be more demanding and complicated. Motivation doesn't come as easily the second time around. Other teams have had a season to work you out and I was also well aware that we'd become the number-one target for opponents. Everyone would be trying that little bit extra against Toshack and Wydad. Unfortunately, as can be the case when working in these places, our biggest problems were non-football reasons and completely out of my control.

We had only played five league games at home when a major crowd incident occurred in the stadium during a match involving our rivals Raja. A lot of people got seriously hurt as groups of fans attacked each other in the stands. The flags they'd been using to show their fantastic support ended up being used as weapons. The local riot police were themselves set upon as they entered the fray. Spectators injured inside and outside the stadium, fighting on the roof of the stands; it's something you never want to see. Three people lost their lives during the disturbance and the stadium was closed. It was a huge blow to Moroccan football, to Wydad and to Raja, with whom we shared the ground. We had to play the rest of our home league games at different venues all around the country – Marrakesh, El Jadida, Safi – all a couple of hours' travel away on unfamiliar soil and in front of only six or seven thousand supporters. It's clearly not the same as playing in Casablanca with 60,000 Wydad fans cheering you on.

A team called FUS, from Rabat, started to push us hard and the race became very heated between the two of us and also the team from Tangier – Ittihad Tanger – in the north. We went through a poor spell, which included a loss away to FUS, our big chance to take over from the league leaders, and, although we recovered to win our last three at home, it wasn't enough to overhaul the team from the capital, who took the championship with a two-point margin. Had we been able to play our fixtures at the Mohammed V stadium in Casablanca, I'm sure we would have completed successive league titles. As it was, the runners-up place gave the club automatic entry back into the CAF Champions League for a second successive season – something that had not been achieved at Wydad for 25 years. The only real negative news came in the domestic cup, the Coupe du Trône, where we went out in our second fixture but we had bigger fish to fry on the continent and, by the time the season was over, we were well on our way in the Champions League.

We had beaten teams from Madagascar, Niger and DR Congo on our way to the quarter-final stage, where we found ourselves vying for one of the top two spots in a group of four with clubs from Egypt, Zambia and the Ivory Coast. With such huge distances to travel, it was a little bit like how it used to be playing in Europe when I was at Cardiff and Liverpool. Accommodation could be basic in the extreme, locals could be very hostile, national officials not always as welcoming and impartial as you'd wish and some pretty long and multi-legged transits to suffer. All in all, playing away meant a considerable disadvantage. These journeys took their toll and there were times when we travelled right through the night. There were long hours in airports and, on one occasion, when we played in Zambia, we were away for eight days including necessary stops over in Nairobi, Kenya, before and after the game. On the way out, my assistant coach and captain had to remain in the airport in Kenya for an extra two days because the person in charge at Wydad hadn't sorted out their visas. The Wydad president even accepted an offer to compete in the friendly Tabuk International Tournament in Saudi Arabia in the middle of all this, which meant an extra week away. It wasn't the ideal preparation for what we were about to face but, still, we won the exhibition contest and picked up the biggest trophy I've ever seen in my life, for what that was worth.

When we got back to Morocco, we were forced to play the first leg of the 2016 Coupe du Trône competition in Fez against against Maghreb Fès, a team that had been relegated the previous season. It was a staggeringly chaotic fixture pile-up. When we arrived, it turned out that my assistant had to remain in the stand because the person responsible had forgotten his coaching licence. Plus, there were international games going on at the same time which meant I was forced to play the tie having seven players unavailable, away representing their countries. In the end, a terrible error by our second-choice keeper Mohammed Akid cost us the game although I was actually quite pleased with a 1–0 defeat under the circumstances. We had debuts all over the pitch that day. We could only manage a 1–1 draw in the home encounter four days later but, at the time, I wasn't too upset to have that one off my plate.

We finished top of our group in the CAF Champions League and had a week to prepare for the semi-final against Zamalek from Egypt. They played in Cairo where we had been earlier in the tournament to face Al Ahly, the other Egyptian giant, who'd won the competition eight times and were recently managed by the

Dutchman Martin Jol. Zamalek had finished second in their group behind the South Africans Mamelodi Sundowns from Pretoria.

Our exit from the domestic cup had not gone down well at all with the president and directors and, for the first time, I got a sense that the pressure was really on and, again, our chances were scuppered by the kind of non-footballing reasons that just shouldn't go on but can often be typical of working in these places. A few days before the semi-final first leg in Egypt, I was told that we would be without a small group of players for the game including my first-choice keeper, Zouheir Laâroubi, who would be unable to leave the country due to military service. I found that one difficult to understand. We were representing Morocco in the biggest football tournament in Africa and I was being deprived of a key player.

The people involved should have seen to it that this didn't happen for the semi-final of the Champions League or, at least, I should have known about it well in advance. This shouldn't be the manager's business. It's got nothing to do with 4–3–2–1 or playing two strikers or whatever. These are players I'd been training with all week and then I was told on the Friday that they're not available. It's little things like that make managing outside of Europe more of a challenge than people looking in might realise. Things like that make it difficult but, despite all the hurdles, all the situations thrown at us and the obstacles put in our way, we'd kept winning. This time, though, it was a step too far.

Akid, our stand-in keeper, had his moments – he could be acrobatic – but was not the kind of goalkeeper a manager wants between the sticks. It was his error that had cost us our place in the Coupe du Trône and I could see that night in Cairo just how nervous he made our defenders. They were uneasy with his presence after that cup exit. They knew he had a howler in him and Akid himself was not entirely concentrated on his game. We were two goals behind after eighteen minutes, both from defensive situations that should never have arisen, and we never recovered. The uncertainty between the players at the back got worse, the lines of communication increasingly scrambled and the Zamalek players could see it. They grew in confidence and walked out 4–0 winners. The tie was effectively over. Everyone connected with the club was utterly shell-shocked. This was the first time the team had conceded four goals in the two years since my arrival. It was soul-destroying. That same evening, after dinner at the hotel, the club doctor informed me that I had been sacked.

Any president worth his salt would come in after a defeat and say, 'OK, let's talk about it tomorrow,' but that's the thing with Morocco. I think it reflected worse on them than it did on me, to come out on the website and say that they'd changed the coach. The Wydad president was involved with the Moroccan FA, thanks to the success of the previous two years, and a Frenchman called Hervé Renard was in charge of the national team. Renard had just made a mess of the job at Lille, but he'd won two African Cups of Nations with Zambia and the Ivory Coast and was very sure of himself. He had his suggestions of who should be the coach at Wydad. They were just waiting for me to slip up. Had I got to the final, I'd have probably stayed on but, irrespective of what would have happened, win or lose the tournament, I was in the departure lounge.

I've parted company from sixteen different appointments over the years, but getting sacked by one of the medical staff was a definite first. One of the directors of the club had travelled with the team but had gone missing after the game. He'd obviously let it slip to the doctor, who'd been decent enough to inform me of what was waiting back in Casablanca. Sure enough, two days later I got my official notice on arrival back in Morocco and my time at Wydad had come to a disappointing end, which was tough given how much I'd enjoyed my first season and how close we'd come to triumph in Africa. At the same time, I wasn't surprised by what had happened. There are not many coaches who last that long in Morocco and I always had the idea there that the minute we lost two or three games, they'd make a change. You know yourself when it's coming. I've never needed anyone to tell me when I've done well or not as well as I should have.

There might come a time when you read in the press that you've been given an ultimatum, but I've never really understood that. Let's say over the next two games you've been given an ultimatum. Well, what if we win the next two and then we lose the third one? Have we got another ultimatum for the following two games after that, then? I think it's better for a chairman to say, 'It hasn't even crossed our minds,' when he's asked by the press and then to just get rid of the manager when he loses the next one. If a chairman does issue an ultimatum, there might be a few players in the team who'd be quite happy to see the manager on his way. I don't say that they'd go out on the field and deliberately lose, but they're not going to play quite as well or with as much determination as they will when the next fella comes in for them to impress.

I try not to use the word pressure, but pressure is something you put on yourself because you have professional pride. I always remember Bill Shankly saying that pressure is what you have when you've got to stand in a dole queue because you've got no job and a mortgage and a family. That's pressure. In football, there's tension and there's responsibility. You're responsible because a lot of people pay money to watch the team play; the cost of travel, of season tickets. For a lot of people, the club is their life, so you have a responsibility to keep them happy in your own way.

Tension is what you have before a big game or if you're coach of Madrid and you're surrounded by your family, your friends and everybody you know is watching, the eyes of the world are on you. Journalists are right up at you with their pens poised; some you like, some you don't, but they all have their jobs to do. You read what they're writing. You know where the bullets are flying. That can bring times of tension and it's then when you've got to remember the difference between that and genuine pressure. That was one thing that was very enjoyable about the job in Casablanca – I didn't know what they were writing about me in Morocco. I didn't know who they were and I wasn't much interested. There wasn't a great deal I could do about it and anyone I knew back in Europe wasn't reading it anyway.

Now, whether I feel the climate is tense or not, generally, if the team doesn't perform, and the results are not positive, then you won't sleep particularly well. You lie in bed awake at night. You're lying there thinking and you know you're not going to sleep. You're waiting to get up the next day and make it right. When that changes – when things are going badly and you can still sleep – then you're out of ideas and it's time to say bye-bye.

I know when it's time to go. You start to see the patterns repeating themselves or you get to a stage when, bang, you simply hit a wall. There's no way around and you have no options left. You know you've seen it before and, no matter what the chairman or anyone else says, you have to tell them that you know where this is going and that it's in everyone's best interest that we resolve this in the most amicable possible way because it's not going to get better. I have to say, of all the places I've ever worked, I most felt like I was swimming against the tide at Wydad. I've had problems in all jobs and I've been able to overcome them. No job is plain sailing. Even at Madrid, when we won the championship and scored 107 goals, and only lost twice, there was a moment in the October where I might have been moved out, but I turned it round.

I think the people at the club read between the lines when I said how important this CAF Champions League thing was for me. I think the president might have known that I would have resigned anyway and he made sure I was pushed before I could jump. Given all I'd faced in the previous season, I'd have sat down with him and told him it was a good time to find somebody new before a third campaign had begun.

I'd got pretty tired of all the problems, all the non-footballing situations which had got in our way, and I was frustrated by the lack of professionalism and intelligence from other areas of the club, but it seems that's what you have to put up with when working in football in places where the professional game is not so long established. A lot of the people who run these clubs have their ideas of how to behave based on what they see of the great football machines of Europe, but they're blind to what goes on behind the scenes there to make it happen. Perhaps I'd been lucky that these things hadn't got in my way in my first twelve months. There were so many frustrations: I remember criticising the groundsman one day because there were no pitches marked out at the training ground. His reply was that he had not been given the money to buy the powder for the white paint. What can you say to that?

I think the closing of the stadium took its toll on everyone. I was ready to call it a day in Casablanca not long after that, but the thought of reaching and winning the final of the Champions League of Africa kept me going. I hadn't won a continental title as a manager. That was a prize worth fighting for.

I stayed on to watch the second leg of the semi-final, which was played in Rabat instead of the Wydad stadium, of course. The side performed with a great deal of energy against a very relaxed Zamalek side and they came close to performing a football miracle by scoring five goals, but unfortunately conceded twice to go out on a 6–5 scoreline. I left the country the following day.

Another chapter done and dusted but, sitting on my Moroccan Airlines flight back to Spain, I couldn't help but feel that this really might be the end. It wouldn't be a bad way to finish – two years' work, league champions and league runners-up, qualifying for the Champions League twice in successive seasons and a semi-final appearance in the same competition. Yes, I was disappointed at the sudden and sad way that it finished but, when I remember how the club was when I arrived, and I looked at how it was when I left, I was more than satisfied.

This was not a new experience for me and I remember the first time it happened in Swansea some thirty years earlier. A lot of water has passed under the bridge since then and I've enjoyed success and good fortune in a number of different countries. My gut feeling this time, though, was a negative one and, approaching seventy years of age, I wouldn't have put money on me being back in the hot seat again. But then I have been proved wrong before. Claudio Ranieri said when he was fifty that he'd finish at sixty, and then, when he was sixty, he said 65. He managed his greatest achievement – when he led Leicester City to the Premier League title in 2016 – when he was 64. I've lasted in this profession a lot longer than ever I thought I would, longer than ever I planned to.

Real Sociedad were playing Betis in La Liga and I was heading back to San Sebastián to watch the game and spend a few weeks in the Basque Country, meeting up with some old friends and enjoying some of the finest restaurants that I have ever come across. Strangely enough, the day after the Sociedad/Betis game, over in Wales, it was Swansea City vs Liverpool. I should have liked to have seen that match but you can't be in two places at the same time, and I'd made my choice on that one a long time ago.

The Moroccan experience had been positive in many ways but I couldn't keep thinking that perhaps Wydad had been my last challenge. There are a lot of coaches out of work and I'm certainly not the spring chicken any more that left Liverpool for Swansea.

Just one year on from that disappointment with Wydad in the CAF Champions League, I found myself in the stands at the Stade Mohammed V watching that side I'd built win the second leg of the 2017 tournament 1–0 to lift the trophy for only the second time in the club's history. Ten of those players who took the field had made their debuts with me and, strangely enough, it was Walid El Karti who got on the end of a cross to score the only goal. Better late than never.

It's been a bit of a theme for me that the person who comes in after I've done the rebuilding goes on to achieve success at the next attempt. It took Javier Irureta another few seasons to turn Super Depor into winners, Del Bosque won the Champions League that I'd already half-done with Madrid, Denoueix finished second in La Liga with my Sociedad team in the campaign directly following my third spell there, Chris Coleman made it to the Euros with those boys that Flynny and I had found and now this Wydad team just one year on. You could say that it takes me to leave for a team to succeed, but the situations have all been different and it depends how you want to look at it. Maybe I'm not the most diplomatic person when things take a dip, as they inevitably have to at some stage when you're putting a side together. Sometimes you get presidents who think that they're responsible for scoring goals and picking the team, and maybe the job involves a little more sweet-talking than I've been prepared to do to ride through those moments. Building a team is a taxing job for everybody and you have to be prepared to take it from the fans, the president and the press, particularly when you're losing players; but I don't need anybody to tell me if I've done well. I know when I've done well and when I haven't.

I've got a championship medal as a player with Liverpool and a championship medal as a manager with Real Madrid. I didn't just get out of bed and pick them up. There's a lot of work that goes in and a lot of suffering. I've lost a lot of matches and had a lot of sleepless nights and I've faced a lot of criticism, but, at the end of the day, when you get tired of answering people and defending yourself to journalists, I just feel like saying – there you are, my debut was in 1965 against Leyton Orient at Cardiff City's stadium and my last adventure was more than half a century later in Casablanca, and you can have a look at what happened in those five decades and judge for yourself. It's very difficult to be lucky for that long. You can be lucky over 52 minutes, but not 52 years.

Epilogue: Iran

SAT AT HOME WATCHING TELEVISION ONE EVENING IN MALLORCA, the telephone rang and on the end of the line was a French agent by the name of Istran Bogner. He introduced himself and spoke of an interest in my services for the national team of Cameroon, asking if I'd like to go and meet the people in charge in Paris. I'd coached plenty of good Cameroonian players before, such as Samuel Eto'o, Jacques Songo'o and Geremi. I was nearly 70 years old and as nice as it is for some people my age to spend their time on the beach, there was part of me that knew I needed more of a challenge in my life than sitting in the sunshine drinking rosé.

When I arrived in Paris, Istran was there to meet me. He had arranged an interview for the following day with the Cameroon delegates but I felt uneasy about this one from the moment I walked into the room. There were six of them in there waiting to appraise me and I thought, 'John, this is not for you.'

When I came out, the famous France international Alain Giresse was sat in the lobby. He'd managed a few French clubs in the 1990s and then national sides all over Africa – Mali, Senegal, Gabon. This was no coincidence. They'd obviously got four or five people lined up to speak to that same day, one after the other, which is not the way I like to do things and that rather put me off. The only interview process I'd had like that before was the one with the Welsh committee in 2004 for the national job, but even then all of the candidates didn't wait in a queue. When one goes in the door and another goes out door and a third is sitting at a table having a coffee just outside, it doesn't make you feel good.

I certainly wouldn't blame the Cameroon FA for taking the time to talk to a few different people after making the trip over from West Africa but when we'd agreed to meet, I thought they'd come specifically to offer me the job. Here I was in Paris, close to 70, being interviewed for a job. I don't know what it was but a sense of sadness came over me that day.

I left Paris saying to Istran that I was not 100 per cent sure that I wanted this and I was back in Mallorca the following day feeling somewhat relieved and much more comfortable. Shortly after, Istran was in touch again, this time with a different offer. It was from the owner of Tractor Sazi, a Persian Gulf Pro League team based in a city in the north of Iran called Tabriz. The owner was Mohammad Reza Zonuzi, an Iranian billionaire businessman who based himself in Turkey. We discussed things in a room overlooking the new Beşiktaş stadium, built on the site of the old one, where I'd walked out with the Istanbul club for their first ever season in the group stages of the Champions League. The hotel we were in hadn't existed 20 years before.

Tractor Sazi was only formed in 1970. It had featured in the country's top flight before the league collapsed during the Iranian Revolution. Then the national competition was suspended during the 1980s because of the Iran-Iraq War. So, it had only been for the last nine seasons that Tractor had actually played regularly in the first division, which they had not yet won. Under new and ambitious ownership, my job, of course, was to change that statistic and take the club into the Asian Champions League and beyond.

I signed the papers then and there and the following day I travelled the two hours' flight on the president's own commercial airline, ATA, which operated flights in and out of Tabriz across the Middle East. The moment I got through the airport doors I was greeted by what, quite frankly, was a frightening reception which I'd neither been warned about nor expected, perhaps naively. The Tractor supporters were there in full force and going absolutely crazy. From airport all the way to my hotel in the centre of the city, it was absolute mayhem. I've never seen anything like it; people, standing up in their cars, swinging their scarves, shouting out of their windows, driving one side of my taxi and then across it to the other. I thought we'd end up in an accident. It was quite the welcome.

As ever, my employers had taken good care of me and put me up in a very good hotel, the El-Goli, from where you can see the city of 1.5 million people stretched out in front of you set in a wide river valley between two volcanic mountain ridges on either side. The sixth biggest city in county, Tabriz had been the capital of the Persian Empire at several points over its history. It's now very much an industrial hub with automobile and heavy machinery plants from where two of the city's biggest football teams had been founded – Tractor Sazi and Machine Sazi, respectively. Both now shared the the 67,000-seater Sahand Stadium where we'd be playing our games from the start of the new season. We had six weeks to prepare.

Istran Bogner was instrumental in getting me settled while I acclimatised to the city and the extremely hot conditions. With temperatures well up into the 30s and 40s it was very difficult for anyone to train, let alone for me to stand on the sidelines. After a couple of days of adapting, I settled down to work after an absence of almost two years since my time in Morocco.

Of course, Iran is a very different country and the Iranian national team was putting in its best ever World Cup performance in Russia, which did take some of the attention away from my arrival, but I was made well aware of the fact that but for Carlos Queiroz, the national team coach, few other football managers with my experience had worked in the country before. All the same, I understood the levels of expectation that went along with that and I must admit to having some reservations about my ability to produce the goods. Like anyone in any job, you lose confidence if you've been out of work for two years. It was the first time that I had ever doubted my own capabilities but, approaching my seventieth birthday, and beginning to notice how some of my old war wounds were affecting my mobility, I knew that these feelings were only normal.

After one week working in Tabriz watching the players and my assistants, and getting used to the habits and customs of the club and Iranian football, my squad and I left for some pre-season work in the more familiar surroundings of Turkey. We were based in a hotel one hour's drive from the capital Ankara and I was very pleasantly surprised by the Turkish people there who remembered me from my time with Beşiktaş. Autographs and photographs were the order of the day and I was pleased to see that this impressed the players and staff of my new club who I think began to look at me in a slightly different light.

Our hotel was thankfully cooler than life in Tabriz, way up in the mountains in a dense area of forest but with some super facilities and pitches for the visiting football teams who frequented the area during pre-season build-up.

We played our first friendly game against Keshla FK from Azerbaijan who had been known as Inter Baku at the time I'd been in charge of Khazar Lankaran, 150 miles over the border from Tabriz. We gave a good account of ourselves with a 2-0 win, then went on to play Gençlerbirliği from Ankara, whom we beat 3-2, and Politehnica Iași from Romania's Liga I, who we drew 2-2. We had time for one more game which was a 1-1 draw against Turkish Super Lig side Sivasspor before finishing our preparations back in Iran. All in all, it was very encouraging: two wins, two draws and eight goals scored, everyone seemed quite happy.

We returned to Tabriz just one day before the opening of the season and, after a presentation game in our stadium, we travelled to a city in the Zagros Mountains in the south-west of the county called Masjed Soleyman to play Naft Masjed Soleyman, who had been promoted from the division below as champions. We flew to the game the day before and stayed in a hotel that certainly wasn't in the top ten that I had been to. It had been a difficult couple of days prior to the match as well. The players had been kept in the offices of the club in Tabriz until virtually dawn 48 hours before the kick off; problems with contracts and the federation apparently, and there had been another setback when my interpreter and one of the medical staff were ordered by the military to serve six months as from the morning of our opening game! There was a terrible sense of disbelief and sadness in the group before a ball had even been kicked. Never a dull moment.

Worse was to follow when it was announced that two of the players that had travelled would not be able to participate, again, because of military obligations. Ridiculously enough, it had been me who had to inform them. The job was becoming a real burden already and I was getting annoyed with a couple of my so-called assistants as well. We could still field a full team but we only had enough players to fill two out of a possible six places on the bench, which was quite the disadvantage given that the players had to get out there and at it in 38-degree heat. We battled away for a creditable goalless draw. I thought I had seen everything during my more than 50 years in the game but this really was something different to anything I'd ever experienced. I soon realised that working in Iran was going to be a real test of resilience. Only time would tell if this was a bridge too far.

Of course, I'd had my doubts before the season began but I was a long way from home here and however difficult things can be on the football side, it's the long hours outside of work that really need to be overcome and this is never straightforward. I'd go into town and sit down in the square and have a coffee or something. There weren't many newspapers that I was able to read. It was difficult to occupy myself. The people of Tabriz were very polite and the club were very kind in making sure that there were staff on hand who could take me round to the shops and the bazaars, but I must confess that I'm not a great one for the tourist attractions.

It wasn't that easy at training either. I was aware that I wasn't the only new face. I was working with people who had all been hired just a few weeks before I'd got there and there was clearly a problem in communication and togetherness. It was all such a new project and there was I, at the head of everything, struggling to find my feet.

The week after our opening fixture, there was also plenty of movement at the club as one of my assistants, the one with whom I had not been too impressed, was moved out and two new players came in, both from the British Isles. I had no previous knowledge of Harry Forrester and Anthony Stokes. Both had played in the Scottish Premier League for Rangers and Celtic respectively and added some much needed cutting edge to a squad desperately short of attacking ability.

Our first home game had to be played behind closed doors because of a ban from the previous season and I couldn't help thinking that things could not get any worse, but they certainly didn't get any better when we could only manage a 1-1 draw against another newly-promoted side. We took the lead in the 44th minute after Stokes got off to a flyer but we conceded with 25 to go and were really hanging on right until the end.

More new appointments were made on and off the field in the first week of August. It was difficult to keep up with everything going on. Two new players arrived on Monday, 6 August from European clubs, both Iranian nationals who had been part of the team at the World Cup the month before. Ashkan Dejagah and Masoud Shojaei brought experience to the squad but it was very much a case of trying to catch up with what we'd been working on. We were a month off being where I wanted but it's clearly not the same to prepare while competing as it is during the calmer period of the pre-season friendlies.

On Friday 10 August, we had one of the most difficult games of the season away from home in the capital, Tehran, against Esteghlal. They were generally regarded as one of the favourites to win the title and, what with the comings and goings in Tabriz, I was far from conformable about how prepared we were, and it was very much the wake up call I feared with us well and truly beaten 3-0. The result could have been even worse. We were that bad. I had decided to play the two new arrivals but it was clearly a mistake as neither of them were able to make any kind of impression and the euphoria that greeted their arrival turned to despair and frustration.

By the end of the month, we had picked up slightly with our first win two home wins, including the derby against Machine Sazi, and a draw away at Sepahan SC in Isfahan. We had a three-week break around the internationals which I was certainly ready for. I returned to Spain to enjoy some time in familiar surroundings but it didn't feel like long before we were back in action and under considerable pressure to improve things but, once again, I witnessed problems that were new to me.

One of our new signings, Iran's left-sided attacker, Dejagah, who has a full sleeve of tattoos down both arms, was summoned to the federation in Tehran to explain himself after he had worn a short sleeve shirt in one of the matches. Players in Iran are warned against getting tattoos and, if they've got them, tend to cover them up when they're representing their country. At the same time, another new player, a Japanese attacker called Yukiya Sugita, was forced to miss two days training while having to sort out a visa problem in Istanbul. It was all organised chaos off the pitch while I was expected to make everything work on it. We were an unbalanced group as it was, and I just could not seem to get things right.

The seven points from the three last games had cheered everyone up though and with Tractor in sixth position in the table, it didn't look as bad as it might have felt.

Our first game after the break changed all that though. It was a cup tie away from home against first division side Sanat Naft from Abadan, a city with one of the biggest oil refineries in the world, right on the border of Iraq at the very top of the Persian Gulf. Its population dropped to virtually zero during the Iran-Iraq War. It was terrible to think what happened there.

Our two Iran national team players were back after a whole two weeks away from the group just for one friendly game in Uzbekistan. I couldn't understand why they needed all that time away. I had been an international manager myself and I was certainly never afforded such luxury. This wasn't right to me but I had been pleased with the way the group had trained in that period all the same, and so I decided to leave out Ashkan and his teammate Masoud from the starting XI. Both would be on the bench instead. Eyebrows were raised within the club but by now I was becoming tired of all the crazy problems every other day; not the best sign given I'd only been there two months.

We performed really well even without our 'star players', but at half-time, with the score at 1-1, I decided to put Masoud, who was the club captain, onto the pitch. We soon went 3-1 up thanks to two goals from Anthony Stokes and another from our right-back. It seemed safe enough to put Ashkan on as well.

What followed was incredible. We surrendered our lead to goals in the 81st and 92nd minutes. Masoud showed an alarming lack of discipline and was sent off, while Ashkan just strolled around as though he wasn't interested. I had to take him off, not something that normally happens after you've just come on as a sub, and our ten men held out in extra-time to take the match to penalty kicks which, unfortunately, we lost.

I ran around and argued with just about everyone. I think that all the frustration that I had bottled up inside for so long just erupted. I left nobody unsure of my feelings. My No.1 target was an assistant who had been brought in by the president a few weeks before. He had been working in London with the BBC, an Iranian who didn't exactly have a CV that excited me. When I saw him shaking hands and laughing with the opposition before the penalty shootout, I called him over and gave him a real rollocking. Not my kind of football man this one.

Everything and everyone was completely negative on the return journey. Nobody spoke. I had seen these signs before. I was on my way. The two internationals would see to that. When it came to a choice between them and me, I knew which way the president would have to go. These two players were powerful figures and the president had splashed out a lot of money to get them. They were part of a so-called 'Top Iran 5' that had performed so well in the World Cup. Masoud had played for Osasuna in Pamplona and Ashkan for Fulham, but you'd think they'd played for Barcelona and Paris Saint-Germain the way that everyone talked about them, and they were 34 and 32; no spring chickens.

I left Iran three days after that cup defeat and I didn't have too much regret, apart from the obvious professional pride that had been dented and hurt.

The Iranians were very, very polite and respectful and I have no complaints about the people of Tabriz. I had been well treated and looked after by the Iranian people – and that's something I'll always be grateful for – but I had difficulty settling there. It was a new club, taken over by new owners, with eleven or twelve new players bought over the summer. The team that went and did the pre-season in Turkey, by the time the season had started, half of them weren't even there anymore. Players would come, players would go, someone new arriving every week. It was very difficult and quite clear that it wouldn't be until Christmas before the whole thing would settle down and start to run smoothly. I'm not getting any younger. I saw those problems coming. Maybe I would have tackled them years ago. Maybe I wouldn't have.

Alongside Lankaran, Tabriz was the most difficult place I've worked, which probably explains why I didn't last four months in either of them, but under the circumstances, the six games, two wins, three draws and one defeat in the league weren't bad given the work we had to do. If we'd won that penalty shootout, things might have been very different but that's always the way in football. The margins have always been very fine.

Extra Time

I THOUGHT IT WOULD BE INTERESTING FOR THE READERS OF THIS book if I put together a couple of teams. One team of players that I played with all those years ago against a team of players that I have managed over the last forty years since my debut in the dugout at Swansea in 1978. What a time that was.

I've been privileged as a player and particularly as a coach and a manager, as we were once called, and I have to admit to being disappointed at some of the players that I have had to leave out. Here we go then.

Players Played With XI – the Reds, Whites and Blue

Goalkeeper: Ray Clemence

Liverpool keeper during my time at Anfield who saved us on many occasions. A full international, he was only unfortunate to be around at a time when Peter Shilton was the regular for England.

Right-back: Phil Neal

Mr Reliable for many, many years with Liverpool and an amazing set of medals to go with it. Scorer of important goals for club and country, not least of which was the opener in the 1984 European Cup win against Roma – the fourth such title for his collection.

Centre-back: John Charles

The greatest player I have ever seen, at No. 9 or No. 5. I was fortunate to play a couple of games in Cardiff City's reserves side as a sixteen-year-old when John was finishing. I'm sure he would do a job at the back for me for this team.

Centre-back: Tommy Smith

The Anfield Iron, they called him. What a fantastic servant to Liverpool he was. Tommy came to play for me at Swansea in his last years and had a strong influence on our success. Like Phil Neal, he was a European Cup winner and goalscorer in Liverpool's first European Cup win in Rome against Mönchengladbach.

Left-back: Džemal Hadžiabdić

I managed to play a couple of games with Jimmy in the Second Division when I was player-manager at Swansea during the 1980/81 season. I played against him for Wales against Yugoslavia in 1976, and when I had the chance to sign him, I never doubted for a minute. Fantastic talent.

Midfield: Graeme Souness

A real Liverpool legend who came to the club in 1978, the same year that I left for Swansea. I was able to play some half a dozen games with him at Anfield. A class act was Souness.

Midfield: Emlyn Hughes

Nicknamed 'Crazy Horse', Emlyn was a huge favourite with the Kopites from the first day he arrived from Blackpool in the late 60s. My roommate during my eight years at Anfield, his passing away so young was a deep shock for us all.

Outside-left: Leighton James

What a fantastic talent. Scorer of that fantastic goal at Preston and a teammate of mine in the Welsh national side.

Striker: Kenny Dalglish

I was fortunate enough to play six or seven games with Kenny when he first arrived at Anfield from Celtic. He was very intelligent with a high level of skill and concentration. He'd be an asset to any team.

Striker: Kevin Keegan
What can I say? I owe him so much. I remember him coming to Anfield from Scunthorpe in 1971 and we just hit it off as a pair straight away.

Outside-right: Steve Heighway
Strictly speaking, a left-sided player, but he had two very good feet. They talked about Toshack and Keegan as Liverpool's main threat but Stevie was so important to us and to that great team.

Bench

Dai Davies
Often unfairly criticised during his time at Everton and as a goalkeeper of the Wales national side, but I was always comfortable with him as a player and later as a manager.

Alan Hansen
Fantastic servant for Liverpool and a super footballing centre-back. Unlucky not to be in my starting line-up.

John Mahoney
My cousin and a hard-working player for Wales and Stoke during the 1970s. You'd never be worried going into battle with 'Josh'.

Ian Callaghan
Another Liverpool legend who I played with and who came with me to Swansea. Ian was part of England's World Cup-winning squad of 1966; a professional of the highest level.

Ron Davies
Look at his goalscoring record at the unfashionable Southampton of the 1970s. I played with Ron in my early years as a Welsh international and was able to see what a classic No. 9 he was.

Robbie James
Robbie had everything but probably never realised his full potential. He was instrumental in Swansea's rise from the Fourth to the top of the First Division and to lose him at 40 years old to a heart attack was terrible.

Players Managed XI
– La Liga Legends

Goalkeeper: Iker Casillas

World Cup winner with Spain and, of course, Champions League winner with Real Madrid. Made his debut when I was in charge at Madrid in 1999 and just shades out the great Luis Arconada, my captain in San Sebastián, during the late 80s; another great international.

Right-back: Carlos Xavier

A fantastically skilled performer, Carlos was one of the best I have ever coached. A youngster with me at Sporting Lisbon and then with me during my time in San Sebastián. No doubts about him.

Left-back: Roberto Carlos

World Cup winner with Brazil and, of course, Champions League winner with Madrid. He was a real favourite with the Madridistas and I was able to see his talent at first hand during my second spell in the Spanish capital.

Centre-back: Noureddine Naybet

Terrific leader and athlete; a Moroccan international who I took to La Coruña with me in 1996. He became a champion with Deportivo; a real player's player.

Centre-back: Fernando Hierro

I signed Hierro as a twenty-year-old from Valladolid in my first spell at Madrid and he went on to achieve everything at the very highest level. His partnership with Naybet would really be special, even against Dalglish and Keegan. What a battle that would be.

Midfield: Xabi Alonso

Liverpool, Real Madrid, Bayern Munich; not a bad career. Xabi made his debut for me in San Sebastián some eighteen years ago and then followed in my footsteps to both Anfield and the Bernabéu. With his terrific vision, Xabi has won everything there is to win.

Midfield: Mauro Silva

What a professional and the perfect foil for Xabi in the middle of the park. Mauro is a real hero in La Coruña where he formed a partnership with Donato – another Brazilian. Another incredible battle – Souness and Hughes vs Mauro and Xabi. Sparks would be flying.

Outside-left: Rivaldo

Played for me in La Coruña before moving on to Barcelona; another World Cup winner and one of the all-time greats.

Striker: Hugo Sánchez

The great Mexican No. 9 was for so long the leader of the Madrid side during the 1980s and 90s. Hugo scored 38 goals in 35 matches when my Madrid side won the title in 1989/90. Just give him half a chance and it's adios amigos.

Striker: Bebeto

I was fortunate enough to manage the great Brazilian attacker and World Cup winner in La Coruña, where I was amazed at his appetite for goalscoring, even in training sessions. Supremely gifted, yes, but an incredible performer who spent hours on the practice ground perfecting his art.

Outside-right: Gareth Bale

Gareth made his debut for me as a sixteen-year-old in the Welsh national team. Southampton to Tottenham, and then only the second Welshman to work at Real Madrid. A pity that so many injuries have held him back.

Bench

Luis Arconada

Bench is not a word Luis would like and he would be right. Great captain for Sociedad and Spain, and maybe should have got the nod over Casillas. Hopefully, he won't come banging on the manager's door over this one.

Oscar Ruggeri

Argentinian centre-back and all-round winner, although with injuries that held him back somewhat.

Ante Rajković

Terrific signing in my time at Swansea. Right out of the old Yugoslav defenders school and a real strong man. I wouldn't have enjoyed playing against him.

Jesús Zamora

Was a one-club man at Real Sociedad and a Spanish international. Revered in San Sebastián and a key player in my cup-winning side of 1987.

Raúl

Many will be surprised that Raúl doesn't make the starting line-up. I have my reasons, though, and it's difficult to argue against Hugo and Bebeto, but Raúl's record at Madrid and later Schalke merits respect.

Bob Latchford

A classic No. 9 out of the old school who made his name at Birmingham City and Everton before joining me at Swansea; an England international and superb professional.

So, there we are, then. Pick the bones out of that lot! There are medals and caps all over the place and I'd love to see these teams play each other. Just writing this chapter makes me realise what a lucky boy I've been to work with this lot; a very privileged John.

Player and Managerial records

Player – Club records

Cardiff City

Season	League			F.A. Cup			League Cup			Europe			Welsh Cup			Total		
	Starts	Subs	Goals	Starts	Subs	Goals	Starts	Subs	Goals	Starts	Subs	Goals	Starts	Subs	Goals	Starts	Subs	Goals
1965-66	7	1	6	0	0	0	1	0	0	0	0	0	0	0	0	8	1	6
1966-67	22	1	10	0	0	0	2	0	1	0	0	0	1	0	0	25	1	11
1967-68	34	1	11	1	0	0	0	0	0	9	0	2	5	0	4	49	1	17
1968-69	41	0	22	2	0	0	1	0	0	2	0	2	5	0	7	51	0	31
1969-70	38	1	17	3	0	1	1	0	0	4	0	2	3	1	2	49	2	22
1970-71	16	0	8	0	0	0	1	0	0	4	0	5	0	0	0	21	0	13
TOTAL	158	4	74	6	0	1	6	0	1	19	0	9	14	1	13	203	5	100

Liverpool

Season	League			F.A. Cup			League Cup			Europe			Charity Shield			Total		
	Starts	Subs	Goals	Starts	Subs	Goals	Starts	Subs	Goals	Starts	Subs	Goals	Starts	Subs	Goals	Starts	Subs	Goals
1970-71	21	0	5	7	0	1	0	0	0	5	0	1	0	0	0	33	0	7
1971-72	28	1	13	1	0	0	1	0	0	1	1	0	0	1	0	31	3	13
1972-73	22	0	13	4	0	2	6	0	1	6	2	1	0	0	0	38	2	17
1973-74	19	0	5	6	0	3	2	0	2	3	0	1	0	0	0	30	0	11
1974-75	20	1	12	2	0	0	0	0	0	0	2	0	0	0	0	22	3	12
1975-76	35	0	16	2	0	1	2	0	0	10	1	6	0	0	0	49	1	23
1976-77	22	0	10	2	0	1	1	0	0	4	0	1	1	0	1	30	0	13
1977-78	2	1	0	0	0	0	1	0	0	1	0	0	0	0	0	4	1	0
TOTAL	169	3	74	24	0	8	13	0	3	30	6	10	1	1	1	237	10	96

Player – Club records (*Continued*)

Swansea City

Season	League			F.A. Cup			League Cup			Europe			Welsh Cup			Total			
	Starts	Subs	Goals	Starts	Subs	Goals	Starts	Subs	Goals	Starts	Subs	Goals	Starts	Subs	Goals	Starts	Subs	Goals	Division
1977-78	13	0	6	0	0	0	0	0	0	0	0	0	0	0	0	13	0	6	4
1978-79	24	4	13	3	0	1	4	0	1	0	0	0	0	0	0	31	4	15	3
1979-80	15	1	5	5	0	3	3	0	1	0	0	0	0	0	0	23	1	9	2
1980-81	3	0	0	0	0	0	1	1	0	0	0	0	0	0	0	4	1	0	2
1982-83	0	0	0	0	0	0	0	0	0	0	1	1	0	0	0	0	1	1	1
1983-84	3	0	1	1	0	0	0	0	0	0	0	0	0	0	0	4	0	1	2
TOTAL	50	5	25	9	0	4	8	1	2	0	1	1	0	0	0	75	7	32	

Player – International records

Team

	Starts	Subs	Goals
Cardiff City	8	0	2
Liverpool	26	0	8
Swansea City	5	1	3
TOTAL	39	1	13

Competition

	Starts	Subs	Goals
Friendly	4	0	0
Home Internationals	15	0	6
World Cup	8	0	2
European	11	1	5
TOTAL	39	1	13

Year

	Appearances	Subs	Goals
1969	8	0	2
1971	5	0	2
1972	2	0	0
1973	4	0	1
1974	3	0	2
1975	4	0	3
1976	4	0	0
1977	4	0	0
1979	5	1	3
TOTAL	39	1	13

Managerial – Club records

Swansea City

Season	Division	Played	Won	Drawn	Lost	For	Against	Points	Final Position
1977-78*	4	46	23	10	13	87	47	56	3rd
1978-79	3	46	24	12	10	83	61	60	3rd
1979-80	2	42	17	9	16	48	53	43	12th
1980-81	2	42	18	14	10	64	44	50	3rd
1981-82	1	42	21	6	15	58	51	69	6th
1982-83	1	42	10	11	21	51	69	41	21st
1983-84**	2	42	7	8	27	36	85	29	21st

Sporting Lisbon

Season	Played	Won	Drawn	Lost	For	Against	Points	Final Position
1983-84*	30	19	4	7	58	24	42	3rd
1984-85	30	19	9	2	72	26	47	2nd

Real Sociedad

Season	Played	Won	Drawn	Lost	For	Against	Points	Final Position
1985-86	34	17	5	12	64	51	39	7th
1986-87	44	19	9	16	59	54	47	10th
1987-88	38	22	7	9	61	33	51	2nd
1988-89	38	11	14	13	38	47	36	11th

Real Madrid

Season	Played	Won	Drawn	Lost	For	Against	Points	Final Position
1989-90	38	26	10	2	107	38	62	1st
1990-91**	38	20	6	12	63	37	46	3rd

Real Sociedad

Season	Played	Won	Drawn	Lost	For	Against	Points	Final Position
1991-92	38	16	12	10	44	38	44	5th
1992-93	38	13	8	17	46	59	34	13th
1993-94	38	12	12	14	39	47	36	11th
1994-95**	38	12	14	12	56	44	38	11th

* Indicates that John arrived at the club when the current season was already underway.

** Indicates that John left the club before the current season had finished.

Managerial – Club records (*Continued*)

Deportivo La Coruña

Season	Played	Won	Drawn	Lost	For	Against	Points	Final Position
1995-96	42	16	13	13	63	44	61	9th
1996-97**	42	21	14	7	57	30	77	3rd

Beşiktaş

Season	Played	Won	Drawn	Lost	For	Against	Points	Final Position
1997-98	34	13	9	12	56	40	48	6th
1998-99**	34	23	8	3	58	27	77	2nd

Real Madrid

Season	Played	Won	Drawn	Lost	For	Against	Points	Final Position
1998-99*	38	21	5	12	77	62	68	2nd
1999-00**	38	16	14	8	58	48	62	5th

Saint-Étienne

Season	Played	Won	Drawn	Lost	For	Against	Points	Final Position
2000-01* **	34	8	10	16	42	56	34	17th

Real Sociedad

Season	Played	Won	Drawn	Lost	For	Against	Points	Final Position
2000-01*	38	11	10	17	52	68	43	13th
2001-02	38	13	8	17	48	54	47	13th

Catania

Season	Played	Won	Drawn	Lost	For	Against	Points	Final Position
2002-03* **	38	12	8	18	46	59	44	17th

Real Murcia

Season	Played	Won	Drawn	Lost	For	Against	Points	Final Position
2003-04*	38	5	11	22	29	57	26	20th

* Indicates that John arrived at the club when the current season was already underway.

** Indicates that John left the club before the current season had finished.

Managerial – Club records (*Continued*)

Khazar Lankaran

Season	Played	Won	Drawn	Lost	For	Against	Points	Final Position
2013-14**	36	12	13	11	44	49	49	6th

Wydad Casablanca

Season	Played	Won	Drawn	Lost	For	Against	Points	Final Position
2014-15	30	16	11	3	48	21	59	1st
2015-16	30	16	8	6	34	19	56	2nd
2016-17**	30	19	9	2	50	24	66	1st

* *Indicates that John arrived at the club when the current season was already underway.*
** *Indicates that John left the club before the current season had finished.*

Managerial – International records

Wales Manager

Year	Won	Drawn	Lost	For	Against
1994	0	0	1	1	3
2005	3	1	5	7	8
2006	3	2	3	11	11
2007	4	5	3	16	13
2008	6	0	4	12	7
2009	4	0	6	10	12
2010	1	0	3	5	5
TOTAL	21	8	25	60	59

Macedonia Manager

Year	Won	Drawn	Lost	For	Against
2011	1	2	2	3	6
2012	0	2	1	1	2
TOTAL	1	4	3	4	8

Player and Managerial honours

Player

Cardiff City
Welsh Cup
1967/68, 1968/69

Liverpool
Football League First Division
1972/73, 1975/76, 1976/77

FA Cup
1973/74

UEFA Cup
1972/73, 1975/76

European Cup
1976/77

UEFA Super Cup
1977

Player-Manager

Swansea City
Welsh Cup
1980/81, 1981/82, 1982/83

Manager

Real Sociedad
Copa del Rey
1986/87

Real Madrid
La Liga
1989/90

Deportivo
Supercopa de España
1995

Beşiktaş
Turkish Cup
1997/98

Khazar Lankaran
Azerbaijan Super Cup
2013

Wydad Athletic Club
Botola
2014/15

Acknowledgements

I HAVE WITHOUT A DOUBT BEEN VERY FORTUNATE SINCE THE DAY that I decided to become a professional footballer, and my success would not have been possible without the help and decision-making of certain people. First of all, my school teacher in Radnor Road Junior School, Roy Sperry, who put me into the Under-11 team when I was only eight years old. He helped foster my love for the game along with that 45 minutes I enjoyed playing football every day in the school yard between 12.30pm and 1.15pm.

When I was sixteen years old, the then Cardiff City manager Jimmy Scoular gave me my debut in the first team and I managed to grab a goal in a home win against Leyton Orient. My goal came late in the game in front of the Grangetown End of the old Ninian Park Stadium. Strangely enough, eighteen years later, my last league goal was scored at the same stadium, in front of the same Grangetown supporters, but this time it was as player/manager for archrivals Swansea City – an unbelievable coincidence.

Bill Shankly was the man responsible for my Liverpool adventure, signing me in November 1970, and I will, of course, always be grateful to Shanks for giving me the opportunity to perform at the highest level; league championships, UEFA Cup victories, a European Cup too; nine winners' medals altogether. Thanks, Bill.

Malcolm Struel was the Swansea City chairman who gave me the opportunity to try my luck in football management. It was March 1978 when I decided to leave Liverpool and drop into the Fourth Division with Swansea. It was a fantastic but difficult learning period for me that really put me in good stead for the years ahead.

Roy Sperry, Jimmy Scoular, Bill Shankly and Malcolm Struel; school teacher, managers and chairman – four men who are no longer with us but who are often in my thoughts. I should say here that there are many other people, especially teammates, who have helped me along the way and it would be difficult to name them all.

Iñaki Alkiza was the president of Real Sociedad in San Sebastián and it was he who took the decision to bring me to his club in 1985. I was the first foreign coach in the Basque club's modern history, so, in many ways, it was a huge gamble on his part. Politically, things have calmed down a lot over the last thirty years, but in those days it was not always easy being a foreigner in those parts. Thank you, Iñaki.

My four years in San Sebastián had brought two runners-up medals and a winners' medal to a club that was on its knees when I arrived, and it was a really important part of my progression. People had taken notice of what was happening and, as happy as I was, it is difficult to say no to Real Madrid. Ramón Mendoza was the president of Real Madrid in 1989 and he was the man who showed confidence and took me to the capital city of Spain, and to what could arguably be described as the biggest club in world football. At just forty years of age, I became one of the youngest managers in the club's history and, after that, it obviously became a lot easier to be recognised and noticed for other jobs.

That's it then, and I must repeat here that, although many others have helped and been vitally important over the last fifty years, these are the ones who, during that time, showed the confidence in me when it was so necessary. All of them, apart from Iñaki Alkiza in San Sebastián, have passed away, but I will forever be grateful to them all.

Finally, I have to mention one other football man who was of enormous help to me. Kevin Keegan was signed from Scunthorpe by Bill Shankly just before the cup final between Liverpool and Arsenal in May 1971. Keegan and Toshack were fortunate enough to strike up an excellent relationship on and off the field. We played together and both captained and managed our countries, while enjoying success not only at home, but abroad as well. When I returned from Leicester after failing my medical in 1974, I was pretty low on confidence but, fortunately, I was able to work my way back into the side and play my part in another two Liverpool championships, a UEFA Cup and European Cup title too. I don't think that it would have been possible without Kevin. Sperry, Scoular, Shankly, Struel, Alkiza, Mendoza and Keegan; thanks for the memories.

John Toshack

BOOKS LIKE THESE DON'T HAPPEN WITHOUT A LOT OF GOODWILL and people kind enough to give up their time for free. Of John's former colleagues and friends, special thanks must go to Carlos Xavier, Hugo Sánchez, Tayfun Ozusakiz, Martín Vázquez, Xabi Alonso, Luis Uranga, Brian Flynn, Alan Curtis, Wyndham Evans, Leighton James, Jeremy Charles, Meho Kodro, Guly do Prado, Mauri, Joe Ledley, John Hartson, Cameron Toshack and Ian Gwyn Hughes all of whom told brilliant stories and helped set the record straight. Thanks to Jonathan Wilsher and Martin Egan for setting up interviews; to Catherine Stephenson, Liam Thompson, Edu Rodríguez Peña, Raúl Rodríguez Martínez for their help with translation and to Sid Lowe for his socio-political insights on football in the Basque region and the unique complexities of Real Madrid. Lastly, thanks to Jonathan Wilson and The Blizzard for getting the project running; thanks to Hugh Kleinberg and James Stables for helping me to getting my foot in the door and to Jen and the boys for putting up with me while I did it. Much obliged to the lot of you.

Dan Sung

www.decoubertin.co.uk